Bombs Always Beep
Creating Modern Audio Theater

2nd Edition: "Revenge of the Beep"

By

Kc Wayland

Edited By

Wendy Lucas & Shanti Ryle

Wayland Productions, United States

Published by Wayland Productions
United States
2020

2nd Edition: Revenge of the Beep

Copyright © 2020 by Kc Wayland

Cover credit: Stanley Von Medvey
Book Formatting: Pacific S. Obadiah
Based on Vintage Book Template by: David Haden.

ISBN-13: 9781648585388
ISBN-10: 1648585388
Print Ver 2.1
www.WaylandProductions.com
www.bombsalwaysbeep.com
Email: kc@waylandproductions.com

Theater for the Mind:
Trademark Reg. No. 5,466,100
Registered May 08, 2018
Int. Cl.: 41
Service Mark Principal Register Wayland Productions
(CALIFORNIA CORPORATION) CLASS 41

Contents

* = New Section for 2nd Edition

Forward
Chapter Outline
What is Audio Drama

Chapter 1 - Storytelling
    1. Choosing your Story   p.17
    1.1 Titles   p.22
    1.2 Creating a Compelling Story   p.23
    1.2a Pacing and Tension*   p.26
    1.2b The Outline*   p.27
    1.3 Story Workshop   p.30
    1.4 What's in a Name?   p.34
    1.4a Character and Story Wrappers*   p.36
    1.4b Natural Character Evolution*   p.37
    1.5 Conflict is Key   p.39
    1.6 Motivation Moves the Story   p.41
    1.7 Conceiving Action   p.43
    1.8 Words on the Page   p.44
    1.9 Workshop Result   p.45

Chapter 2 - Storytelling through Audio
    2. Starting the Story   p.49
    2.1 Perspective   p.50
    2.1a Audio Aesthetics and The Sound Palette*   p.52
    2.2 Characters   p.54
    2.3 Scenes   p.56
    2.3a Creating a Scene for Audio*   p.58
    2.3b Audio Scene Transitions*   p.61
    2.4 Creating Dialogue and Narration   p.64
    2.5 Forcing Visualization   p.67
    2.6 Language Mechanics   p.69
    2.7 Writing onto the Page   p.69

Chapter 3 - Starting Production
- 3. Pre-production Ends — p.81
- 3.1 Stages of Production — p.82
- 3.2 Key Positions and Roles — p.84
- 3.3 Low Budget Productions — p.86

Chapter 4 - Logistics
- 4. Budgeting — p.89
- 4.1 Funding — p.94
- 4.2 Contracts — p.96

Chapter 5 - Actors
- 5. Casting — p.99
- 5.1 Descriptions — p.100
- 5.2 Casting Notices and Submissions — p.101
- 5.3 Holding Auditions — p.102
- 5.4 Casting for Audio — p.103
- 5.4a Casting Audio as the Actor or Director* — p.104
- 5.4b Keys to Success Working with Hollywood Talent* — p.108
- 5.5 Selecting Actors — p.111
- 5.6 Deal Memos and Contacts — p.112
- 5.7 Payment — p.114
- 5.8 The Table Read — p.115
- 5.9 SAG/AFTRA — p.116
- 5.9a SAG/AFTRA Rates* — p.119

Chapter 6 - Scheduling
- 6. The Fight Against Time — p.120
- 6.1 Script Formatting — p.121
- 6.2 Reports and Breakdowns — p.123
- 6.3 Creating the Schedule — p.125
- 6.4 Further Adjustments and Considerations — p.132

Chapter 7 - Preparing to Record
- 7. Recording Preparation — p.133
- 7.1 Recording Scripts — p.135
- 7.2 Titles and Credits — p.137

Chapter 8 - Recording and Directing

8. Approaching the Material	p.140
8.1 Warming Up	p.144
8.2 The Recording Space	p.145
8.3 Active Listening, Guiding, and Participation	p.149
8.4 Recording out of Order	p.151
8.5 Generics	p.153

Chapter 9 - The Tech Side of Recording

9. Suspension of Disbelief	p.154
9.1 Choosing the Recording Space	p.156
9.1.1 Low-Budget Spaces	p.159
9.2 Signal Flow & Audio Hardware	p.163
9.2.1 Low-Budget Recording	p.169
9.2a Hierarchy of Sound Recording*	p.171
9.3 Recording Formats	p.178
9.4 Session Setup	p.180
9.5 Audio Script Supervising	p.182

Chapter 10 - Post-Production

10. The Story Comes to Life	p.185
10.1 Post Workflow	p.185
10.2 Post Hardware	p.188
10.2.1 Low Budget Options	p.190
10.2a Post Software*	p.190
10.3 The Art and Tech of Editing Sound	p.193
10.3a Noise Reduction*	p.195
10.3b Advanced Audio Editing Samples*	p.196
10.4 Post-Session Setup	p.200
10.5 Assembly Cut	p.208
10.6 Voice Cut	p.211
10.6a Performance Selection and the Editor*	p.214
10.6b The Pacing Cut*	p.216
10.7 Rough Cut	p.217
10.8 Sound Effect Libraries	p.218
10.8a Foley vs SFX*	p.219
10.9 Sound Design	p.221
10.9.1 Establish Location	p.221
10.9.2 Sample Scene	p.223

10.9.3 The Sound of the Scene	p.223
10.9.4 Aural Design Techniques	p.225
10.9.4a Audience Digestion, Limitations, Lufs, and Levels*	p.227
10.9.4b Dissonant Sound*	p.229
10.9.4c Mixing to the Voice*	p.230
10.10 Foley	p.230
10.10.1 Footsteps	p.232
10.10.1a Sampled Foley*	p.234
10.10.2 Editing at the Mic	p.234
10.10.3 Equipment	p.235
10.11 Modifying Audio	p.235
10.11.1 Cleaning up Audio	p.236
10.11.2 Enhancing Audio	p.239
10.11.3 Aux Track Effects	p.242
10.12 Fine Cut - Adding Music	p.234
10.12.1 Theme Music	p.234
10.12.2 Composed or Stock Music	p.244
10.12.3 How to use Music	p.245
10.13 Finishing	p.246

Chapter 11 - Publishing

11. Out to the Public	p.247
11.1 Podcast Hosting and Websites	p.250
11.2 Marketing and Social Media	p.252
11.3 The Community	p.255

Chapter 12 - Theater for the Mind

12. The Movement	p.256
12.1 Conclusion	p.257

Additional Resources

xx. Equipment Index	p.258
xx.1 Concepts and Phrases	p.261
xx.2 Photo Credits	p.262

Forward

Hello, and welcome to <u>Bombs Always Beep: Creating Modern Audio Theater</u>. I, Kc Wayland, shall be your host. Over the course of this book, I will explain the technical and artistic side for all things concerning this unique and born again medium. As you read this text, keep in mind that anything recommended in this book isn't "carved in stone." Rules and guidelines can be bent or creatively broken, but the tips and techniques contained within provide the foundation for what I find generally works best when creating aural entertainment. If you're using this text as a guideline for your production, be sure to read the entire book before beginning your project, as there are tips presented later in the book that could apply early on.

My intention in writing this book is to set new standards in all aspects of production- from inception, to writing, editing, and finally, publishing. I've spent the past 8 years creating one of the largest and longest-running modern audio productions, <u>We're Alive</u>. At the time of this writing it's received over 60 million downloads, as well as numerous accolades, including a nomination for an "Audie" from the Audio Publishers Association, and "Best of iTunes" in 2012. I have presented and participated in multiple conferences, conventions, and seminars, all focused on audio theater as well as actively mentoring and assisting others in the audio drama community for a number of years.

Audio-only entertainment has undergone tremendous changes with the advent of modern production and distribution techniques. Over the past several years I have been vigorously developing and documenting the advanced production workflows from various audio theater projects. One of the most notable and groundbreaking projects I have done would be producing *Bronzeville*. This unique experience allowed me to refine and test the workflows against the standards and restrictions presented when working with top Hollywood talent.

I have an extensive background in both the creative and technical sides of the industry. I received "Top Graduate" and "Distinguished Honor Graduate" recognition with two Broadcast Engineering Certifications from the Defense Information School in Fort Meade, Maryland. During my deployment in the Army with the 222nd Broadcast Operations Detachment, I helped set up "Freedom Radio" in Baghdad, Iraq, where we produced a live FM broadcast to the troops throughout the entire country. When I returned, I completed my Bachelor's Degree in Fine Arts in 2008 in Writing and Directing from Chapman University, and was awarded "Cheverton Graduate," (Chapman's version of Valedictorian). I recently returned to Chapman in 2017 to teach my own course in audio theater.

Lastly, and most importantly, what I bring to this book is years of audio-only entertainment experience. I have accumulated more than 10,000 hours working in this medium in every production position, including Foley, Writing, Editing, Recording, Marketing, Social Media, and Production Management. It would be difficult to find someone who has dedicated more time and effort working in audio theater. By writing this book, I hope to ensure its continual development and growth on the professional level, along with the advancement of artistic aural experimentation. It will be exciting to see what productions will follow in the next few years. The advent of new technology and distribution may have spurred an entirely new independent movement and wave of productions, but the rebirth of the medium is still in its infancy.

Chapter Outline

What is "Audio Drama"?
This first section is the introduction to the medium, a brief history, and an in-depth analysis of the various styles of audio-only entertainment currently on the market.

Chapter 1 - Storytelling
This first chapter demonstrates how to create a story that's told through only audio means. Every aspect of a sample story is flushed out in a unique way through a *Story Workshop*. The building of a story then grows from the exploration of natural character motivation. Lastly, this story section contains tips for exploring and writing onto the page, and helpful brainstorming techniques.

Chapter 2 - Storytelling through Audio
What are the things that are unique to audio-only entertainment that need to be considered when writing a story? What are other aspects that help enforce the visualization of the story? Environments and setting choices become the equivalent to "framing" in cinematography. Lastly, the section ends with the guide on how to transfer all of these ideas onto the script page formatted specially for audio-only productions.

Chapter 3 - Starting Production

Pre-production for audio entertainment consists of assembling a team and completing assets before starting production. This chapter outlines the stages in the workflow to complete an audio production, followed by the key positions and roles required to run larger productions. Contained here is a low-budget section that details tips and techniques for cutting corners and saving money, while still achieving high-end results. These are more of the "guerilla" styles of production.

Chapter 4 - Logistics

Presented here are the aspects of production that no one wants to deal with, but everyone should know. How much does everything cost? What are potential costs of production that aren't normally anticipated? What is the range of budgets for this medium? Story rights need to be examined for royalty considerations, including detailed contracts worked out in advance. How can this audio production be funded? Kickstarter and other crowd-sourcing options can be risky and time-consuming, but also rewarding. This section covers all the aspects of the production machine, and how the process is facilitated by the fuel of capital.

Chapter 5 - Actors

Getting the right person for a role is not an easy task. How does a production handle finding that perfect actor? What sort of qualities should be scrutinized for an audio-only actor? How are call-backs dealt with? There's a lot to consider and know ahead of time when finally casting someone for the role, including dealing with their agent, unions, payments, contracts and deal memos.

Chapter 6 - Scheduling

Audio-only entertainment is typically lengthy, and the recording times short, making scheduling actors complicated. This section goes through the process of properly formatting scripts for reports, then transforming that information into data for the schedule, as well as various considerations for recording order adjustments.

Chapter 7 - Preparing to record

There's a lot that goes into setting up an efficient recording session. Proper actor communication needs to be established and handled appropriately. Included here are other logistical aspects that need to be considered before a recording session begins.

Chapter 8 - Recording and Directing

With pre-production complete, now the recording sessions begin, and with it the role of the director and how they influence the performances. There are various ways in which a director can warm up the actors and help prepare their voice. It's part of the director's responsibility as well to set up a relationship and workflow on the recording stage, knowing how to operate and perform in the space with other actors. An audio-director needs to be actively listening and participating, keeping up the energy and momentum for continuity. They are also the guide, helping actors switch to various places in the story while giving them the needed information to know what's going on in their upcoming scene.

Chapter 9 - The Tech Side of Recording

Recording is complicated. There are many components involved with perfecting the capture of sound-neutral performances to ensure the most accurate aural representation, while minimizing the additional amount of noise and artifacts. There are various pieces of hardware covered in this section, and also low-budget options as well. Each session for an audio drama is set up uniquely, to optimize the workflow through post-production.

Chapter 10 - Post-Production

The longest and most involved part of audio drama production is Post, and this chapter's length reflects that. Every step of the workflow is covered to ensure a smooth process along with how to utilize specific team members. There's also an inherent deeply artistic side to sound design: the clarity and use of sound to build an aural image and how Foley can be used to connect the audio world with the audience.

Chapter 11 - Publishing

How to be heard is the constant struggle. This chapter covers the various platforms to launch the project, where to host them, dealing with marketing/social media, and the community as a whole. An audio drama needs listeners to be successful, and these are the steps to get started in reaching an audience.

Chapter 12 - Theater for the Mind

As the medium grows, so too does the need to start finding ways to promote quality over quantity. The movement involves special branding control for productions that focus on aspects to create vivid aural images, and truly creates *a theater in the mind* of the listener in being part of that world.

Additional Resources

Additional pieces of information regarding an equipment index, along with key concepts and phrases are included.

Introduction

What is an Audio Drama?

"Audio Theater" or "Audio Drama"? Similar to saying, "Film," or "Movie," or "Cinema"? Terminology can be confusing, and many artists who work in the medium don't always agree on which is better to use. You might hear the term "Art Film" and not "Art Movie," because one term has a bit more style and substance over the perception of the other. Every cinematic narrative is a *movie* but not every one is considered a *film*.

Similarly, in the audio world, there is a comparable relationship with "Theater" and "Drama." Audio Theater denotes a more specific use of theatrical storytelling elements and performance, while Audio Drama is more general, covering a wide variety of different types of aural storytelling. If your production is looking to create an aural image of sound which is based on a script with character interaction and dialogue, "Audio Theater" might be the more accurate categorization.

Certain aspects of Audio Drama are shared with Cinema, and there have been attempts to try and combine the branding with phrases like "Audio Film" or "Audio Movie" for marketing purposes. This just further muddies the classification because terms like "Film" is derived from the physical stock in which cinema was first recorded, and "Movies" comes from *motion* pictures. It may be easier or eye-grabbing to use these classifications in the short term for advertising purposes, but in time this can cause brand confusion, especially at this crucial point for the medium.

Audio drama is having an art renaissance. The ease of access to the technology and the distribution platform of podcasts is turning up the volume on this form of aural entertainment. The growing listenership and metrics of reach are driving advertisers to these shows, injecting funding into the medium again, luring new creators to the field. This source of income is something that we must embrace. In the real world, art cannot grow without profitability and support.

Advertisers often struggle with pitching audio-entertainment because of the labeling/branding that corresponds with the particular programming. If one were to assign a certain dollar amount for advertising against audio programming, it becomes critical to know the differences between Audio Theater and something like that of a multi-cast audio book. The cost of advertising is typically proportional to the quality of entertainment, and the "star-power" that is attached.

When trying to explain the various intricacies and forms of audio drama, most people are familiar with the term "Radio Drama," which refers to the golden era of the medium which gave access via the AM/FM dial. Mentioning a show like *The Shadow* or *Gunsmoke* recalls the time when radio relied on live performances from producers like RKO, with actors and Foley artists flying by the seat of their pants to create the soundscape. Radio Drama is still the term most familiar and commonly used, even though few are still actually broadcast over the radio. For that reason, online creators and distributors of this medium will often promote the phrase "Modern Audio Drama" to describe their productions. The term, however, is so loosely used, that much of what's created might not even be considered an Audio Drama. In fact, many publishers will use the terms interchangeably for books on tape which contain multiple readers, causing further branding dilution.

With so many different labels and varying styles, it's been difficult to clearly communicate how the different forms are classified. Through collaboration and coordination with various publishers, I have worked to help better define classifications of styles of the medium in the following ways:

- <u>Audio Entertainment:</u>
- Book-based: This section pertains to text that is directly transferred from books, meaning that the dialogue and format hasn't changed significantly from the first published materials.
  - Non-Fiction
  - Audio Book (Non-Fiction): Single-narrator reading of a non-fiction book.
  - Fiction
    - Audio Book (Fiction): Single-narrator reading of a narrative book.
    - Enhanced Audio Book: Book with single or multiple readers, enhanced with SFX (sound effects) and/or music.
    - Multicast Audio Book: Book directly translated into audio with multiple performers reading different roles

- <u>Audio Drama</u>: This section pertains to narratives that are specifically written and designed solely with the intention of an audio-only final product.
  - Radio Drama - Term used for narrative dramas produced during the "golden age" of radio (1930~1960)
  - Audio Play - Term used for multiple actors performing roles with minimal narration and SFX.
  - Audio Journalism - Non-fiction news reporting style (e.g., <u>Serial</u>).
  - Audio Mockumentary - Fictional news reporting style and found footage (<u>Welcome to Night Vale</u>, <u>Black Tapes</u>, etc...).
  - Sound Art/Experimentational - Fictional miscellaneous aural category. There's a lot of room for using sound solely to tell stories, with varying amounts of VOX.
  - Audio Improv - Actors create a story specifically for audio, but don't have a pre-existing narrative to follow. aka Bat Improv - just like a bat that cannot see, the improvisors rely only on their voices to tell their improvised story.
  - Audio Narrative - Term used for single-to-multi-cast stories that rely on the story to be told via narration/monologues, with possible accompaniment of Foley, SFX, and music (<u>Alice isn't Dead</u>, <u>Scotch</u>, <u>Mabel</u>).
  - Audio Theater - Term used for multi-cast narrative stories that follow a dramatic script; uses narration, SFX libraries, and music.
  - LIVE Audio Theater - Term used for multi-cast narrative stories that follow a dramatic script; uses narration, SFX libraries, music,

and possibly LIVE Foley (<u>Wildclaw Theatre</u> in Chicago).
- Theater for the Mind - Term used to describe multi-cast narrative stories, recording a majority of the cast at the same time. Minimal narration, advanced sound design techniques, custom music, and Foley are used throughout the framework of the story. (More information on this unique category in a later chapter.)

By creating a clear definition between the different styles, the audience can better select the sort of entertainment they'd like to listen to, rather than lumping everything together into one "Audio Drama" designation. Also by properly categorizing the productions, advertisers and funders can have a better idea of what is being created, further helping fuel the industry.

Why is this medium important, and why are we talking about it now? Because it's growing. The BBC has never really stopped producing Audio Drama since the golden age, but the scope of influence was mostly limited to the United Kingdom. Outside of that, it has been a very small amount of producers still exploring the medium. In the last several years we've seen the percentage of independent online audio dramas grow exponentially. The reason we're seeing more and more productions come to the table is because of the direct-to-audience approach of podcasts. A few years ago, no one knew what a podcast was or how it worked- now they are mainstream.

The varying degrees of professionalism in these productions range from public radio empires, independent studios, mom and pop productions, to even high school student summer projects. Advertisers have started flocking to the space, because many people are tuning out of conventional FM dials, and have moved to the download-on-demand availability with a few clicks from a user's phone. Most of the podcasts on the market currently are talk shows and can become dated very quickly. Audio stories are evergreen content, though, and thus represent massive potential for marketers. This recent turn of events has started to make the medium more financially viable, drawing in even larger producers and studios from the film industry.

But still, why? Why is it that more people are listening to Audio Dramas? Because they are powerful, at a very basic level of human-human connection. Oral storytelling is one of the oldest forms of human communication. Picture sitting around a campfire, sharing stories of fact and fiction. This verbal tradition connects with a listener in the most primitive of ways. Hearing the story allows the audience to visualize and use their imagination, creating their own images of the story within their head.

Audio drama has an important place in-between books and film. With only written words on the page of a book, a writer creates characters and a world, requiring the reader to cast and produce the story in their own mind. Films provide everything, the audience only has to sit back and enjoy the ride. Audio storytelling falls between the two, offering a unique opportunity to be far more intimate. The listener becomes an active participant and part of the story.

Changes in social lifestyle is another reason people are starting to tune in more. With new exciting life possibilities, we are constantly on the go, increasingly driving more time than we spend at our destinations. It is refreshing and newly inspiring to be able to escape the monotony and dive into another world. Be it while creating, working, traveling… audio is the perfect companion for modern living. So much of the world we occupy strains our eyes with a constant bombardment of screens. TVs, phones, computers, and even books add a level of visual fatigue. It's nice to be able to sit back and let the world dissolve, and become swept away into an aural experience.

Chapter One

Storytelling

1. Choosing the story

When coming up with a concept for any sort of audio drama, it's important to pick a topic, story, or genre that is compatible without the use of visuals. Theoretically, you can make an audio drama on just about anything, but there's a varying degree of difficulty that comes with making sure that the audience clearly understands what's going on in the story. That brings us to the <u>number one rule</u>:

"Confusion is the killer of audio dramas"

The audience needs to be able to follow and understand what's going on in the story in order to enjoy what they're listening to. This concept might seem like a no-brainer, but it can become difficult without visuals. And there are always tradeoffs. If the characters or narrator goes into explicit detail of what's going on, the audience can become bored and/or the momentum of a scene slowed to a grinding halt. It also sounds very awkward to have characters in the scene over-specify who's doing what, as in, "…just a minute now, while I go open this crate." [Sound of crate]

The skill in writing for this medium is about finding a balance of exposition, writing techniques, and plot devices to fully illustrate what's going on without having to resort to painfully awkward dialogue. I pulled the crate quote above from an old 1934 radio play, "Calling All Cars." This play even included other gems like, "Look out, Russ! He's got a gun!"

Most of the classics from the golden age of radio drama tend to follow the same principle of letting the sound effects (commonly abbreviated as SFX) only accent what's going on in the story, rather than using it to explain the action and amplify the performances. Many of those shows required a Foley artist (defined in section 10-10) to reproduce the SFX live, because of the limitations of recording and technology. These restrictions greatly influenced the style of writing and dialogue, and consequently was accepted for most productions of the era. You had to *tell* the audience what was happening.

This historical age of radio dramas ended with the advent of television. TV was stunning in comparison and engaged people more by their being able to see the faces of actors as well as the settings. Radio storytelling couldn't compete and the advertising dollars migrated to the visual mediums. "Showing" instead of "telling" became the principle driver of narratives that would last for the next 70+ years. The popularity of the audio-only story was replaced by the increasing hunger of the visual monster... that is until now.

To return to the telling of stories with only using sound is a difficult principle to master, and many still don't have the full grasp on how to do it effectively. Some writers want to look back at the dialogue and story setups from the "golden age" for help, but modern audio dramas **should not** directly borrow or mimic the styles from the past. The tastes and sophistication of the public audience have evolved to something very different over the last part of the century. Films made even 20-30 years ago would fail in most current markets. Just as film has evolved, so too has audio drama.

Over the last few years I've started to develop a methodology to assist audio drama writers. Whether you're someone transitioning from film or are just starting to experiment in this medium, many of these concepts and tips are crucial to be able to communicate as effectively as possible with an audience through the use of sound. Think with your ears. Use all the tools at your disposal. From early on in the concept phase to the last second of the production:

"Sound needs to be the driving force of the story, and its biggest character."

Throughout this book I will refer to the term "aural image." "Aural," by itself, describes the artistic interpretation of audio. When I describe something as having vivid or lacking an "aural image," I'm referencing how clear the vision is in the audience's head. What sort of imagery comes to mind when hearing a particular sound or combination of many? Audio captured in downtown New York would have a distinct aural image of the city: the metro system, the traffic, the commotion, and the people. Every environment in every scene presents itself with unique opportunities to use Sound to connect to the listener. The beginning of that relationship starts with the initial concept.

"Why should this story be told as an audio drama?" "Does Sound play an integral part in the core concept?" These are questions to ask in the early concept phase when creating or adapting a story. Some genres and archetypes translate well, while others can struggle for clarity. The "golden age" took advantage of this, selecting concepts that strategically took advantage of enhancing the "aural image."

1. Suspense/ Thriller/ Horror/ Mystery

While I've received criticism in the past for creating a "horror" type story instead of something more serious, I have actually chosen the best genre to take advantage of all the elements of audio. Sound has a great deal in common with our own internal threat response system. A car screeching, a cry for help, a distant gunshot... all trigger a response that's very instinctive. We are alerted by hearing something before we ever see it. The genre also contributes to the idea that the aural image created in the minds of your audience is always more terrifying than anything that could be reproduced onscreen. It's not what is in front of you that's terrifying, it's what you don't see. In this case, the monsters are uniquely tailored in the imagination of the listener. They create something terrifying, specific for them.

Crime dramas are also in this category. The detective storylines with "suspect interviews" and "stakeouts" can verbally illustrate what's going on and create vivid aural images; similarly with mysteries and suspense. A large portion of newer podcasts tend to fall into this category.

2. Comedy

Everyone loves to laugh. It's one of the most unifying concepts, and is generally what can make or break most films nowadays. Plot sucks?

Horrible sets? Low production value? Doesn't matter if it's funny. We'll forgive most everything else, as long as we have a good time. I remember my days in film school, sitting through the extended waves of bad films- and the ones that received the most cheers at the end were those that hit the funny bone in the right way. The flip side is it's very difficult to pull off. Comedy writing is something that almost can't be learned. Collaboration can help in this genre. A group of writers to bounce off jokes and collaborate becomes a testing ground for what works and what doesn't.

3. Fantasy ... Sort of

This one is a two-sided coin, and generally one of the most mistake-prone genres of audio drama. The plus side: you can do *anything* and go *anywhere* with sound. You want to go to the moon? Easy. 5,000 leagues under the sea? Climb aboard. Rothgar 12 in the Galrack system... um... beam me up? There are lots of audio dramas that dwell in this genre. The series I created, We're Alive, can be considered fantasy, but the difference is that I chose a story and a reality that were grounded in concepts already established. I molded a world that was already familiar to the audience, with the realities and rules of that world built on top of.

> **"An audience needs to have at least some pre-existing concept of the world you are creating."**

A picture can be worth a thousand words, but that is also a concept that does not work within the realm of an audio drama. If an audience member has to imagine TOO much, then they will have a difficult time fully understanding and visualizing the created reality. They will be easily confused if the story jumps into an entirely new world and culture, without having a clear foundation.

Picture a mid-west farm in your head. I bet you see a barn, could be red. Maybe some animals, a white house with a large porch, and so on. It's easy to conjure up an image because most people already have a sense for what that environment looks like. And thus it's easy to build off of. The audience doesn't need to hear every detail about it.

Now imagine Rothgar 12. **Nothing** comes to mind, and that's the problem. Of course it's possible to include this information in the initial stages of the story, but it's far more difficult to do successfully. The story must spend a great deal of time explaining details of the setting, when the story is just getting off the ground. If you choose to go further into this world and deep into Rothgar 12, then beginning on the farm could be the first part of the journey. Start somewhere familiar to the audience, and it'll be easier to take them somewhere completely foreign.

4. Historical or Adaptation of existing works

If you're using a story that people are already familiar with, then visualization might not be as difficult. Selecting a character that's been portrayed thousands of times like Ebenezer Scrooge requires less description. Historical adaptations or events can be handled similarly. If the story takes place during World War II on the beaches of Normandy, in Egypt during the pharaohs, or in Rome during Caesar's reign... then there is a pre-conceived setting that's likely to be clear to the listener. And then there is the issue of *accuracy*. It's far easier to get things right by sound alone and not have to deal with styles, sets, or wardrobes. The difficult part comes with the character's accents, and making sure the dialect is consistent with the correct time period and location.

5. Action/ Adventure

This is a fun category, but requires a lot of sound design, Foley work, and music to pull it off. There's a lot more that needs to be done overall to make this genre clear to the listener, but it does lend itself well to the medium. There's a lot of room for Indiana Jones-like epics. Action in the story requires that the scenes are blocked out in the scripts. It also needs significantly more VOX work that isn't necessarily written dialogue, including extra grunts, breathing momentum, and such.

Then there are some genres or base concepts that are just **incredibly difficult to do right**, and/or they come with extra caveats to consider:

1. Sports-related stories. There's nothing like listening to a game of basketball being played, right? Throw in an announcer, sure, but it's still exceedingly difficult to create a clear aural image if you're focusing on the characters performing the action. Sports were created to be watched, so fundamentally, there are hurdles, but can be done with the right story and characters. A sports-story adaptation of "Remember the Giants" would work well in audio, as the focus of the story wasn't necessarily on the field.

2. Solo acts. To write audio drama is to write dialogue, and if there's only one character, there's no way to communicate outside of the character's head. There are devices to make it work, but overall it's a challenge to not make it sound awkward.

3. Fan Fiction. Those light saber SFX and Han Solo storylines that you think you'd love to expand upon will only generate Cease and Desist letters. Why? Because in order to maintain control of a copyright, the copyright holder has to ensure that they maintain control of their IP (Intellectual Property), otherwise it can be construed as public domain. There's nothing worse than to create an amazing audio drama that you can't share with the world due to legal reasons. They can be successful in the short term because of pre-existing fan bases, but in the long run the IP-rights holder will find out. If you still want to attempt making something based on an existing story, **get permission first.** If it's a parody, there are protections also in place, so check with an entertainment lawyer if you plan to monetize in any way.

4. Stories that overly involve fantasy effects as the foundation. Sound effects that provide the framework for the story that aren't naturally occurring must be explained. An audience won't be able to identify what blaster beams are from laser streams to plasma pistols. Super Power "sounds" from comic stories are an example of this. If the effects are established slowly and with careful sound design, "Signature Sounds" can become part of the character of the story. Crafting these can require a great deal of sound designer expertise.

1.1 Titles

One of the most difficult choices you will have to make will be concerning your title. The title is your brand, the first thing that people associate with your story. It has to be clear and catchy, and also not already being used. Be sure to check search engines to ensure that your title is your own. Also, you might want to check online for www.thetitleofyourproject.com, to make sure the domain is clear. Is your title clear when spoken? If you tell someone the name as a web address, will a user be able to easily find it?

Once you pick your title, you're stuck with it. So take your time, and test it. A short title can become lost in search engines, and a long one can get truncated. "The new adventures of ..." Twenty-two characters are wasted for just that part of the introduction alone. In this modern era, the online visibility and availability of a title can be a major factor in its marketability and success.

No pressure, right? I include this section not to deter anyone, but only to emphasize that the decision in creating a title is long-lasting, and should be considered seriously.

1.2 Creating a compelling story

How do you tell a story that captivates someone? There has never been one right answer, and the taste and appetite of an audience constantly changes over time. No other way to say it, they must love your idea. What is it about your story that is the hook to grab a core audience? That's for you to find out, and then spend a lot of time developing, because an "idea" is not a "story." We all have those friends… "I have a great idea for a movie!" And often within that statement is a concept, one or two characters, but that's it. There's a lot more to telling a story than an idea or a concept. There are story arcs, conflict, pacing, character growth and discovery, ticking clocks, layering, plants and payoffs, etc… Writing is a process, it's work. You'll have to do research, interviews, and even travel on occasions to try and connect with what it is you're creating.

My process is different from most, but I feel that it might be beneficial to certain writers who are looking at different ways of approaching "story crafting," or if you prefer "word engineering," as my mechanical brain tends to think of it. My intention in this section is to show ways to root out what's important in a story. I will give examples of developing the simple concept to a more complicated arc that carries several characters on an emotional journey. While the book objective is to create scripts for audio drama, these concepts could apply to manuscripts and novels as well.

Let's get back to that notion of the idea. All stories start with this initial concept, and require brainstorming. You have to take time to *think* before you *write*. Prepare: scribble notes, outline, record voice memos, whatever you need to fully understand what you want to write before starting the script format. It's not impossible to come up with a good story by jumping directly into creating it, but I find it is much harder to then adjust the big arcs and ideas that are the pillars for the story.

Ideas and concepts are flexible, come from many directions and sources, but seem to never show up when you're trying to find them. So when they do come to life, no matter where you are, when that spark lights up in your head, don't let it get away. Jot your ideas down on paper, or with voice recording software on your phone (Voice Memo in iOS). It doesn't matter how it's done, as long as it's somewhere permanent. Sometimes just the process of annotating it is enough to cement it into one's brain.

I've spent months and even years thinking about certain storylines and characters. And then the time would come when I would be in the shower, and the idea or solution to a story problem would pop up out of nowhere. I'd rush to record it onto my phone, sometimes still dripping everywhere. Often times I'll continually flesh out ideas of multiple storylines at the same time, and shelve a lot of undeveloped concepts. Once I've finally found that last piece of the story puzzle, that concept is ready for the next stage of development. If you rush trying to make a story, it will feel like it was created that way.

Inspiration comes from all around us, and sometimes you might have a concept or idea that's similar to something already created. Well, so what? Just because a genre of story-archetype has been told previously doesn't mean it can't be told again in a unique way. How many times has someone told a "alien" story? What about Anne Rice's Vampires vs. Stephanie Meyer's Vampires? Even though many of us might clearly favor one over the other, it doesn't matter because there's an audience for both. I sometimes hear the argument that, "Every story has been told." Well, if that's true no one would keep writing. What's the one thing that's different? **Your perspective.**

Ask yourself, why it is that you want to tell a story? What is your unique perspective? Why are YOU best fit to write about this?

There's only two ways you can write: you either have to write what you know, or learn what you want to tell. I originated the concept for <u>We're Alive</u>, clearly a zombie apocalyptic story, and it's obviously something I haven't experienced. However, the unique perspective I brought with it was being a combat veteran soldier, having the experiences of war, the tension, the stress, and what sorts of tactical planning might be involved. This background was unique to me, and something special I felt I could bring to the genre.

When brainstorming the kinds of things you would like to write about, a simple launching point could be to figure out a "journey" that one character needs to go on. You can always add more supporting cast members, but keep it simple for now. And for this journey to begin, you need to know where you're going first. Writing a story can often be like a maze, it's easier to start at the end. The writing will be constantly working towards that goal and it will feel natural and connected, rather than disjointed and stuck trying to figure out how to "end it."

Another reason for this preparation is because **endings matter**! I've had friends and colleagues tell me how much they loved a particular story that followed people whose plane crash-landed on an island, but that didn't end as succinctly as they hoped. Some would justify it by saying, "It wasn't the ending that made it enjoyable, it was the journey," while others felt like their time was wasted because of the overall inconsistencies in the conclusion. You don't necessarily have to cater to what people want in your writing, but you can make the journey AND ending work with each other, making the last impression carry on after the finale.

The "it was all a dream" stories sometimes work, but not often, and the process of making them work becomes much more unforgiving with audio dramas. The audience for this medium generally spends more physical time tuning in than they typically would for movies. If the entire 6-hour epic is based on a contrived "lie," i.e., a dream, then the audience will feel their time is wasted because they weren't experiencing something real to the characters. There are ways it can work, but generally one of the biggest mistake with new writers is that they want the "gotcha" ending which can leave listeners feeling cheated.

Keep it simple. Many writers try and shoot for the moon and create a huge epic without first spending the time to understand and complete simple stories- an essential step before moving on to the more complex ones. All writers have to start somewhere, but it's best to start small and work your way up. Be warned, even the simplest stories can be the most complicated to write. But also, simple stories with natural and compelling characters often win Oscars.

Every author writes for two: for themselves, and for the audience. If ever an author emphasizes exclusively one over the other, the story can suffer. A writer might enjoy killing off every character, but the audience won't. The audience might not want anyone to die, but the author might need to. It's a balance, a give and take. Treat the audience as someone who deserves to be entertained, with a balance of positives and negatives, ups and downs. There is a relationship that develops between the creators and consumers, and they need to trust you as a storyteller.

I want to address a few more concepts, and the best way to cover them is through the story workshop. This is something that I've done with beginning writers who struggle to get a concept off the ground. The process can start with something as simple as a one-line plot.

1.2a Pacing and Tension*

Whether writing or editing a scene, the speed or anticipation of an event determines the story's pace. Pacing is a simple concept with infinite variables and an area where an editor's experience shines. By knowing when or how to draw out or shorten narrative situations, the writer inevitably changes the impact it gives the audience. The pacing can be adjusted in editing too, completely changing performances by shortening or lengthening lines.

In the audio world, editors don't have as many limitations as the film world -- they can change time and space to almost infinite degrees with the recorded lines. They can make the person seem further away, change every variable of the distance between dialogue, add sound effects to accentuate a performance, and replace fragments of sentences or words. Editors can manipulate even the tiniest inflection of a syllable. Those adjustments happen within the first few stages of post in the vocal cut by a sound dialogue editor.

Editing experience guides how timing assists the dramatization of the scene. How fast does a character respond to a question? The length of silence before answering could be an admission of guilt or nervousness when it's too quick. The actors often set the pace and rhythm of a conversation in recording, but editors have the ability and freedom to change things. When the actors participate in an aural-only scene, they have no idea what actions or sound effects go between the lines, or how long those actions should take place in the world.

Pacing speeds up the action or draws out the tension. In a bank heist scene, for example, a ticking clock emphasizes the impending doom of getting caught. The longer spent in the bank, the more likely the robbers fail. Yet, the moment they first enter the bank should be accelerated, heightened with fast-paced movement required to do the job correctly. By having moments of action, tension, and then release, a rhythm is created that involves the audience and draws them into the experience. The listener will then become more a part of the story. The rise and fall of action also allows the audience to take a break from focus, so they can relax from the tension and breathe. Constant tension will snap the engagement of the audience like a rubber band. It has to be released at times to let the pressure moments have greater impact and value.

- **TENSION** - Bank robbers prepare to rob the bank.
- **ACTION** - Bank robbers come into the scene and secure the location.
- **TENSION** - Bank robbers hold all the witnesses, while they slowly crack the safe.
- **RELEASE** - All the money is in the bag, the plan is perfect at this moment.
- **ACTION** - Run to get to the exits and getaway car.
- **TENSION** - The robbers exit is blocked; there is no easy way out, a standoff ensues.
- **RELEASE** - The robbers make it to the car, lose the cops, and breathe a sigh of relief.

1.2b The Outline*

To capture and retain an interest in a narrative, the events of the story must be organized and paced to fit the story and the audience best. As such, an author should create an outline to ensure that the overall emotional structure guides the plot's development. The emotional arc — while limited to the insides of the character — is essential to what happens outside of the character. Placing the proper events at the right emotional junctions ensures that what is at stake is truly valuable both to the story and the characters. It's all an elaborate entanglement of ideas and feelings that is ultimately up to the audience's interpretation. The author wants to create a captivating emotional rollercoaster for the audience.

Let's use that theme-park coaster as an analogy. First, stories begin with all the semantics: the wait and anticipation for the ride to start, and loading/securing people into the individual carts. This is the introduction, the opening credits. It establishes audience expectations and builds intrigue. Seeing the coaster in action before they get on draws them to joining the ride's queue and climbing into the cart: the equivalent of an inciting incident that propels all else.

As the coaster gains steam, it often climbs a large hill to build momentum. This is the story's building phase, where the world and characters get established: their routines, the questions, and introductions to everyone and everywhere. This section may not seem exciting, but it's necessary to achieve the highs and lows of the story's trajectory.

When the carts make their initial descent, it's fast and exhilarating: something has happened, and the passengers are on the ride of their lives. Energy has been released, and now the audience is rushing through unexpected, breathtaking twists and turns. The author has set the stage for the story's central conflict. These are the thrilling adventures the audience wants to experience. Nothing should come easy, and the struggle should be engaging and exciting in a new way.

Don't forget the loops! Defying expectations is all part of the game. Sometimes the audience doesn't know where they are, but they'll soon find their way and enjoy the state of disorientation from which they emerged. Stay too long upside down, however, and the audience might fall out. Defy expectations, but don't derail the track of the story for the sake of spectacle. Keep the audience guessing what's around the bend.

Eventually, the momentum may hit a low moment and need to be picked back up. What goes down must go back up. A roller coaster often has a track segment that takes the cart higher one last time to reach the final thrills needed to complete the journey. This is the build to the climax of the story. There's usually a natural low moment when the Hero is at their lowest and must find a way out of it. If the ride stays at a constant speed, it becomes repetitive for the audience. A change in variation and tempo allows room for anticipation. What is coming over the last horizon? What will happen to our hero? Will they get out of their predicament?

Finally, we reach the denouement: the last chapter where the climax reaches its conclusion and the audience experiences a final thrill before going home. To make a lasting impression, the narrative conclusion must justify the length of the journey, often including more spins and loops than most of the previous track. How the passengers feel as they step off the coaster is often the most important.

Did they enjoy the ride? Will they tell their friends? Word of mouth is one of the most potent forms of motivation in feeding art. Those who are moved by or connected with something will often tell others about their experience. And, of course, those who don't enjoy the ride after investing their time will complain about their experience.

No matter how the ride was intended and designed, it could ultimately produce smiles on some and frowns on others.

Almost every story breaks down into a basic three-act structure, one of the most commonly used in media. While the three components can apply to a single episode or series of episodes (season), they also apply to an entire series.

Act 1. Establish the world
Act 2. Live in it, establishing the problems
Act 3. Solving them.

Outside of this format, others have created their own story formulas, a simple narrative structure and character arc that follows a particular order of events that dramatically pays off. Dan Harmon, the creator of *Rick and Morty* and *Community*, came up with what he calls "The Story Circle," an eight-stage process in which the narrative ultimately follows:

1. Establish the Protagonist (You).
2. Establish their need.
3. Go! Cross the threshold to get need (The chaos side of circle).
4. Search! Road of Trials. All the ways Step #3 didn't work.
5. Find! Find what they were looking for.
6. Take! Pay the price for what was found.
7. Return! Bring it home, new need.
8. Change! Test the change, the final showdown of Hero.

The full circle ends with the character returning to where they started, perhaps outwardly seeming the same but with significant inner change. Looking back at *Goldrush*, I can see this pattern in my personal storytelling:

1. The lives of the soldiers are established. They have fun, enjoy their world.
2. They long for adventure and excitement, and not being the lowest in their world. They believe that the gold would change that.
3. They must first collect info on where the gold is, arrange transportation, and head out on their journey.
4. The helicopter must be fixed up under pressure, and time is of the essence.
5. They found the gold, and ultimately feel like they succeeded.
6. The helicopter breaks down and they pay the price for their journey, nearly dying. Finding other survivors puts in perspective what value gold actually has in their world.

7. They realize that the people of the Atlas are of more value than the gold and their new need is to escape and return home.
8. We test the climax' change by testing whether they truly value people when weighed against material things. Everyone's distorted view of the gold exacts a sizable price to remove, and, in the end, what matters comes full focus. The soldiers return home, the same way they were before, but having undergone so much and learned together. They've become a better team.

Many stories can be broken down into similar patterns. They all attempt to provide a satisfying emotional journey for an audience. Not all art is meant to satisfy, as well. There are pieces where the intended lasting impression is horror and unease rather than resolution or peace. In the end, the artist/writer determines what the audience is supposed to feel at any given moment.

Characters won't have a sense of accomplishment without any sacrifice, and there is no winning without losing first. These are the trials and tribulations that we mimic in our own lives. We strive for independence and success and want others to experience that as well. Everyone wants a sympathetic character to succeed, but the entertainment comes from watching them struggle to achieve their goal before obtaining success.

1.3 Story Workshop

The simple story concept:

A road trip with a young boy and his group of friends go to a concert several states away.

If we focus first on style and theme, it feels to me like it might be a light-hearted, friendly adventure. I use the word "feel" here intentionally, because you, as the author, have to interpret the story you see in your head. Explore the ideas and concepts that fit the world you're creating. You are the master of this customized universe.

Think about this group of friends on a journey across several states. It's going to be a long way, filled with drama and road bumps, literally. Already at this point, I can start to recall my own personal experiences with extended driving trips. What sorts of things do I recall that might become obstacles for my characters? More of the story starts to fill in, inspired and connected by personal life events. The more ways the story connects to the author, the more authentic it will feel. And the more unique and natural will details start to shine through.

What are some of the road-bumps?

The group heads out, and there's drama soon after; someone left their cell phone on top of the car at the rest stop. That was a huge headache, but they got through it. Then they found an abandoned house on the side of the road that night, and they stopped to see it. One friend swears he saw a ghost, and then later gives everyone a scare when he jumps out at them. At the next gas stop they meet Jim Carrey, and they all took a picture with him.

Ok, so maybe not all those things have happened to me, but as the writer you need to keep things unique, and meeting a celebrity is entirely plausible. Continuing to feel out the story, I'm already starting to wonder how their journey is going to end. Thinking about all these upcoming hardships, I don't see it ending the way the character has planned.

Finally, they make it to the concert- and the event has been canceled. Everyone has to head home.

Even though the ending might be a let-down to the characters doesn't necessarily mean it's an unfulfilling ending for the audience. Life is full of disappointments; it's realistic. And any journey that is predictable becomes uninteresting very quickly.

How the characters respond is what will provide the satisfying conclusion, and an opportunity to defy expectations. My first brainstorm provided only the foundation of events, but nothing yet about *who* will be on the trip. After all, the characters should be the focus of any story, not the plot.

Let's start talking about the young boy mentioned in the first concept-line. Start asking "what ifs?" to flush out the reason WHY anyone in the story does what they do, looking for their true motivation. A character's motivation should be the driving force for what happens, and it's the best way for everything to feel organic. That there is a "journey" to go on in the first place should be inspired internally from the people in the story. Something has to be at stake. The larger the prize, the more character motivation and audience interest.

What if the result of going to the concert was more of a life-altering event than expected for our main protagonist (the good guy)? What if this concert is the first time the boy gets to meet his real father, not knowing before who he was? That he was actually *the star* of the rock band he was going to see. How would that encounter change him?

That would be a big character arc, and in terms of an emotional passage, it's feasible under the right conditions. If you choose an arc that pushes a character too far, it won't be believable. Too small of an arc, and the events leading up to it won't matter. What do I mean by a "character's arc"? It simply describes the change that one character undergoes over the course of a story. Does the character improve his behavior in some way or become worse (great example: Breaking Bad). How does a person change from the beginning to the end of the story? If everyone stays the same, you have just a plot piece, not a character piece.

I see a lot of potential in this "real father" option for the storyline, so let's keep exploring possibilities. With this general character arc and story closure, we can further scrutinize the road-bumps along the way and make sure they all contribute to the ending in some manner. We can do this, and start to construct the framework of the story by using tools called *Plant & Payoff* (P&P) and what I call *The Establishment Principle* (EP).

Plant and Payoff: When most writers think of Plant and Payoff, they typically think of "Chekhov's Gun," where the weapon itself appears early on to establish its existence with the audience. "If, in the first chapter, you say there is a gun hanging on the wall, you should make quite sure that it is going to be used further on in the story." - *Anton Chekhov*

"Plants" aren't limited to just physical objects. It can be a line, a metaphor, concept, or anything established early on that will grow into something by the end.

If there was ever a time you watched a movie and thought "where did *that* come from?!," then it wasn't established properly. You can get away with almost anything as long as you prepare for it early enough in the story. People tend to accept change slowly, in both real life and in the stories they love.

Enter The Establishment Principle. I like to think of The Establishment Principle working like poison. A little exposure over a long period, and your audience will accept anything; they build a tolerance. The frog and the hot water story...

The Establishment Principle: The more outlandish the concept, the earlier it needs to be established.

Our story about the boy could feature extraterrestrial aliens if we show them early enough. Stories that don't follow the EP can break their own narrative. If you're doing a film about magic elves but don't establish any magic in the story until the end, then the story will be disingenuous to the audience.

Same goes with a plant and no payoff- it can become a "red herring," or something meant to mislead the audience (good and bad). For long-form stories or a series format, these plants and payoffs can be spread out over entire seasons of content. They are the foundation for open-ended storylines, and provide consistent questions requiring listeners to continue to tune in for answers.

Since the boy meets his father for the first time at the conclusion of the story (the concert), we have to establish early on why he doesn't know him. Otherwise the conclusion could be the ride home.

We establish the relationship he has with his mother, and perhaps hint that something isn't quite right between them. This gives an opportunity to add conflict with his step-dad; maybe the boy is not even aware that the step-dad isn't his real dad.

The protagonist and his step-dad don't share the same passion; the boy loves music, the stepfather loathes it. The protagonist has natural musical talent, an innate gift that neither his step-father or mother have. The mother opposes the journey, but for other reasons. The real reasons stay hidden.

The best plants establish a balance of being concealed initially, but become obvious later on. If the mother's hindrance to the boy's journey is too strong, it could clue the audience in on the subtext too early.

How does this change the perspective of our young boy? How can we further develop his emotional arc? An audience wants to see characters change, for the better or worse. Answer the question, "Why are we following this person?"

The boy is longing for something different in his life. His goals contradict his parents, and his rebellious nature will force him on this journey without his parents' consent.

Conflict is starting to come to the surface. All stories need some struggle in order to be interesting, but it needs to come naturally. If you force conflict, the characters don't have clear reasons for why they do anything, only that the plot needed it to happen. At all times, continue to ask why a character does something. As well as asking "what ifs?"

- *What if...* the boy's rebellious nature is the internal drive that brings him to his real father at the concert, and the boy realizes that his rebellious nature parallels the same thing his father went through, which ruined his father's life?
- *What if...* his mother's efforts to keep him from seeing his father wasn't really about control, but was about her trying to protect him?

The boy's character arc and themes for the story become clearer. We now have established a strong starting and ending point where the boy undergoes a large transformation with an eye-opening experience. Arriving at the canceled concert may be the physical completion of his trip, but the real journey is more about his emotional transition and character growth.

When the boy meets his father, the protagonist realizes who really cares about him. He returns home to his mother and step-dad, having grown wiser and more understanding, and improves his relationship with his real parents.

The intention and goals of the story are now clear, and we can move on to fleshing out more of the supporting details and develop the characters further.

1.4 What's in a name?

First time writers love to go online and use name generators to identify their characters. I just attempted the first one that came up and here's what was computed: Ammar Vitale Pastore. Try again: Víkingr Keshet Lowe . Name generators don't work. *Ever.* Why? Because people don't name children randomly. Names are careful selections by the parents, reflecting and honoring people from the family, culture, or are just trending and become common for the location and time period. A name tells a lot of information about a character without them speaking a word. Brevity is important not only in scripts, but all writing. Spend time to develop a name that's lasting, important, and means something, because you'll be working with it for a long time.

The greatest "name-smith" of our generation and my favorite author, J.K. Rowling, said in an interview that she often has more fun coming up with names for characters than she does writing for them. One of her methods is very advanced word-smithing.

Albus Dumbledore: Dumbledore=bumblebee in Old English. Rowling says that it "seemed to suit the headmaster, because one of his passions is music and I imagined him walking around humming to himself." Albus also means "white" in latin. He may have been named for his white beard or maybe simply in the description of a good wizard. Character qualities can be established before anything has been written about them on the page.

One of my secret places where I collect ideas for names of my characters is in a cemetery. By finding out when and where a person lived gives me a sense of accuracy and depth without an intense amount of research. When using gravestones, I recommend to swap the names around so that the graves are only references to keep anonymity. After all, this "likeness" must be coincidental for legal reasons. Surnames (Last names) have such rich history, sometimes positive and negative. They often come with connotations and associations that an author may not be aware of, so be sure to check against records of any real person.

For this story, I'm going to use some cultural references as clues to discover the boy's name. We'll use "A" for now. Starting to think about the timeframe of when the rockstar father met A's mother, I imagine them to be hippies. If I chose "Moon Beam," an informed audience could fill in the extra details, but that name is a bit too close to identifying a real person.

Looking up "Moon Beam" and other "Hippy Names" on Google, I found an association: "Ty." Digging a little further into flower-power-inspired names, I selected "Dawn" for the mother. And for the step-father, "Phil," which just comes from my gut reaction for a very straight-edge/uninspired/plain name. For the biological father Ty meets at the concert, I decided to create two names: his stage name and real name (he's a rock star after all). "Sky Wolf," seen on concert posters fit perfectly, with "Trent" as his real name. I used Trent because it reminded me of "Trench," as if he's stuck in something and can't get out, and it fit for Ty because it's common for families to use similar starting letters for names.

1.4a Character and Story Wrappers*

Stories are meant to communicate with audiences in ways not always apparent on the surface. As with any art form, added levels of subtext lurk underneath every scene. What a character says vs. what they mean merely scratches the surface of what's genuinely being conveyed in a scene. Authors have perspectives and strive to create meaning behind every action and character. Aural symbolism (comparable to film symbolism) describes what is truly meant by the various designs and features of narrative audio. The heavy drop of bass in the background or a door's closing at a particular moment could be intended to communicate something to the listener beyond surface dialogue. The deeper the levels of complexity in symbolism and subtext, the more audio storytelling's overall richness. Sound should always tell the story.

Similarly, the plot and overall events of the story are the actualizations of the narrative, the surface, but the underlying symbolism could be different. Like a candy bar, a wrapper presents a reality to the world, but the truth lies underneath. The message and themes of my "zombie" story are not the surface events of violence, but the underlying choices of the characters in a world that continues to oppress them. The infected themselves have vastly different meanings behind their existence and intentions. The characters, on their own, present an outside wrapper: their portrayal to the audience. Their actions hint at inner motivation, but once the veil recedes, the listener experiences the insides and understands the character's truth. Humans are fascinated with the unknown motivators of our fellows, and a narrative must indulge in all the aspects and layers of both truth and story reality.

The characters all mix, like a bowl of candies, where each character adds their unique flavor. Too many of the same becomes bland, and variety is key. The wrappers may all look similar if not the same, like soldiers wearing a uniform, but the ingredients within matter most.

Characters, like real people, CHOOSE to present their own wrappers to the world. Who they are underneath is hidden, often guarded and secret. Everyone has an aspect of themselves that they don't want to be known. However, the author must comprehend and understand what motivates their creations. The author knows all this, takes appropriate measures, then presents the mystery bowl to the audience, leaving a sense of discovery as each candy is unwrapped.

The author controls the audience's experience in how everything is created and heard, but the flavors of each are up to audience interpretation. Everyone's taste is different, and not all stories are compatible with specific palates. Others don't often know what they want until they've tried something new: a combination of flavors they didn't expect. All authors should strive to achieve a refreshing story that cleanses the palate for any stale medium.

1.4b Natural Character Evolution*

What makes a person tick? What makes you tick? What drives you to get out of bed in the morning or complete a task? Motivation lies inside every person and prompts every action. Otherwise, no one would do anything. A character eats when they're hungry, defecates when they are full, and requires sleep at the point of exhaustion. The more writers respect the reality of the world that they create, the more authentic their stories. The goal of all writers is the suspension of disbelief, and reality drives audience interpretation. Anyone who subscribes to true crime understands that the element of truth promotes the genre's intrigue.

How does a writer create a person? In a way, they don't. Your parents created a *person*; writers create *characters*. Understanding the difference allows liberties in how all stories unfold. A character is *fabricated*, engineered, and designed. At their essence, they are made up and explicitly tailored to act and feel a certain way at the most opportune moments in a story. A person is real, a character is not. Essentially a writer can do whatever they want with a character, compelling them to work in favor of the story to act the way they are when needed.

Every character has a birthday. When were they born? At what age were they exposed to events that influenced who they have become? Characters do not have age ranges; they have a year they were born — a date, a time, and a place. What environment they grew up in at that time and everything around them influenced their development. A child who witnessed the moon landing could have a far different life perspective in their adult future than a child who didn't. Instead of focusing on creating a character to serve a purpose, create a character whose purpose arises naturally from the events of their past.

Let's take a villain, for example. All good villains are sympathetic, and they believe that their perspective is more valid than anyone else's. What "bad" they are doing is not wrong, but instead justified by their reasoning. Why do they feel that way? Answering this question often serves as a subplot of the story, but a writer should define the background that informs a villain's reasoning when first creating them. While random acts of violence occur in the real world with people, we are establishing characters to which NOTHING should be casual or random.

There are many villain cliches. These tropes are occasionally fitting to use — specific stories are often interwoven into the themes so densely that the style is lost without them. A few examples:

1. My family/home was destroyed, and I must get revenge on who did it!
2. Some unknown force is making me do the things I'm doing unwittingly (passive storytelling)
3. I am defined by my ability (superhero tropes)
4. Stock historical villains like Nazis
5. Thugs, just following orders and as substantial as paper
6. I'm just evil and I like it.

The list can go on and on, In fact, there are so many villain tropes, that it is almost tricky NOT to create a character that follows one. Instead, start by ignoring the tropes and dive into the heart of the villain. What makes them tick? Why are they evil? The pursuit of money is often uninteresting. Stereotypical mobsters, gangsters, thieves, or thugs all want gold or money, but that motivation is relatively thin for characterization. There needs to be more.

One recommendation: do some research. Find a character in history that might resemble that of the intended villain motivation. Scandals are littered throughout history, where people who have exploited others and done horrible things for personal gain. Sometimes the intended outcome conceals events that happened in their past. Villains' motivations dictate their actions: those who rise from the ashes rarely want to return, love makes people do crazy things, early family issues often echo throughout someone's life, and even instances where villainy is a matter of perspective.

If love is the intended motivation of a villain, then we can understand their brokenness by stepping back and creating a history of negative love-related incidents. Perhaps early in life, a traumatic event of rejection grew more substantial, like flowers tossed in the face of a teen at an emotionally vulnerable state. Specific traumatic incidents will leave wounds that fester and worsen over time. Even if properly treated, trauma leaves scars behind. No human alive lacks an event that shaped who they are. Those conditions and experiences are what a writer gets to create. It's a constant formula and never-ending equation of what circumstance occurs in a character's past that will culminate in the intended reaction later in life. This formula is how a writer can truly manifest the mind of their character to find their ultimate goal or their "want".

Under the right circumstances, many people would toss away *money* for *love*: the unachievable, ideal compatibility of a lifetime companion. A character who wants love desperately enough to be willing to hurt someone else to achieve it is by all definitions a *villain*, lacking a sense of empathy and not seeing how their actions affect others. This doesn't necessarily mean they are a bad person, but in the case of story-fabrication, they are simply creating the obstacle that hinders the hero. Anyone against our hero(protagonist) is the *antagonist*, commonly referred to as a *villain*.

In this sample scenario, our protagonist has found their true love, but the antagonist also has the same love interest, and they feel they cannot live with the competition of adoration. This conflict is genderless and ageless and prevents the hero from fully attaining love. The "love-triangle" setup has been used time and time again throughout narrative storytelling since the first dramas in history. Regarding plot and emotional conflict, some would argue that every modern narrative could trace its roots back to Shakespeare's dramatic pieces. The simplest breakdowns of emotional conflict come from man vs. man, man vs. himself, and man vs. nature. The difference in every instance are the chosen characters, their background, and the plot vehicle that drives the story. By creating genuine characters born into their own world, they live and grow inside the narrative, flushing out the rest of the world and their motivation in a natural way.

1.5 Conflict is Key

I had a writing professor, Ross Brown, once tell me a great example of what makes a compelling conflict, and how it's all about *what's at stake*. If you watch sports, then you know how much excitement comes from watching a pre-season game. What about a regular season game? How about the play-offs, or the Super Bowl? The level of excitement increases with every advancement, because more is at stake. Raising the stakes adds more flavor to conflict, but like all flavoring, there can always be too much or the wrong proportions.

Let's dive into the main conflict. What is the driving or motivating factor that starts the story?

Ty is at an age where he could move out. He's been planning the concert trip for a long time; it's the farewell tour of his all-time favorite band, Sky Wolf. His step-father, Phil, responds by saying, if he goes, then he will "have to find someplace new to live."

A bit extreme, maybe a bit too much sauce on the plot, but we could balance it out by supporting the conflict with circumstances like: Dawn and Phil rely on Ty to help run the family business, and his leaving puts them in a financial strain, possibly worker scheduling complications, or, the one we'll go with: **Ty, by going to the concert, would blow off an interview for a good college. A life that Phil wants Ty to explore.** That one fits, as it equalizes the perspective of both sides of the argument. This choice also contributes to parallels drawn later between Ty's mistakes and the mistakes of his biological father.

The spear-head of the conflict, "Kicking Ty out," needs to elevate progressively; it shouldn't be the first attempt to solve the problem. Elevate the conflict gradually and organically by using different *tactics*:
- **His mother, Dawn, tries to give him simple reasons not to go.**
- **Phil tries to back up Dawn, offering alternatives.**
- **When that doesn't work, the parents escalate to more extreme methods.**

We know that Phil and Dawn are just trying to do what's best for their son, but sometimes the worst things can be done with the best of intentions. This helps establish an empathetic relationship with the audience.

There also needs to be more than one conflict in a story. Conflict layering is how real life develops. We deal with multiple things at once.

Ty's friend, Sam, is the one who leaves his phone on top of the car and loses it after they drive off. What sort of ideas would make that conflict worse/more interesting? There could be baby pictures on his phone that only he has. *OR...* **He has provocative pictures of his girlfriend on it. The phone is not locked with a passcode, and his girlfriend also happens to be on the trip as well, a very pissed-off girl named Erin.**

What sort of additional conflicts could arise from that one mistake?

1.6 Motivation moves the story

As you continue to block out and create additional scenes, remember at all times that each character needs their own *motivation* and *objectives*, and how they achieve them is defined by their *tactics*.

When characters' motivations oppose each other, natural conflict is created that organically fits in the story.

That one concept is the foundation of why people watch movies and relate to stories in general; they either sympathize *with* or *against* a character. Characters feel more genuine and real when you, the author, can always answer the questions, "why is the character doing this?" or "why is the character in this scene?" No matter how large or small a character, they need a reason to do something. It can be simple or complex, but no one just stands there to say a few words. On the other hand, the world is continuing on while the audience is focused on a small bit of it. What is someone doing "off-scene"?

Ty's friends, Erin and Sam, who will be accompanying him on the journey, need to have some motivation to be there too.

Sam loves the band, Sky Wolf, and is even more of a hardcore fan than Ty. Sam is also the "devil on Ty's shoulder," always causing him to get into trouble. Sam just wants Ty to let loose and have fun in life, and also feels Ty's parents are too overbearing. Erin is coming along with Sam because they're a couple, engaged, and soon to be married.

Unbeknownst to Ty, Sam and Erin are going to be moving away after they get married. Sam was offered a job somewhere else, and this might be their last trip together.

These motivations compliment the main story because they don't obstruct the main conflict. They only further add dimension to the other characters and what they want out of this trip. Everyone wants something different.

Always continue to raise the stakes. Can you make the bumps along the way be more difficult to overcome? Are conditions at their worst? Dig a hole in front of the characters, and the deeper you make it, the more enthralling the climb out will be.

In our story, we can have **the characters run out of money, get lost, car breaks down, and even be forced to ask Ty's parents for help, all the more difficult because he ran away from them.**

But there *are* LIMITS. Know the story you're telling. If all of a sudden Ty needs a bone marrow transplant from his biological father to save his life, that would be trying to put too much into the story. Everything in the story so far fits the confines of this world's reality.

One of the largest limiting factors to any story is how to use DEATH. A character's demise is, after all, the ultimate stake for any person. But death will only have power in the story if it means something. Too often I find stories using death as just a way to remove someone from the page, budget, or is meant solely for shock value. Remember: *We're supposed to care.*

This is the key to every successful story. The audience must care about the people in the story. They need someone to root for, to be sympathetic towards.

Creating a large-cast show like We're Alive, I was able to bring in a variety of characters from different backgrounds, and develop a very diverse show. One thing that I find interesting is that many of the fans' favorites were the villains. It's a tricky thing, but the audience should care about them, too, or at the very least want to understand them.

HOW DO WE CARE ABOUT VILLAINS? Everyone must have a reason to do what they do, even if they're bad reasons. Pure evil is boring, and unrealistic.

In We're Alive, I created a group of prisoners who essentially had the same objective as our main characters, but what made them different was the means and the extent they were willing to go to achieve their goals. Proper and clear motivation makes the characters, good or bad, *believable*. From a certain point of view, they can be relatable. Phil may just want the best for Ty. What good father wouldn't?

1.7 Conceiving Action

We have established our general arcs, are familiar with our characters, but where do they go? What *exactly* do they do?

Action that supports conflict needs to occur throughout the story; it will move the narrative forward in a direction that contributes to the ending. As a writer you always want your characters doing something, and with every event there are ways to build the relationships between them and advance the plot.

If you're stuck, then look for inspiration on these sorts of specifics and the story environment, which can greatly help dictate how events unfold. In the case of <u>We're Alive</u>, the places where the adventures occurred completely controlled the storyline. I found a great deal of inspiration from looking at reference photos, documentary and video segments. Even Google Maps can be a great way to put yourself in the location of your story while writing. Just dropping the little man onto the road of the map and looking around can help spur all kinds of new ideas. What do you see? What would the characters experience? Any additional physical obstacles they might have to overcome?

When I visited a jail for <u>Lockdown</u>, I had no idea that there were no buttons in the elevator, that someone else controlled where it went via a camera in another part of the building. Those sorts of details are writer's gold. I could use those restrictions to further enhance the story, adding a sense of authenticity and personalization that's often missed. If we trace the route that Ty and his friends go, maybe there's a place along the way that could inspire **the haunted shack scene**.

As you start to figure out *what* and *where* events take place in the story, the next key step is to figure out *when*. When dealing with the journey's structure and pacing, **timing is everything**. Your audience can become tired or bored if nothing happens for long periods, or worn out by a constant barrage of action. Alternating between action and set-up/build-up gives the audience time to relax and absorb more of the story. Varying the levels of tension can heighten the impact. With Ty's journey, the order of events can enhance the arc of the characters, by putting the physical locations of conflict (blown out tire at the side of the road) at the same times of emotional conflict (Realization that the phone is missing). Like the motion of a wave, alternate between tension and release, and use choice moments to surprise the audience by changing the tempo. Once you feel you have chunks of action, or what are referred to as "sequences," then start to organize those moments into an outline. You have just created the roadmap of events in the story.

1.8 Words on the Page

All the ideas are in place. The outline is completed, and you know the characters, the arcs, the conflicts, and the ending. Now comes writing words on the page. It's not necessary to figure out everything about the story before you get started. Understand and know that every writer's process is different, and the amount of prepared materials needed will vary from person to person.

At the same time, all writers should give themselves the flexibility to explore the scenes when creating drafts. Sometimes writers don't know if something in the outline works until they explore it with the characters and their own dialogue. Don't be afraid to change things if necessary, and explore new scenes if the story is flowing in a new direction. If a scene feels too long at first or may not make perfect sense, keep on going. You can always adjust or cut it later; getting a first draft requires a lot of exploration. However, sometimes a writer needs to turn back and stop a scene that's derailed too far. Trust your instincts. The more a writer writes, the more they know when something feels on, or off target.

Writing is like exercising a muscle- the more you do it, the stronger you get. And one can only get better by reading or watching the best examples. Audio Theater is created from scripts, which is closest to the screenplay format, and similar to TV and Film. There's many downloadable screenplays online that can help beginning authors understand how to translate action onto the page.

Watch the movie, read the script- do both at the same time. How is action conveyed? How does the script go from one scene to another? To write audio dramas, as well as for film, is to write dialogue. Focus carefully on what's being said and how it's said. When watching a movie, close your eyes, focusing closely on what they're saying. Pay attention to sighs, grunts, any sort of Vox. Just as important, focus on when they're not saying anything, the spaces between the characters talking.

The more you pay attention, the more you realize you've already been exposed to the cadence and style of dialogue heard a thousand times over. All those movies, tv shows, and plays. With each viewing you've been developing instincts to know what is good vs bad dialogue, when a conversation doesn't sound right. Unknowingly, you already have an ear for it; you just need to tune it properly.

A technique that I use to help me write dialogue is to develop a sense of what that character sounds like in my head. Instead of trying to create one from scratch, assign a celebrity voice for each main character. You have to be able to recall them clearly, so choose actors that are familiar. To me, Ty sounds like Malcom, from Malcom in the Middle. This "celebrity voice" technique helps tremendously by helping keep the dialogue consistent. But be careful- don't just copy the character that is portrayed. Only use the voice as a guide.

Write as you hear the characters speak, including their slurs and grammatical mistakes if appropriate. Dialogue can be unclear or rough, but it can never be technically *wrong* as long as it fits the character saying it. The way people talk isn't perfect and shouldn't be perfect in your script. Sometimes the wrong way sounds better in the scene than the correct one.

The goal with any writing for dialogue is to be specific and true to the individual. You can test this by reading the dialogue and swapping characters lines. If the words said by one character can be swapped with another and it doesn't seem to matter, then the dialogue wasn't unique to that person.

And with that, the pieces from the Story Workshop are ready to be put together into a coherent story. I changed a few storylines as I worked out the details, but this was the result:

1.9 Workshop Result

A young teen named Ty is enticed to go to a rock concert with his two best friends, Sam and Erin (who were recently secretly engaged). They're all going to see one of their favorite bands, "Sky Wolf," several states away. When Ty seeks permission from his parents, Dawn and step-father, Phil, they try to come up with reasons to restrict him from going. First it was "College Applications," so Ty stayed up all night to finish every one of them. Then Phil lined up a special interview into a prestigious college in which he's an alumni, on the day of the concert! Ty's mom continues to make more excuses, and warns of the dangers of traveling so far when he is only 18 and has never been on his own like this before.

Ty continues to push, after trying to jump through the various hoops they have created, and pulls the "I'm 18" card. His parents react with an ultimatum, "If you leave, then don't come back." Ty doesn't understand how they could be so against him going. He doesn't even want to go to the college Phil is so set on. It didn't even have a music program, the real drive for his going to college. But he is also receiving constant encouragement to go from Sam, not only his best friend, but super-fan of Sky Wolf. So Ty, Sam and Erin all sneak out one morning before dawn and leave for the concert. It's time to become his own man.

Ty is enjoying his newfound freedom with Sam and Erin, but on the trip they are constantly running into problems. Sam's cell phone went missing, along with some provocative pictures of Erin that Sam said he deleted. They work it out since they decide the phone was most likely lost forever. After a fun/crazy night staying in an old, abandoned, creaky house, they come back together and watch "Ace Ventura" on Erin's phone. It's Erin's favorite movie, and they all bond together while viewing it in the middle of the scary shack. All becomes right for a short time. Then things start to go downhill again.

They can't get Ty's car to start, and they're so close to the concert! At the same time, someone found Sam's phone and sent Erin's pictures to all his contacts. Erin gives the engagement ring back to Sam, and heads to the bus station to go home. Sam reveals to Ty one of the reasons he pushed so hard for this road trip. After they returned, Sam was going to move away for a huge new job and marry Erin, but now everything is a mess. Ty swallows his pride and calls home. His mother, Dawn, answers and is sympathetic; she will get money to him.

She knows she can't stop him now... so she says to go to the box office when they get there and give them his name. Ty's confused, but accepts the "wired" money. At the service station, they run into Jim Carrey! His car broke down too! Erin would go crazy to be there, he's her favorite actor! Jim, known to be a wildly fun and crazy guy in real life, ends up getting in the car with them, and they find Erin at the station before she leaves, mend things, car's fixed, and they head to the concert... Jim goes on his merry way.

At the concert, Ty finds a special all-access pass waiting for him at the box office. He and his friends get to go backstage, and he finds out who Sky Wolf *really is*. His birth dad is a mess. Years ago Trent left the family when he was young, with a few eerily similar traits to what Ty has now. In the end, Ty leaves the concert early, disillusioned. He realizes the person he might be becoming. And why his parents wanted something different for him.

They go home. Ty works things out with Phil and Dawn, and Phil surprises him with an interview to a really great music school. That school just happens to be in the area where Sam and Erin are moving…

All is right in the world.

In the epilogue, Sam and Erin take Ty to another concert, and introduce him to their new favorite artist… The Jim Carrey Band.

It may seem a little cheesy, and maybe it is, but it's a succinct story with lots of ups and down, character growth, and even a happy ending.

All stories are different, but at their core, they all employ writing strategies to make compelling and relatable stories. You want people to care about your story and characters. That becomes the key to everything. It should be what most authors strive for. Artists make stories to entertain, to influence, to inspire, to expose others to things they may have never noticed. For some it even offers the opportunity to identify with something in a story that could ultimately help them deal with problems in their own lives. Art can heal.

I've received a lot of e-mails from people who have been touched in some way by what I have written. When I started, I never imagined someone could be impacted in a life-changing way through a story about "zombies." Here are a few examples:

- Someone recovering in a hospital, giving them something to "see" while undergoing eye surgery.
- Getting over the loss of a loved one through death or a breakup; a character reminded them of the one they lost, and they feel close to them when they hear that voice.
- Even two people, in different states, finding love in each other

and getting married, with the initial common interest being a "zombie audio drama."

Writing is hard, and clearly it can be a lot of work. And at times, it may not even feel the least bit rewarding. But if what you write can influence just one person in a positive way, then it's all worth it.

Chapter Two

Storytelling through Audio

2. Starting the story

You have 30 seconds to grab your listener. With the distribution format of podcasts (something I'll get into later), listeners tend to bounce from feed to feed looking for something to listen to. You don't have much time to connect with the audience and keep them tuning in. Starting the audio story with a five minute conversation involving two people at a coffee shop might not be the best idea; it'd have to be really compelling dialogue.

The first scene is an opportunity to establish what kind of story you are telling. It should set the tone for the entire piece. If this is an action/adventure, it makes sense to start out with that intensity. If this is Horror, start with something scary. There's a term used in film called the "inciting incident," where an event takes place that propels the rest of the story. This could be that scene. Out of all the sections of a story that deserve the most drafts and polishing, it's definitely the first ten pages.

Most films usually try to do this. They have an opening sequence that sets up what's going on, and if it's a James Bond film, then it involves a large amount of action and effects. Many concepts of story and dialogue are shared across the mediums, so where does audio drama start to break away in terms of writing and storytelling?

2.1 Perspective

You found him... "Mr. Tall, Dark, and Handsome."

Is that all you want to give as a description of this man to your audience? Sometimes a listener wants to know a character's exact appearance, and sometimes they don't need to. How, then, would you communicate how someone looks to your audience using only words and sounds? If you're using that exact line of dialogue above, *who* is describing them as "handsome?"

In order to create an audio drama, you have to understand where the story is coming from, otherwise you won't know *how* to tell it. Does there need to be a voice to fill in the blanks, or can the scene by itself provide enough contextual clues for an audience to understand what's going on? If so, as far as audio drama is concerned, there are three different options for the perspective of a narrator.

Omni-Narrator: The "god" perspective of the story. This "omni—presence" can go in and out of the minds of any character at any moment, sees all, knows all. But at times, this viewpoint can be extremely overpowering and pervasive. The omni-perspective knows all the events and choices that will happen before they transpire. This is more indirect and global which can actually be less interesting than someone who has a more limited scope.

Limited-Narrator: One person's perspective at a given time. Right, wrong, or indifferent, this is how they see it. We experience the world through their eyes. These were the men and women who lived the moments. It's far more interesting to hear the tale told by those who were there, giving the story more depth. It also gives the opportunity for trained interpretation of the events unfolding, i.e., a cop would have a far different perspective describing a car than a mechanic.

No-Narrator: The only way you know who is speaking is for someone to identify them. There's no breaking of the scene perspective, just raw dialogue of what's happening accompanied by sound elements. It's difficult, but it can be done. When written poorly, dialogue can become clunky exposition and the audience might not understand what's happening. Not all scenes need to be set up or described vividly- you don't always need to know how many tables are in the coffee shop. But then again, in some stories you do.

There are additional types of narration, but most of those have to do more with literary writing than an audio-drama perspective. The choice to use or not use narration is an important one because a writer can't necessarily switch mid-project if all of a sudden something requires clarification. You can always use *less*, but if a narrator hasn't been established, then they can't be added without confusion.

In all the audio dramas that I have written so far, I have chosen to go with the limited perspective narrator. Choosing characters in the story to give their own version leads to more exploration and allows the audience to get inside their heads. Sometimes there's a lot that someone won't say outloud, and narration is the only time the listener can tap into that raw cognitive network.

More than one narrator can offer further character definition. In We're Alive, I wasn't tied down to just one perspective, but was able to switch to other characters' vantage points. It's similar to what George R. R. Martin does in the series, A Song of Ice and Fire, and it adds a lot of versatility to change environments. This is something that can be very handy in aural storytelling.

Now that you've established the perspective of who's *telling* the story, next you have to choose how the story is being *heard*.

SPOV: the Sound Point of View.

The camera is related to film as SPOV is to audio drama. It is the location where the sound is perceived to be heard from the audiences' perspective.

Typically the SPOV tracks the story as it takes place, but it can change greatly, depending on the scenario. Is the SPOV inside the closet with a man trying to hide from the murderer? Or are *we* outside, following behind the murderer's approach to the closet? The scene is the same, but the SPOV reflects the vantage point and completely changes what the scene would sound like. It's only necessary to note during the writing stage if there's a specific change of reference, like the example of the murderer above. The perspective of sound is incredibly flexible and can explore areas that normally aren't possible with a camera or the story. We have the ability to hear things as an audience that aren't necessarily known to the active narrator.

The careful identification of narrator perspective and SPOV makes for a much more clear and enhanced experience for the audience. When written in a script, it could be noted simply in brackets: [SPOV is from Character A].

2.1a Audio Aesthetics and The Sound Palette*

Aesthetics represent the artistry of any process. This is how creators choose to communicate their ideas to an audience regardless of medium. For audio, aesthetic choices aren't always easy to discern. When talking about aesthetics in film, observers often discuss how the framing and content of a shot evokes meaning and feeling, or how the editing of the sequence of particular events convey some meaning intended by the film-maker. There are several dimensions with which to interpret visual mediums. Audio has that same ability. The dimensions within audio may be limited to what can be heard, but that doesn't mean artistic choices are limited. In the palette of sound, many elements can convey many different feelings to the listener.

The Sound Palette

Each dimension of the sound palette presents its own ideas and communicates something different according to how they are used.

Vocals, Sound Effects, Foley, Music, Synthesized, Processed, and Silence

Vocals: The strongest communicator in the aural spectrum are the voices. They portray the characters in all their emotions, and typically communicate the necessary exposition to fully understand the audio story. Someone's dialogue, breathing, screams and cries pull an audience into the story and character's experience more than anything else. Any emotion conveyed in a dramatic piece needs a sympathetic conduit with which to sympathize: that is achieved through the voice.

Sound Effects: The next strongest element of the sound palette is sound effects. These are sometimes referred to as "hard" elements that are pre-recorded and used as needed in production. These sounds lay the framework for a scene: a door opening or closing suggests who is coming or going, a gunshot claims the lives of characters. These elements are often difficult to record on their own, and are more cost-effective to stockpile, pre-record, or buy. Sound effects tell a lot of the story on their own. Even the simplest of choices such as the roar of a car engine denotes a time period or age of the vehicle, a character of strength or weakness as it putters or struggles along, and the motion and speed of the scene as the car races out of control, swerving over the concrete and spraying bits of gravel on the road. So much of a story's emotion and exposition can be conveyed through these specifics, be it as subtle as the intentional click of a gun or as large as the arrival of a helicopter through the pouring rain.

Foley: The partner to sound effects, Foley deals with the customization of sound for a specific scene. Whether it shows up on screen or in audio only, the speed, weight, and quality of a Foleyed effect tells the audience a story. Everything from how a character shuffles his feet as they walk down the street, turning and checking behind him, to the way the chair creaks back when the character hears bad news conveys particular emotions. Even the way a jacket unzips in an intimate, sensual scene shows how effectively Foley can add nuance to a scene. These actions have infinite potential for customization. Some foley sounds can be pre-recorded. However, performing the actions in real-time with the voices further grounds the characters in the sound-reality, and doesn't make characters sound like floating heads with voices that move without intention through the scenes.

Music: Music taps into the subconscious of emotions. A person can recognize a song in an instant the shortest of samples. By itself, music has the ability to soothe the soul or enrage the beast. In film, music is used to enhance the emotions of a moment, as well as also tell us pieces about the story. It can set the mood, tone, and even establish familiar themes. For example, the audience can recognize a western in the twang of a guitar or a horror through the sharp, suspenseful strings. Through the advanced use of leitmotifs, or musical scores and beats can associate with a character or action and can foreshadow and recall elements just beneath the consciousness of the audience. Music can further push the narrative by setting the pace, slowing down actions or speeding them up. Music can accent the swipe of a knife, or the dying momentum of a car engine. Used in conjunction with storytelling, music can illustrate things that might be invisible to the audience.

Synthesized: Post production has changed how audio dramas are created. No longer trapped by what could be done live, more utilities and tools are available to invent and manipulate artificial sounds. Footsteps can be created in real time, with variables like speed and weight, by pressing a few keys on a musical keyboard. Even synthesized voices of robots —such as those used in *Wall-E* — can be pre-sampled and manipulated with human-to-computer input devices such as digital pens to create the variable tones of their robotic voices. MIDI software can generate anything from lengthy hits of bass tones to samples of previously recorded clips, and it can save a lot of time in the search for the perfect sound.

Processed: How can sound live in its own space and create its own sound-reality? If a voice is recorded in a neutral space, without reverb, then it can be placed in practically any environment thanks to processing power. Reverb samples can be captured in any room space and then applied to that neutral voice to mimic the sounds of that environment. At the press of a button, a character is transported to a restroom, a concert hall, or even a cramped cargo van, all in real time. These natural reflections give the voice a new sense of space and location. The black box of recording doesn't limit where its story can go. Sounds can be also processed using total filtration and manipulation such as radio-like compression effects or complete sound reformers that can combine a lion's roar with the crunch of an apple. A human can easily sound like a monster with the right flanger. These various amounts of processing all reflect an ability to better fill out a desired sound palette to better fit and support the audio narrative.

Silence: Last but not least: the lack of sound. What is NOT being said or heard vastly impacts the audience. The emptiness after a moment of high tension preserves and solidifies the impact of the event. The silence between moments dictates a scene's pace in how a sound is received. Our ability to interpret sounds depends greatly on the timing between them. Longer moments can heighten the emotional stakes in a scene. Too, after a heavy moment of large impactful sounds, a break of silence allows the audience to digest what happened without overloading their interpretive bandwidth. Even a long pause before someone responds to a question could be an answer in itself.

2.2 Characters

Nothing is more limiting or frustrating then trying to create a distinct cast of characters for audio drama. The writer is admittedly restricted by forcing diversity through the voices. Simply said:

No one can sound alike.

Vocal choices start at the script writing stage. This doesn't necessarily mean you should fill your entire cast with characters having accents from places all over the world. Obviously, that would be unrealistic. Find organic ways inside the story to vary age, gender, and ethnic backgrounds, or use a combination to help add diversification. Take advantage of any opportunity to create as many *distinctive vocal patterns* as you can. Casting is the final choice for how a certain voice will sound, but who the role calls for starts on the page.

What makes a person's voice unique is often referred to as timbre, or frequency pattern. Young boys who have a higher pitch have shorter sound wavelengths in their voices, resulting in higher frequencies. If you were to do a coming-of-age story with teen boys from the same grade, their voices could potentially be much harder to differentiate than a cast of boys from varying grades. Knowing that, you can plan accordingly to set up more variety from the story inception rather than having to deal with confusion later.

Keep the cast as small as possible

Being able to distinguish and identify a character by their voice takes more time to register in the listener's brain than having a visual reference. The more voices the audience has to distinguish, the harder it becomes to differentiate them. It all goes back to the Number One Rule: *keep it clear*. Writers can fight this concept, explaining reasons why they need a character for this role or that, but often characters with smaller roles can be combined into one.

What do you do if your story does in fact require many characters? <u>We're Alive</u> (WA) had over 88 different characters, but that was over the course of four seasons. The way an author can make sure they're distinct and clear is to take the time to introduce them.

There's a lot more space to do things in the audio drama world than in the film world; don't be in a rush to put everyone who is in the story into the first scene. The audience also needs a decent amount of time to familiarize themselves to a new character, so one or two drop-in lines for an introduction isn't going to be enough. We should connect with that person and know who they are in their first scene.

In Audio Drama, a *name* is to a character, as a *face* is to a person on screen.

We discussed this in the workshop section, but there are a few more aspects to consider in the audio-only world. A character's name becomes their aural signature. It's the only way an audience can concretely identify who someone is, because a voice isn't always a clear designation.

Is a name hard to pronounce? Cut it. Similar to another character phonetically... Kelly, Shelly? Change it. Even if it is remotely close... John, Joseph, Joe, Jill. There are so many other options for names, don't risk confusing identities.

Phonetics plays a huge part of name selection for audio dramas. The way a name sounds (linguistic enunciation) can contribute to characterization, providing an efficient way to understand what kind of person they are. Pronounce the name "Lucious Malfoy." The first name alone comes out almost slimy and the last name screams malevolence or malfeasance ("mal" meaning bad). It's not important for listeners to know exactly what it could mean. But it does help in painting a clear aural image in the listener's head. A character's name is the first concept they "see."

2.3 Scenes

Who's in the scene? Names are important in the audio world because they have to be used a lot more than in a visual production. Character identification in a scene has to come from either utilizing someone's name, voice, or story device to help establish who is there in the room.

This could be determined by having the characters address one another at the beginning of a scene, using a Voice Over (VO) to say who's there, or if we're already familiar with the voices and scenario, it could be as simple as letting them speak. Keep in mind that if a character is going to be present in a scene, they need to be an active participant in the conversation. One line of dialogue per character for every two pages is a good rule of thumb, otherwise the audience might forget that someone is present.

Scenes and Action: "Well, don't just stand there. DO something!!" Talking head scenes are boring. Like any form of drama, characters just standing around talking don't contribute to the energy. There's also very little one can add to this soundscape. Footsteps can shuffle and the floor can only creak so many times before they've lost all meaning!

Choose moments of action that can compliment the scene or dialogue. Even the smallest change can contribute to the aural qualities. Often it's better to discover the action of the scene before starting to create the dialogue. Writing action in an audio drama scene is like writing the physical blocking for film. Where do the characters go in the scene? Someone could be at a desk typing while another stands; someone could be actively searching for something in room, or even doing every-day chores like washing the dishes? Action needs to be created early and included in the script, so that the actors know ahead of time what they're doing in the dialogue. Without any movement, the scene will become stagnant. Whenever possible, you always want to:

Let sound drive the scene. You have only two main tools for audio dramas, Spoken Words (VOX) and Sounds. In the golden age of Radio Dramas, sound effects had to be done on the fly. The only sounds added were the obvious ones: gunshots, doors opening and closing, thunder sheets for inclement weather, and so on. Complicated sound environments were intentionally avoided because of the limitations of what could be performed live. With modern audio drama, this isn't a factor any more. There are some technical hurdles when doing complex scenes, but nowadays you can sound design practically anything.

Words aren't always necessary. There are moments in We're Alive that we had to create complex action without dialogue. In the second season, for example, there's an assassination attempt. The setup was that a prisoner is being murdered... in front of someone who is literally blind. The story setup may sound outlandish without the context, but because of this creative design the audience was allowed to be with the person who was blind, and experience *exactly* what they're going through. The audience is in the scene, and every cloth movement, footstep, breath, and even the lack of the shell casing hitting the floor (hint, hint), is a clue as to who committed the atrocity directly in front of us.

This is an example of choosing a situation and plotline that enhances the story through its aurality. Your characters need to dig a tunnel through a jail wall, build a bike, change a tire, crawl under a bus to retrieve a toy... Whatever the story, make choices early in the script that allow for a diverse and more enriching sound experience.

Another way to improve the soundscape is to constantly vary the setting. It communicates with the audience where they are without using dialogue, and doesn't require as much exposition from the characters. By transitioning to different environments, the dissimilar aural footprint makes it clear that we are in a new location.

Some examples of unique aural footprints:
- Cave - dark, damp, echoing depth.
- Farm - animal sounds, farming equipment, workers.
- Ocean - lots of wave sounds, birds, boats.
- Transportation Centers- airports, train stations.

One aspect of aural footprints that can become difficult is "walla." Walla (or "rhubarb," if you're from the UK), is ambient background dialogue. Sometimes it's a crowd at a baseball game, or a market, or perhaps at a preschool. Because we work in an audio-only space, the background details are more focused for the listener. I make this point because this single element is one of the more limiting factors in modern sound design. If the scene is set in a generic time and place, it's far easier to create the background sound elements than a place so specific as an ancient viking funeral. Supplementary written walla should be added to the script when selecting complicated story locations. Walla may be challenging for a specific environment, but when used correctly, the additional voices creates authenticity and brings the aural world more to life.

2.3a Creating a Scene for Audio*

When creating a scene for audio, there are three stages in which the construction takes place: the writing, the recording, and the editing. Writing the script is the first stage which lays the foundation for the content, the recording is next where scenes adjust through the acting process, and editing is last where the pieces are rearranged to form the final version of the content. Each stage allows for creative liberties in the scene-building of an aural story.

Scene-building is comparable to the construction of a house. The script builds the foundation and studded walls that contain the scope of the story, limiting where everything is supposed to be, and what will ultimately take place in the space provided. The recording of the voices becomes the insulation, drywall, and stucco, giving the house definition and shape past the shell it once was. Editing comes last, which finishes the rest of the house details by painting and decorating everything and making it livable for the occupants to enjoy fully.

While it's not a perfect metaphor, the above is meant to convey how it becomes difficult to completely change what's happening in the scene after the previous stage is completed. The recording can't drastically change the script's content, and the editing can't recreate entire scenes from the recorded material. The artist must use what elements are present and determine what's possible.

The goal of every stage in scene creation is to communicate effectively with the audience. If some aspect is confusing at the writing stage, it should be re-written. If the spoken words don't "sound right" at the recording stage, they can be adjusted on the fly with adlib/improvisation or minor line changes. At the editing stage, what's confusing from the recorded dialogue can be accented with sound effects, and lines can be cut or re-arranged.

The writing stage allows the most flexibility as it establishes the foundation for the content. Pre-planning will assist in accurately conveying what is needed to communicate scenes best aurally. There are five questions the listener will subconsciously ask when first listening:

Who? What? Where? When? Why?

Who is in the scene?
What is going on?
Where is the scene occurring?
When do these events happen?
Why is this scene important?

In audio-only entertainment, these aspects need to be conveyed in some creative way as they are invisible to the listener. With visual narratives of film, all these questions can be answered in a matter of seconds with one shot. Audio takes time and crafting to communicate these key elements and to allow audiences to understand the context of the scene fully.

Who? The characters involved in the scene need to be forcefully established outside of only dialogue, and continuously reiterated for full comprehension. Names become essential to repeat, to understand and associate who is speaking at certain times. Without faces, the name and voice become the only explicit identifier of the character. Whenever someone new is introduced, (if they are recurring), a name within the first few lines is vital for listener discernment. A character who is considered "background" or a walk-on doesn't always need a name sometimes, being left out is beneficial, as the listener need not mentally keep track of another name. Find creative ways to establish a name in the scene so that it doesn't sound awkward or unnatural, as it's not always common to mention someone's name continually. Call-to-action lines are great ways to hide a name-drop like this: "Hey Al, you mind handing me the paper there?" Also, identifying oneself through communication devices are also natural and expected: "Hey Tim, it's Pablo. How are you doing?"

What? What is occurring in the scene? Are the characters traveling somewhere? Are the characters cleaning, building something, or performing their daily routine? If the characters play a card game, the scene can start with a simple introductory line such as "Alright, all bets are in. Show your cards." The context of the scene comes up quickly, as the dialogue jumps to a poignant place with exposition. Efficiency is key in any dramatic scene, so beginning further into the action often allows better contextualization. Another example with characters baking: "The recipe calls for five eggs, Josh, you mind grabbing them from the tray in the fridge?"

Where? Where is the scene taking place? In a film, an establishing shot would show where the characters are, but in audio, locations must be established either with dialogue or sound effects. Whenever details can be established with sound, rather than words, it will do more for the audio immersion of the listener and the medium's utilization. Keep this in mind when writing a scene up to the editing stage. If a scene takes place in a train station, the listener can learn this through sound effects before the first bit of dialogue occurs via a blowing whistle from a background conductor. Repeated music can also help establish locations as an introduction for various settings, becoming a *leitmotif*. Also, building scenes with sound exposition before dialogue contributes to better pacing, allowing more space after the last scene ends and before the next begins.

When? If the scenes are occurring in sequence, one after the other, the story's time isn't always important to establish for context. However, when jumping out of order into the past or future the audience will need additional information for context. Narrators can determine when and where the scene begins, but so can other various auditory devices and dialogue. Additionally, in flashbacks, a slight reverb in a conversation can suggest that the events have already occurred in the past. Creative dialogue can also bring an audience up to speed on the date, "It's been four months since you talked to her, get over it." Using significant events of the known calendar will also establish the passage of time. If the last fight between characters happened on the 4th of July, and their next encounter at Christmas, this transition would suggest a new timeline.

Why? Narratives all try to be as efficient as possible, going from one important scene to the next. While the pacing of audio dramas tends to be slower than that of film, there is still a necessity to keep the story moving forward economically. *Why* is the audience listening to these characters at this place and time? How does this section of action and dialogue move the narrative forward? What new necessary information appears that progresses the overall story or arc of the characters? The author is the ultimate authority of what is pertinent in understanding the perspective of the story. Moments that may not seem overly important, like a comedic aside, could be vital to the pacing and cohesion of the narrative.

These various questions, while meaningful to interpret context, allow for some artistic impression. Unanswered questions such as these can be a creative outlet for audio, perhaps playing on a limited perspective. If someone is blindfolded in the scene, the scene's WHO can cleverly unfold for dramatic purposes. Maybe a character is present at the location that doesn't want to be recognized. This aspect of audio production can give new meaning to the artistic license of the story. The narrow dimensions of audio can be used to enhance the mystery of the narrative further. However, the artist must balance how they stretch these rules, as it can go too far. Remember, "Confusion is the killer of audio dramas."

2.3b Audio Scene Transitions*

"Get to the meat of the story."

It's a common phrase used by storytellers all around. It means to cut the fat out that is unnecessary to the drama and only serve the delectable, edible portions. To modernize the phrase a bit (for my vegan wife's sake) and make it more appropriate for the medium, "Why are we hearing this?"

Ask yourself, does this scene support the central theme and narrative? Can it be combined with another to keep momentum moving? Most pages are written with purpose, but sometimes a writer will add excess to the intro and outros of the scene. Why slowly ramp up an argument when it's faster to jump into the crux of the conversation? Not every scene needs a fade in, but the narrative shouldn't jump around so much that it disorients the audience. Confusion is the killer of audio dramas.

So how does a project find ways to cut those corners creatively? Transitions. By jumping in and out at the precise narrative points, transitions allow a hyperfocus of the events experienced by the audience. Often, there's too much information irrelevant to the plot that distracts from what requires the audience's focus. In audio, it can be tricky to maintain comprehension as a scene transitions from one time and space to another. The easiest way to create transitions is to build them into the script and not assume the scenes will naturally work from one to another with music beds.

To illustrate the various examples below, Scene A is the scene we're coming from, and Scene B is the scene that is taking its place.

1. The Alley-oop. One method that works in both visual and aural worlds is the verbal "alley-oop" or a setup between two scenes linked by dialogue. Scene A might include dialogue that connects to Scene B through a shared theme, target, or juxtaposition. A: "He did not say *that*," cuts to B: Him saying "*that*." Or A: "We need to get to the location" cut to the location at B: "Did we HAVE to come here?" The dialogue bridges the harsh cut between the two scenes, but the scenes' atmospheres can be completely different. In fact, the more unique the chosen locations, the better aural contrast it provides.

2. The long fade/music transition. There are moments where it's best to slowly exit a scene and let the audience digest what they just experienced. The quicker the story moves to another location, the lessening of the lasting effect. Let it resonate with the audience and allow the music carry one scene into another. While this transition is not particularly unique, the selection of Scene B can lessen or heighten the impact of A. The long fade also depicts the passage of time. Headed on a long road trip? Skip some time by letting the car fade away then pick up when it's most important in the journey.

3. Cut through sound effects. The slamming of a book in Scene A, cut to the slamming of a door in Scene B, can act as a sound bridge between both scenes. Sound effect transitions can combine spinning tires in A with a spinning lottery wheel in B. There are infinite varieties of where to include those transition moments in a script. A notable example: Alfred Hitchcock transitioned the scream of a woman into the whistle of a train.

4. Sound-Space-Transition. The scene can change the SPOV (sound point of view) from one place to another, like a camera on film. In *We're Alive: Lockdown* this was done as the perspective shifted through an air vent from one area to another in the prison, exploring the space yet keeping a consistent track of time and proximity location. One thing that often gets lost in transitions: WHEN the story is now taking place in B, in contrast to when it was in A. By having the SPOV teleport from one space to another in the same time, you minimize confusion and can enhance the progression of the scene. Other times the same momentum can be achieved by "flying into" the scene, such as the movement from an audio cassette to full-audio spectrum as done in *We're Alive: Goldrush*, or even through the CB radio from one vehicle to another, never dropping the time progression or momentum of the scene. Even in simple scenes where the characters move from one room to the next, it's a transition to a new place in the script, and the SPOV should follow it.

5. The Aural Waltz or Background/Foreground swap. In audio, it's not difficult to change perspectives from one conversation to another in the same space. Scene A and Scene B might be more like Conversation A and Conversation B, or possibly C or D. In *Bronzeville*'s club scenes, various sub-conversations occurred separately in same time and location. The focus of the SPOV then moves like a dance, parading from one conversation to another. The writer chooses when the partner's switch, creating an aural waltz.

6. The Montage. Nothing moves time faster than a good old montage. As long as the transitions are clear, it's possible to move from place to place with ease, so long as there is consistency. Montages follow a particular pace, where the segments must complement and add to each other as they build the narrative sequence. Often, this means that each scene chosen for the montage should take the same amount of seconds. Other times, it's all about the coordination of the action when the lines cross between a specific point. *Goldrush* used this technique at various moments, including starting and repairing the car and truck in the last chapter. Instead of spending a lot of time during the process of fixing the car, the progress is quickly moved forward, but still illustrates the delay in time. Building the suspense for the elaborate chase scene required the proper orchestration of events to make sure they logically and dramatically crossed at the same time. The peaks of tension in drama are controlled by timing, enhanced by choosing those moments that always build and don't collapse.

7. The cross-cut. Some scenes continually cross back and forth but maintain relative connections in time. Scene A Action 1 cuts to Scene B Action 1, cuts to Scene A Action 2, cuts to Scene B Action 2. Hopping between two scenes allows the trimming of excess information and focuses on the actions that are necessary and relevant to the others. Time is less important here as long as the order of operations maintains consistency.

8. Multiple Timelines. When dealing with a narrator-style audio drama, there is always a sense of two different times: the present time of the narrator and the past from the narrator's perspective. Having those two clear timelines makes it possible to jump back and forth between various as long as they maintain relative order. In *Goldrush*, this method is used in several places as gags and jokes to move along the narrative but also to translate the perspective of what is occurring in the scene. With these breaks in the scene, the narrator skips through time. Also, visualizations or narrative in Scene B can be reinforced by the narrator in A. In *Goldrush*, where we danced on the edge of a fantastical genre, the narrators continually grounded the story by questioning its authenticity, just like the audience would. If the story challenges its own reality, the narrator can always keep it in check.

9. Voice-over passage. Every so often, a voice-over can be very helpful in a scene. Sometimes, giving the time and date at the start of a scene can help establish context before a word of dialogue is spoken, providing information that would otherwise be difficult to convey. An emotional interpretation of a scene via narration or even simply mentioning the time of day or location, helps establish the story's present, past, and future.

2.4 Creating Dialogue and Narration

To write audio dramas is to write DIALOGUE. For most authors, this can be one of the most difficult aspects of writing. I find that the best approach with the characters is to keep it honest and genuine. I encourage writers to lift people from real life as inspiration. And the more you know a person, the more you know how they typically sound. There's nothing more real than the people you know or knew from your past. Dig deep for inspiration- that third grade teacher, your first manager, perhaps a past love. Let who they are come through, and with that guiding inspiration, the character will become real. Like the "celebrity voice technique" from the Story Workshop where we assigned a known actor to the role, these are all methods which will help you become more familiar with the voice and heart of the character.

Audio dramas rely on "telling rather than showing," which requires imagination and creativity to balance out hefty amounts of story exposition. It's easiest to hide plot details in conflict and arguments:

> TOM
> I ain't going in there man, you can't make me.
>
> JERRY
> Why not?! It's just a house.
>
> TOM
> Yeah, but someone got murdered in there. I know.
>
> JERRY
> Who told you that?
>
> TOM
> Somebody.
>
> JERRY
> Well, that somebody got it wrong.
>
> TOM
> Oh. Well okay then.
>
> JERRY
> It was more like 3 someones. They just never found the bodies of two.
>
> TOM
> What?!

Fig. 2-4-1 Tom and Jerry Sample Scene

There are many other ways to creatively hide exposition in the scenes. Dialogue can sometimes be replaced with sound effects, or even through story setups like introducing a newcomer to pre-established concepts. For instance, we learn about the rules of the wizarding-world through a famous fictional character as both he and the audience experience everything for the first time in Harry Potter and the Philosopher's [UK]/Sorcerer's [US] Stone. The more you write audio-narratives, the faster and more natural it will be to create dialogue that weaves into the story what needs to be told. And then there's times when dialogue just can't give enough information effectively or quick enough, and would then rely on the fallback of **NARRATION**.

Sometimes there's no other way to clearly communicate what's going on in the scene, but to add narration. It can be as simple as a voice meant to convey a passage of time or name a location. Through Voice Over (V.O.), characters can share the thoughts that are only in their head, communicate what's happening, and/or anticipate what might be coming next. There is still more in-depth exploration that narration can do, that normal dialogue or sound can't. For one, it's the only way to hear an internal perspective, and thus dive into the head of another. Other useful instances are when you need to intimately describe something, or to set up a scene with details that are necessary for the story to make sense. From <u>Lockdown</u>:

Simeon's VO's are the foundation for the narration in Lockdown, but it is a very limited format. His dialogue is designed to be one long interrogation interview. By setting up this narrative device, the story uses the perspective of the character to deliver the exposition as naturally and organic as possible.

In many instances, having an additional perspective can be very helpful. **BUT**. Narration is like a diluted poison for audio. A small amount won't hurt anything. Too much, and it could kill. Overall, narration is considered the language of books, not audio theater. The problem with narration is that it's often either unnecessary or that it can stall the story's momentum. If something can be communicated through dialogue or sound design, then that is always the better choice.

```
            SIMEON (V.O.)
Jeremy was kind of a pretty boy,
tall, sort of looked like a
greaser, slicked over hair, thick
eye brows, in decent shape. Hell,
most of anybody in there was. You
had a lot of time to work out in
the cells. He was in a blue
jumpsuit, low threat. Everyone had
colors for their classification. I
was tan, general pop.
```

Fig. 2-4-2 Simeon VO Sample

2.5 Forcing Visualization

The audience needs to "see" what's going on. Every story will need some physical description in order to understand details of the plot. At the same time there are plenty of things that *don't* need to be described in the story. This is another instance where **balance** is key. The color of the jumpsuit mentioned in Simeon's narration may not be the most crucial detail of the plot, but it does give a visual representation for the listener. This is the basis of the wonderful partnership with your audience, in that a great deal of the story will be developed by the listener's imagination. The author only needs to assist by providing enough framework for them to be able to step inside this created world.

Ways we can further offer images of the characters will come later on in Production, in the form of sound design. For example, the sharp sound of expensive leather shoes on the tile floor and can be used to illustrate their financial status. This adds details about the character without using words.

There are some things that are difficult to illustrate without narration, a few of those being:

- **Character descriptions:** We need to know a bit about what someone looks like.
- **Colors:** There's no visual cues in audio, so describing colors is the only way to insert them.
- **Settings:** Knowing a specific location is necessary unless it is a generic place.
- **Action:** Without context, the details of what's going on can be unclear.

There are a few tricks that an author can use at the writing stage to help illustrate these aspects without using VO.

1. Let the characters plan: by figuring out how to do something as a collective group and vocalize their actions before the events take place. This allows the audience to have a foundation for what they expect to hear. When the plan changes, as it usually does, the listener already knows what was supposed to happen, so the scene progression is easier to keep clear.

2. Use devices to force visualization: if character #1 is on a walky-talky or telephone, then the person receiving the call cannot see what #1 sees. The required dialogue that would follow becomes a device then, that can enhance and clarify information.

>   CJ (RADIO)
> Pegs has them held back in the
> stairwell. It looks like they're
> taunting her- hang in there Pegs.
>
>   KELLY
> What now? Can she make it up the
> stairs, to the 7th? Those windows
> aren't blocked.
>
>   CJ (RADIO)
> I think she's afraid to. They shot
> through the stairs, once- they
> could do it again.

Fig. 2-5-1 Radio used to force exposition

3. Recalling what happened, later: the characters can recite what wasn't clear, after the action is completed. The longer the time between the action and explanation, the less effective this is. In the following scene, knowing exactly where Saul stabbed "the infected" might not seem like a necessary detail, but it further clarifies the incident for the aural image, and also gives an opportunity to set up a joke.

>   ANGEL
> Did the others hear?
>
>   SAUL
> No, they're still outside.
>
>   ANGEL
> That was really fucking stupid,
> those others could have-
>
>   SAUL
> But they didn't now, come on, we
> should head out the back while we
> have a chance.
>
>   ANGEL
> Good call... I'll follow you...
>
>   SAUL
> Gotta admit that was pretty cool
> though. I stabbed him right in the
> eye.
>
>   ANGEL
> Yeah I know, he didn't even see it
> coming...

Fig. 2-5-2 Recall Sample

4. Write ways to introduce the scene's location with sound: give us some sort of cue to know where we are. On a train? A horn blows, followed by lots of train movement sounds as the cars rattle on.

As the audio drama medium grows, more of these techniques will be developed, and maybe you can create some as well. In essence, it is any method or device that forces characters or sound to further explain what's happening.

2.6 Language Mechanics

Lastly, when you progress to putting words onto the page, avoid duplicate words that are close together in dialogue. In recordings, they pop out as continuity errors. They're noticeable to an audience and for whatever reason can disrupt the focus of the listener. One small paragraph might contain the word "that" multiple times. On the page it can be glazed over, but once heard aloud, the repetition become glaringly obvious and will sound awkward.

Words have a flow and rhythm, so be aware of heavy words that can throw off a scene, or a character. Reading your written dialogue aloud is an important component in understanding how words translate to the ear. It will help identify where tongue twisters or verbal stumbling blocks might be hiding.

A key note to remember is that dialogue must "sound right," even if doesn't make perfect grammatical sense.

2.7 Writing onto the Page

When you're ready to start putting words onto the computer, whether in the outline phase or the screenwriting phase, there are a few tools of the trade and some writing standards of which to be aware.

First, let's talk about outlining, and building the "story bible." It's an old industry term meaning that you have one central place for all your ideas, rules, character outlines, arcs, etc... There's no real limit to what can be contained here.

Personally, I have volume after volume of notes, pictures, maps, multiple outline versions, thrown out concepts and stories- mountains of information. For years I struggled with organizing it. I had folders from an old PC, and then went to a Mac, had multiple versions of the same files in different places, and also overwrote some things accidentally. It was a mess. Then one day I discovered Scrivener.

I tested out a few other writing tools, but this one really worked for me. It held everything inside its own database, as well as letting me import all my old PDF exports and original final draft scripts. Everything in one place! It really helped keep my thoughts organized, and made sure I didn't lose anything. Trust me when I say, I get nothing for this endorsement. The product is just that helpful for me to keep everything organized.

Here are also a few potential downsides for those who want to use Scrivener. There's limited collaboration tools because the database is on one system, and at the moment the data can't be shared easily without issues. The software also lacks encryption or password protection. You can always work around these by requiring a password to unlock your computer, but I feel it is something that should be noted.

Outlining doesn't have any standard to follow; it's however you want to organize your information. Some people work best with Post-It notes, white boards, voice memos, Google Drive, etc… (I still do all those as well). Whatever way works best for you, go with it.

"How do you create a script?" There may not be any template for your outline, but you better believe there are comprehensive standards when it comes to formatting a script. The techniques I share here are what I have tested and feel work best for the medium through my numerous recording sessions and years of experience. It includes an extensive process of testing what does and does not work well. This will also will be helpful later throughout production management.

First things first, however. I want to talk about the primary reason *why* we write the way we do, and it's very simple:

Scripts are written to convey the story as clearly as possible. There are standards and templates, but with all scripts, there's still inherent flexibility. On a project I recently mentored, I was asked how I could write in a transition from one perspective to another in the same space and simultaneous time frame. I had used this device when writing <u>WA</u>, and looking back at the original script, the only thing I wrote was [Switch to X character's perspective]. No one had previously established any rules for how those sorts of things are written; and it is how I thought it was communicated most clearly and efficiently.

Writers always have the freedom to manipulate the standards to fit what they're choosing to write, but first it's best to learn what those standards are. Currently there are two main templates that people use when scripting for audio drama.

There's the US/BBC Radio Drama format, and the US Screenplay format.

```
U.S. RADIO DRAMA FORMAT                                          1.

Scene One: Int. Location #1 - Day

1.  MUSIC:              ALL CUES ARE NUMBERED.  SOUND AND MUSIC
                        APPEAR IN ALL CAPITALS UNDERLINED.


2.  CHARACTER #1:       Character names appear in all capitals.  A
                        character is designated by either their
                        first or last name, but a role designation
                        may be used instead.  The designated
                        character name should remain consistent
                        throughout the script.


3.  SOUND:              ALL SOUND EFFECTS SHOULD BE USED SPARINGLY
                        AND WORK WITH THE DIALOGUE.


4.  CHARACTER #2:       Dialogue begins on the same line as the
                        character name in normal upper and lower-
                        case text with double-spacing.


5.  SOUND:              IF A SOUND OR MUSIC CUE INTERRUPTS A
                        CHARACTER'S SPEECH ON THE SAME PAGE...


6.                      Then continue the dialogue without
                        repeating the character name.


7.  CHARACTER #1:       Split dialogue between pages only if at
                        least two lines appear on the first page,
                        and only after a sentence.

                        CHARA #1/CONT'D OVER...
```

US/BBC Radio Drama Format

                              MARK DYKSTRA (CONT'D)
                    Inmate walking! Dani- grab the keys
                    to the holding room. Any problems
                    with the other transfers?

                              DANIELLE
                    No, seems like a pretty mild bunch,
                    not like the last group.

                              MARK DYKSTRA
                    Good. I need a quiet day for once.

Another guard comes up.

                              DEPUTY ELOISE
                    Here's Jeremy Andrew's transfer
                    papers.

She hands them over, they continue walking.

                              MARK DYKSTRA
                    Thank you. I'll add him to the
                    list.
                              (beat)
                    Your bus won't be here for another
                    two hours. Might as well get
                    comfortable.

Danielle moves in quickly with the keys.

                              DANIELLE
                    These are the ones, right?

                              MARK DYKSTRA
                         (annoyed)
                    Yes- open it up.

Danielle starts to open the door.

6   INT. T-BLOCK HOLDING CELL - CONTINUOUS

                              SIMEON (V.O.)
                    They stuck me in the holding room,
                    filled with benches that chain you
                    to the floor. We were supposed to
                    wait things out in there till our
                    ride came. It was way worse than my
                    normal cell. Not much else to do
                    aside from staring at the wall.

                              CJ (V.O.)
                    We?

US Screenplay Format

Most people today who want to write audio drama first search online, then find and use the old format from the radio drama days. The problem is that this format didn't exist during this new era of post-production. The old style script included sound effects and elements that were needed to be performed live with the actors. Not so now.

After the golden age ended, the more prolific medium in narrative storytelling became film and TV. The screenplay format eventually evolved into what it is today, cutting out the excess notes not needed in the script and focusing solely on the aspects that are important to understand what's going on in the scene.

Notes for music and sound effects can be written down in the margins and decided on later by the person in charge of those departments, rather than including them in the script pages for everyone. Often amateur screenwriters will write in extra elements, like directing notes or camera notes. A good director will read over the piece and decide how to inspire the performance they want in the scene rather than having the writer instruct the emotions for the actor on the page.

The sample page using the screenplay format above is from <u>We're Alive: Lockdown</u>, and is an example of that minimalist approach, giving the general descriptions and blocking (location mapping) in the scene. Include any sort of interaction that's important, and the speed or energy in which they do it. A good method to minimize those extraneous elements is to ask the question, "Do the actors need to know this to understand what the character is doing?"

Another reason to use the screenplay format is because actors are more used to reading those types of scripts. They have practiced and are familiar with this format because film and TV currently use it. In terms of page layout, it's easier to focus on only their dialogue, as their lines are clearly noted in the center and the character names are easy to find above the dialogue. Directors, producers, and even editors are so accustomed to this format, that using any other may cause added stress and confusion.

The industry standard computer application for writing in the screenplay format is Final Draft. Yes, it's somewhat expensive, but it is what most all screenwriters use. There are outliers and templates in Microsoft Word, but most of those are missing some of the more advanced functions that make production management easier. Know that the writing process can be slowed down with complex templates. There are cheaper options from Movie Magic and Celtix, but Final Draft is still used the most among professional writers.

Your first step to become successful at writing a properly formatted script is to read several before ever touching the keyboard. By reading a full screenplay, you will get a good idea of the general format, how scripts are written, and how transitions from place to place are incorporated. It's not difficult to discern these characteristics, and the more diverse the seasoned authors, the more you'll discover how the format of a script is used to convey a certain writer's style. Some of the best scripts I've read know how to use clever hooks to go from one scene to the next. But before you can do any of that, you need to know the basics.

To find good scripts to read, look up either award-winning ones, or one from a favorite movie. Be sure to find the *actual* shooting script, and not a transcription. Transcriptions don't contain the original screenwriter's formatting and intentions, which are what a writer should be analyzing. The WGA (Writer's Guild of America) has a library in LA where you can read any source script. In fact, most of the scripts from We're Alive are located there, but visitors are not allowed to copy them or take them out of the building.

Assuming that you have read a few scripts and have an understanding of the basics, I'll move on to some of the nitty-gritty moments where the screenplay formatting for audio drama can be unique.

```
Mark comes out of the office in the distance.
                    MARK DYKSTRA
                 (in the distance)
          I don't care about block eight.
          What the hell is going on!
          Central!?
                 (no response)
          Central! Central!

                    DANIELLE
          Call them over the phone-

                    JEREMY
                 (calls out)
          What's going on!?
                 (beat)
          Hello?!
```

Fig. 2-7-1 Parenthetical Statement example

Parenthetical statements (like this) can be used in a variety of different ways in a script. In the audio drama world they can help convey simple directions to be contained inside of dialogue blocks. How far away someone is from someone else significantly changes the way a line is read.

There's an old saying that "no one reads the descriptions," so using parentheses ensures that the actors are aware of how they should deliver the line. In the example above, the parenthetical phrases dictate the position for Mark's line, and also the energy level for Jeremy, so he knows to project his voice. The last line of the excerpt above has a (beat). This is something I use all the time in my scripts. It informs the actor to take a break at that moment, to split up the dialogue with a pause. These assist the actors in slowing down the moments, and not just making everything slur into one run-on sentence; something that is greatly beneficial during recording sessions.

Another use of parenthesis is in the Character Headers:

```
        GAVIN (RADIO)
There's nothing left to eat here
either...

        MARK DYKSTRA
Hold on- the inmates are asking for
us again.

        GAVIN (RADIO)
I'm just saying, it's something to
try.

        JEREMY
Who is that? Is help coming?
```

Fig. 2-7-2 Parenthesis in Character Headers

The (RADIO) addition to the character name clarifies that this voice is coming over a radio, and not inside the scene. This can be done on other occasions such as Voice Overs (V.O.). (Cont'd) means the dialogue is continued from a previous line- this is typically automatic in screenwriting software. (CLEAN) is used for alternate foul-language-free lines, and (RAP) or (SINGING) for obvious reasons.

Other times I use in-line parenthesis is when mixing languages.

```
              JODI
         (in Spanish)
    Can you stop staring at me?
         (in English)
    Seriously, stop it!
```

Fig. 2-7-3 Mixed Language Sample

In this segment, Jodi says the line in Spanish, but it is written in English. For simple dialogue I tend to use this method, but if it's a longer, more complex line in another language, I use the dual dialogue screenwriting option:

```
[IMPROV] Their arguing escalates until:

              CHUCK
         We have rights!

         FREDO (EN)                    FREDO (SP)
    You're all nuts.              Son una bola de locos.

              JEREMY
         Shut up, for a second-

              MARK DYKSTRA
         No, you shut up! All of you! I gave
         you a chance- and
```

Fig. 2-7-4 Dual Language Option

Dual Dialogue is a tool built into screenwriting software that allows dialogue to occur simultaneously on the page for alternate takes. Normally it's used for characters talking at the exact same time, but in this case it can be used to give an alternative dialogue without adding to the page count. This is crucial for figuring out accurate runtimes, and for scheduling recording sessions.

Another use of dual dialogue: In this section you can see the normal version, as well as the "clean" version on the right. Instead of trying to replace one or two words into a very confusing mid-sentence alternate line, it creates two distinct dialogues.

                    JEREMY
          Easy Chuck. Not worth it, not
          today.

          CHUCK   CHUCK (CLEAN)
Been here a couple months?   Been here a couple months?
Surprised you lasted that   Surprised you lasted that
long. My block would eat you   long. My block would eat you
alive.   alive.
   (beat)   (beat)
Try seven years in this   Try seven years in this
shithole. You learn a few   place. You learn a few
things, manners for one, and   things, manners for one, and
who the fuck some people are.   who the hell some people are.

The place is silent.

                    CHUCK (CONT'D)
                (clears his throat,
                 changes attitude)
          So. Anything new out there, Jeremy?

                    JEREMY
          Just someone else checking in on
          the padded cell.

Fig. 2-7-5 Two versions of the script in the same document

Brackets are used for those moments when the writer wants to include something important in the script for the production team, but there's no clear way to do it:

Jodi and Gavin chuckle.

                    JEREMY
          Again... NERDS.

The screen appears. **Everyone reacts. [IMPROV]**

          JEREMY (CONT'D)   JEREMY (CLEAN) (CONT'D)
Holy shit!   Ho! look at that!

                    BOGART
          There it is!

                    GAVIN
          I'm impressed. That was a really
          good idea.

Fig. 2-7-6 Brackets used in a script

77

The direction I wrote, [IMPROV], is something for the director to note, so that when this scene is recorded, they know that there are lines that are not on the page- and that the actors will be improvising dialogue. Having everyone speak at once would be difficult and limiting for the actors if it was crammed into the script, and this is just easier.

Another example of using brackets can be when switching perspective internally within a scene [Switch to X character's perspective]. When you want that script to contain something that normal formatting might not allow, brackets are the way.

Scene headings are used to note exactly when and where we are starting out a scene. They contain a lot of information in a small amount of space, and clarify the end of one scene and the start of another. You'll notice the addition of a number to the left of the heading; this is the scene number. Audio dramas tend to have a very large page count, so by having a number organization to every scene, you can easily communicate which specific scenes you're referring to throughout recording and post-production.

SCENE #	SCENE HEADING	PAGE #	LENGTH
0	WE'RE ALIVE: LOCKDOWN (1)	1	1/8
1	EXT. RUINS - NIGHT BURT (21), CJ (3), GUARDIAN ROCKWELL (10), MUG (11), MURPHY (6), PUCK (22), ROGER (1), SIMEON (8), WEASEL (18)	1	8 2/8
2	INT. SWAT VAN - CONTINUOUS BURT (22), CJ (23), GUARDIAN ROCKWELL (3), PUCK (21), SIMEON (28)	9	8 1/8
3	INT. COLONY INTERROGATION MONITOR ROOM - ... CJ (6), PUCK (6)	17	1 2/8
4	INT. COLONY INTERROGATION ROOM - CONTINUO... CJ (32), JEREMY (3), PUCK (1), SIMEON (28)	18	6 2/8
5	INT. TWIN TOWERS JAIL - T-BLOCK - DAY DANIELLE (3), DEPUTY ELOISE (1), MARK DYKSTRA (5), SIMEON (2)	25	1 4/8
6	INT. T-BLOCK HOLDING CELL - CONTINUOUS BOGART (19), CHUCK (56), CJ (1), DANIELLE (4), FREDO (3), GAVIN (1), JEREMY (30), MARK DYKSTRA (20), SIMEON (36)	26	14 2/8

Fig. 2-7-7 Scene report sample referring to scene headings

It also helps significantly to create scene reports from inside Final Draft. The reports generate a detailed breakdown of who is in what scene and become the foundation for the recording schedule later on.

Lastly, one of the most important aspects in creating any script is the ability to revise and change the words. Final Draft includes a "Revision Mode" as part of the toolset. This allows the author to change the script over and over, while keeping track of what has been changed:

```
                PVT CARL THOMAS
      Yes I did Sergeant, right after I         *
      told you the black number thing-          *
      maybe you didn't listen, but I            *
      definitely described what they            *
      looked like-                              *

                MICHAEL                         *
      I would have remembered something         *
      like that!                                *

                TANYA
      Hey, now-

                MICHAEL
      I took notes! And I would have done       *
      something if-                             *
```

Fig. 2-7-8 Revision Mode Sample

Nobody wants to read the entire script again unless they have to, and Revision Mode annotates what lines have changed by altering the color, and adds an asterisk at the end of the line. When I send a script to be proof-read, I make sure that the editors have their own revision level/color so that I can see what changes they have made to the script, and if I agree with all of them. Final Draft by default allows for four revision levels. More colors, additional revision modes, and how they are annotated can be customized to best fit your production.

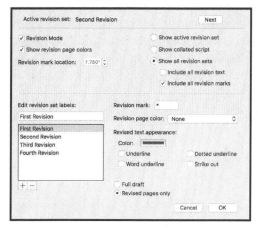

Fig. 2-7-9 Revision Mode Options

All these tips and techniques are helpful in completing your script, but the best way to learn is by doing it. Writing muscles need to be constantly worked to be most effective. Creating something in a new format and medium takes

time to learn and to maximize your efforts. It took me a while to find my voice as an author. It's something that I had been working on long before We're Alive, and continue to work on. Give yourself time to learn. If it was easy, or with instantaneous results, then everyone would be doing it.

Running Time? So how long does an audio drama have to be? How do you calculate program time in minutes relative to page count? It depends on what you're trying to create.

Episodic: 30-40 pages each episode.
A decent-sized episode, roughly a half hour in length.
Standalone: 60-70 pages.
An hour long self-contained drama.
Feature length: 100-110 pages.
The length similar to a standard movie.

An audio drama tends to take more time to reveal itself given the amount of exposition taking place, and requires longer scenes to introduce concepts and characters. When doing a multi-part series, I don't recommend going longer than hour segments, due to listener fatigue. Recognize that there is a fair part of the work done by the listener, and sometimes keeping the segments shorter to contain the story helps your audience. Another way is to have an intermission, inserting commercial breaks to relax the focus required.

To calculate page count for audio drama: 1.2 pages per minute is generally the average, but it all depends on the writer's style, and how much dialogue or action happens between the lines. I ran the numbers on Lockdown against the final cut. It was 379 pages long, and runtime was approximately 5 hours, or 300 minutes. Doing the math, 1 page of written material was 48-50 seconds after post-production.

Chapter Three

Starting Production

3. Pre-production Ends

Pre-production ends when the script is mostly ready, some of the casting is perhaps identified, and the green light for funding begins. How you now proceed depends a bit on the material already created. There are two likely scenarios that could apply, each with some advantages and disadvantages.

- Write on the Fly: The scripts are being created as the series is being produced. Instead of one large block of recording days, the selected episodes are broken up into groups. A typical season of 10-12 episodes could be broken in half, with multiple recording sessions possibly months apart. This model lets the writers feel out the characters more based on their performances, and allows for further adaptation and adjustments in the future scripts. The downside is that by breaking up the recording sessions you'll most likely have to deal with scheduling conflicts of the actors. The logistics for two sessions can also cost more than just one booking

- Write everything at once: All the scripts are prepared in advance for the entire project (season, mini-series, or one-off), and are ready to record in one single block of days. The advantages are that the cost of logistics is less since everything is captured all at once, the time commitment is easier for the actors, and the scheduling can be optimized so that there's minimal down time for actors. Recording in one specific time block also allows for further development as the actors spend more concentrated time in their roles. The major disadvantage is that the entire script has to be created first. Revisions can be made after, but for the most part everything is locked in place. It also <u>requires</u> that ALL the funding is in place as most of the costs occur during recording.

The biggest factor in both of those scenarios is time, and how much you have before the production begins. The more prepared you are, the easier it will be. The momentum of the project needs to be continually moving forward and thus requires making whatever adjustments necessary to accommodate this goal. No matter what the production, you will always be fighting the clock.

3.1 Stages of Production

Here is an overview of the different stages of audio production. Sections later in the book will include more details.

1. Scheduling
When does the project need to be finished? How much time is needed to edit? When is this production going to record? These dates are typically handled by the Audio Production Manager working with the requirements of the cast and crew.

2. Casting
It is vital to know every actor the story requires, and their character descriptions to start the process of casting sessions. This is typically handled by the Casting Director, with guidance by the Director.

3. Table Read
Whoever is cast reads together for the first time to get a general sense of chemistry, and to determine if any re-casting is needed. This is typically run by the Director.

4. Raw Recording
This is the continuous session of recorded audio. Script Supervisors make notes with timecodes for every take, and pass notes and raw materials on to the Assembly Cutters.

5. Assembly cut (AC)

Post-production starts as raw recording materials are cut down by the Assembly Cutters, based on the detailed timecode notes of the script supervisor. All the unnecessary recordings are removed, followed by the combining of all the good take options onto multiple tracks in the audio editing software for the vocal cut.

6. Vocal cut (VC)

Each scene is spaced and timed-out for action, and the best vocal performances are selected by the editor or sound designer. The cut, at this point, is ready for pickup notes from the production heads. Rough musical compositions can begin.

7. Vocal cut review

The VC is received by the director for notes. Any dialogue or performance that needs to be replaced is annotated and given to the post-production team for pickups to be made. The important notes at this stage are all regarding the flow of the story. Do the scenes make sense by only what's being said? Is it clear who is saying what in the scene? Is there any specific part that doesn't make sense, a technical problem, major adjustment or re-recording that will need to be made?

8. Pickups

If there are sections of dialogue that needs to be re-recorded based on the vocal cut, then pickups are arranged.

9. Pacing Cut

The best dialogue performances and complex sound effects are in place to set the master time.

10. Rough Cut

Most of the sound effects and Foley work are in place. Pickup lines and any additional dialogue are timed-out. Notes from the director are given and adjustments are made. The important notes at this stage are in regards to the sound effect elements that are now in place. Are there any sounds that don't fit the scene? Is there something missing that needs to be added in for clarification? Is the action and dialogue of the scene clear against all the other audio elements in place?

11. Fine/Final Cut

All of the music elements and sound effects are locked in, and any final adjustments should be minor. Does the music work as is, or are there additional places music is needed? Final approval is made.

3.2 Key Positions and Roles

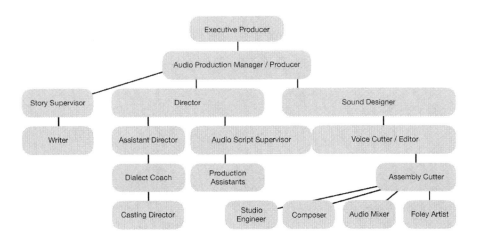

Fig. 3-2-1 Audio Production Key Positions

Audio productions can be as complicated as film productions. There's a lot of work to be done regarding contracts, schedules, editing, etc., and require a significant crew in order to create a unique aural experience.

Not all of roles listed here are necessary for every project, but as productions increase in scale, so too, should the crew. Ultimately, each role should assist the other, because in the end, it's the quality of the production that matters the most. It's a good idea to let everyone know what they are responsible for at the beginning, define what's expected in the contract stage, and establish a proper chain of command.

Many of these positions are responsible for set management, and to make sure the production goes as smoothly as possible. Be prepared that green crews are rocky at first, but after a while they'll get their groove.

Executive Producer - The amount of involvement of the EP tends to vary. Some are more involved with creative producing, while others tend to deal more with production management. And then there are others who are the financial backers. At the end of the day, the EP is the person in charge of everything, and often there is a hierarchy of EP's.

Audio Production Manager - The line producer of the audio production world. This person is in charge of scheduling, contracts, SAG/AFTRA paperwork, and most legal things that have to be in writing. Because of last minute actor reschedules or incidents, the APM is constantly making adjustments to the schedule.

Director - There are two different types of director: the lead creative head of the project and/or the person who directs the actors for recording. While not official titles, a Creative Director is ultimately responsible for the story that reaches the listener's ear, while a Actor Director would be more like a coach for the day-of recording, and doesn't stay on with the production past that role.

Assistant Directors (optional) - ADs are responsible for the production schedule staying on time, tracking what scenes are coming up, reading catch-up sheets before scenes, and monitoring safety on and off the set.

Dialect coach - Specializes in the words and accents heard in the production, and can read lines with actors to help them with their vocalization.

Story Supervisor - Used on larger productions, the person in this role would be in charge of the overarching story, and also managing the team of writers.

Writer - The person who puts the words on the page. And most of those words are dialogue. There can be a hierarchy when multiple writers are involved, depending on the production's organization.

Sound Supervisor - This is the manager of the audio production process, making sure the audio recordings are handled properly from start to finish. This position is especially important when there are multiple people working on the same production.

Assembly Cutter - This very detail-oriented position takes all the raw recorded material and reduces it into only the pieces needed.

Voice Cutter/Editor - This role is specifically responsible for the dramatic timing and selections of the performances, under the guidance of the director, creative producer, and/or sound supervisor. They will often pace out segments of audio, leaving empty areas, knowing how long certain actions will take. This person is also often the Audio Script Supervisor.

Audio Script Supervisor - Monitors and logs the recording takes, timecode, and director's choices. Often referred to as "script sup," but has a much different role than that of a film script supervisor.

Sound Designer - This significant role is responsible for creating the soundscapes of the audio theater. They should also be able to identify what sounds can be obtained from a library, and which ones need to be created with Foley.

Foley Artist - Works with the sound designer to specially tailor the recording sounds needed to match the action of the scene. Lots of footsteps.

Audio Mixer - The person who takes all the elements and makes sure they're balanced and leveled. This makes the difference between something being heard, or not.

Casting Director - This role is responsible for finding the actors needed for the story. Works with the director and/or creative producer to make the choices of who best fits the character.

Composer - The person who creates the musical score and themes.

Production Assistants - The crew members who are the miscellaneous task holders. Sometimes in charge of signing in cast members, running for coffee, or putting together call-sheets for the next day. PAs are on set running the production outside of the recording room. They are responsible for greeting actors, taking them to the green room or recording stage. Post-Production Assistants focus solely on the miscellaneous tasks in the editing process.

Studio Engineer - is responsible for running the technical setup of the recording. They are also responsible for the Pro Tools Session management while recording, often renaming the tracks for file/character management.

3.3 Low Budget Productions

On low budget productions, there are fewer crew members so everyone wears more hats of responsibility. The tips that follow are for the guerrilla approach. There are always ways to deal with obstacles like contracts, equipment, and recording spaces. When the *We're Alive* project started, our first budget was only $150 for the pilot. I borrowed everything necessary to record the first few episodes, including using some alumni connections for the spaces, and friends to help fill in the blanks for staffing. That has never changed. I still rely heavily on those who are close to me and I can trust. Pull people who have passions together for your team. Productions of any kind are far more difficult, if not impossible, to be done alone. You either have money, friends, or followers.

Keeping this in mind, managing anyone without paying them *is* the most difficult part. There needs to be a head of the production who manages the team and the project. That ultimately means telling people what to do. Without the incentive of payment, conflicts can easily arise around the simplest of things. On other occasions, people drop out, don't do what they're supposed to do, not pay attention or even care. Not everyone treats a project with the same professionalism. Remember that communication is key. Talk about issues that come up rather than burying them. Work around schedules as best as possible, set realistic goals, and give extra time for delays in the schedule. Working together successfully with friends can happen. And then, again, friendships can also be destroyed by business. The friend-side and worker-side of every person is different. And one doesn't really find this out until that friend line is bridged into a working relationship. Communicate goals and objectives with each other, and make sure that expectations are fulfilled. Before the project begins, outline what these things are in writing, and make sure the terms are agreeable to everyone.

My last bit of advice when attempting a low budget project is to learn how to do **everything**. Learn how to edit, how to write copy, schedule, and get the craft services. Logistics is involved with even simple things like getting coffee for a crew. Being able to step into any position at any time is vital when a project essentially has no budget. Everyone should be able to help pull each other's weight a little, and by knowing all the jobs, it's easier to help those who might need assistance. I'm a firm believer that everyone involved in an audio production should know how to edit, even a little. Editing is such a vital component to audio production, and can sometimes be the largest burden. Many editing hands can make light work.

Remember: money does not equal talent or passion. As this book continues into other areas of discussion, there will be sub-sections that cover the low-budget possibilities alongside productions with a standard going-rate budget, particularly in regards to recording spaces and equipment. There will be some sacrifices in quality at times, but these sections will provide lower-cost options for those who wish to start creating audio dramas from home.

Chapter Four

Logistics

4. Budget

Dealing with logistics is the tedious part of the business, but also tends to be the most important. Whether you have a huge production involving mega-studios, or are operating out of your garage, you will need to put together contracts, a budget, and secure funds in order to pay for everything. The first step in all this is to find out how much money you will need.

The Budget

There's a lot to consider when trying to figure out everything that needs to be paid for in a production. For this next section I went through the last few budgets I've made, and annotated what I think are the fairest wages and reasonable cost estimates. Every line item listed doesn't necessarily apply to all productions. For instance, if you're writing your own story, you wouldn't need to buy or license it.

Wages scale with experience... and prices grow with project size.

The rates listed below are starting wages for a single low-budget, union, narrative series production ($50,000-$200,000). There are some crew positions which have a film union counterpart (DGA ,

WGA), that may come with additional contractual obligations, pay rates, and other various pay stipulations. Be sure to check current union guidelines for specifics.

Many of the positions who are part of the creative team and logistics, such as producers, writers, and directors, are considered "above-the-line." These are typically the people who put the project together and have their contracts negotiated before pre-production begins. Royalties/residuals are sometimes paid out in lieu of upfront payment, and they receive a percentage on the backend which is sometimes referred to as "points." **Who owns the "project" after it's done?** These considerations are typically negotiated at the project's inception.

A contract should be made outlining the details of partial ownership for the recordings and produced materials, and any coverage needed regarding story rights/intellectual property (IP). This is important to explicitly outline, because all contracts and rights need to be in each person or company's name. It is critical for legal reasons, residuals, and also for any future property adaptations. This is especially important concerning:

Story Rights
There are a few options when securing rights for both fiction and nonfiction:

- The production company is licensing or buying the rights of an existing story, and paying someone to write the words on the page.
- The production company is browsing story options and hiring the original writer, or another writer.
- A script is chosen by the production company and is being produced.

These are just a few possibilities in what could be a variety of scenarios. Depending on the source of the story and the writer involved, the cost could be as little as $0 to $50,000+ depending on the author. There might be negotiations for partial ownership of story rights as well. Written serialized audio programs are typically much longer than any screenplay, so having multiple contract writers working on individual episodes is an option as well. Writing for one episode (40-60 pages), should pay anywhere from $100 to $10,000+, depending on the author's experience.

Producers
Executive producers, Audio Production Managers, and Line Producers are next on the list in the budget. Smaller productions might only have one producer, but for larger projects which require a lot of

coordination, there might be several. Typically most of these positions are above the line, as part of their role is to determine and maintain the budget, and then to hire out the rest of the positions on the project. Pay rate also is flexible depending on roles and functions.

Pay rate per project: $2,000 - $35,000+.

Directors

The director for a project can sometimes be determined above or below the line depending on what role they have in the production. If you have creative producers, the directors can be hired out on a per episode basis; or they can be above the line and responsible for the entire creative vision of the project.

Creative Directors pay rate per project: $10,000 - $35,000+.
Day-of director: $250 - $1,000 per day.

Cast

The actors on the project can have a large pay range depending on the fame and skill of the actor. Rates can be determined based on individual contracts and negotiations with the actors according to the SAG/AFTRA New Media guidelines. What this means is that the producers have the ability to negotiate points (royalties) on the back end of their contract. For smaller productions, or passion projects that don't have a lot of capital funds to start with, sometimes it's more beneficial for an actor to receive payment after the completion of the project. If a project goes big, so does the actor's paycheck, incentivizing larger names to come on board to a project with "set potential." Royalties aren't necessarily required, but check union guidelines, as there are requirements if budgets exceed a certain amount (currently $25k per minute).

When working with unions, also take into consideration that productions need to contribute a certain percentage based on the total pay for the actors' SAG/AFTRA health and pension fund. Currently, in 2017, that amount is 17.1% of the total amount paid to all the actors for all days. So if the pay is $1,000 to the actors, $171 additionally goes into their health and pension plan, for a total cost against the budget of $1,171. On larger productions this can be a significant amount, and can crush the budget later on if unanticipated.

New Media guidelines state that pay is negotiable, but cannot go below minimum wage by each state's standard.

Cost per Actor: $150 - $350 per episode, per day; $50 minimum for each drop-in/small role.

Production Staff

The production staff are crew members who can be budgeted hourly, or for an amount of work determined by a contract. These roles include the Production Assistants and Post-Production Assistants. Producers can negotiate the hourly wage necessary for each of these roles.

Cost for Production and Post-Production Assistants: $10 - $14 Hourly (adjust for inflation, and follow local, state, and federal guidelines).

Assembly Cutter

This stage is a lot of work, but doesn't require high level editing skills.
Cost for Assembly Cutter: $100 - $200 per episode.

Editor/Voice Cutter and Audio Script Supervisor

The "editor" of the post-production process is in charge of picking takes and timing out the performances. The Audio Script Supervisor is often also the Editor, who makes sure all the performances are captured properly on the computer or other recording device. Depending on who is performing the role, this position can also be budgeted together with the sound designer. This person is also sometimes referred to as a "Sound Engineer" or "Sound Recordist."

Cost for Editor/VoiceCutter: $100 - $400 per episode.
Cost for Script Supervisor: $100 - $200 per day.

Sound Designer

This position is heavily weighted in terms of responsibility and skill requirement. A significant amount of work is involved to build entire worlds of sound and to make everything feel believable.

Cost for Sound Designer: $500 - $4,000 per episode.

Foley Artist

This position is partnered with the sound designer creating the sounds specific to the scene. Because this position is variable depending on the amount of Foley required, it's best to pay this wage either per session or per hour.

Cost for Foley Artist: Hourly $20 - $40 or $100 - $400 per episode.

Composer

Music is a huge portion of the medium, and fills in the spaces to complete the picture. There's often a lot of sound gaps, making musical accompaniment necessary, which then requires a large amount of material to be created. When budgeting costs for composers, look ahead and see if any additional music packs or special samples are required for your project.

Cost for Composer: $1,000 - $3,000 per hour/episode.

Set photographers

Budget a set photographer for promotional materials, or video behind the scenes.

Cost per Photographer: $100 - $500 per day.

Props

Anything that might be required for production, e.g., special shoes for footsteps, or unique sound effect materials for Foley.

Cost: Variable.

Craft Services and Supplies

The snacks on set, water bottles, drinks, plates, napkins, utensils, etc...

Cost: $25 - $50 per day.

Meals

In an 8-hour day, it's necessary to feed your cast and crew a meal. Each and every person needs to be accounted for and fed.

Cost: $10 - $20 per person/meal per day.

Printed Materials

This is often an unexpectedly significant cost, but to print the huge volume of script pages (all of which need to be single-sided for actors), can cost up to $500 depending on the amount of copies and who is doing the printing. Having so many pages requires binders for actors that contain the entire script, which can also get costly. There are various printing businesses and office supply places, so be sure to price out accordingly. Sometimes it's more cost effective to buy a laser printer for the production, or locate a facility with a laser printer where the production can pay for or provide toner.

Cost: $150 - $500.

Recording Studio

This can become the bulk of the budget, depending on how much studio time you need. An 8-hour recording session (9, if the studio you rent charges during your lunch break), can run typically anywhere from $1k to $2.5k a day. Hourly rates range anywhere from $100 - $400 an hour. If you don't have a Foley recording facility, that, too, might need to be budgeted for studio time.

Costs: $1,000 - $2,500 per day.

Additional clearances and licenses

Want to use the really popular song that is on all the radio stations? Or license any segments of films for diegetic sound fx? It's always more difficult to deal with purchasing rights in this area, and can limit distribution. Be sure to get price quotes from publishers way in advance.
Costs: Variable.

Sound FX Libraries

Productions are going to need to buy a few libraries of pre-recorded "sound fx" to get the project off the ground. It'll save time and money not to have to re-create all the sounds in the project. It's possible to buy per sound effect, or in bulk packages. The benefit of buying SFX libraries, is that they are typically licensed to the production house, and come with the ability to be used for multiple productions.
Costs: $1,000 - $10,000.

Marketing Materials

The sky's the limit when approaching potential costs for marketing materials, but the feed will need at least one piece of artwork to be on any podcast directory: cover-art. At minimum is to have one square logo large enough to reproduce for print (3000 x 3000 px).
Costs: $100 - 2,500 per contracted artwork.

These are just some of the possibilities for expenditures. Every production is different. Be sure to plan accordingly for the story and production requirements. Some of these costs can be combined, roles can be doubled up, and some work can always be done for free or donated. Many hands make lighter work.

4.1 Funding

Once it's been calculated how much money the project will need, start setting the funding goals necessary to begin production. There are plenty of possible sources for obtaining Capital, and sometimes a combination of each will be helpful in reaching your target.

Kickstarter, Indiegogo, Patreon, and other crowd sourcing

For <u>Lockdown</u>, we used Kickstarter to raise 55k for our 5-hour long production. Our budget was still thin, and relied heavily on donated hours and facilities. Raising that much money on Kickstarter was an arduous process, and added an entirely new level of work to get the project off the ground.

The process of planning and creating the startup pitch video is challenging, and is required by crowd sourcing websites. Before the campaign launches, you must determine the rewards and tiers offered, create custom artwork for the campaign, and develop the social media marketing to draw in donations from listeners. Add to that all the additional work that comes afterwards to get the rewards out to everyone, as well as having to budget the creation of physical assets with the tiers. These were just some of the additional steps required to launch the project. Also know that the process of crowd funding can be risky too. If the campaign fails, the online perception of the project could become negative; and if funded, the backers may not be so forgiving for late rewards, or delays in production. Essentially, you work for the backers.

Another consideration is that the type of public release and rewards offered could conflict with any possible future licensing from publishers or advertisers. There are a lot of factors and also drawbacks, but the major benefit is that project will be funded, and the published materials will be your (or your company's) property, open for future sales, expansions, and licensing.

If you do choose to go the crowd-sourcing route, be sure to budget accordingly. Make sure to triple check that there are enough funds to take care of manufacturing and shipping of the rewards along with the amount needed for funding, minus the percentage that the funding website takes, plus a little buffer for those small oversights. Many campaigns have ended with backers not receiving their rewards due to poor planning. Crowd sourcing can be a financial risk for the backers as well, so be sure to plan the campaign thoroughly; otherwise it can result in online negative backlash and comments.

Self-funded

It's possible to afford and fund an audio drama project by oneself, or with the help of family or friends, and even with credit cards. With any donations or gifts, however, get in writing any stipulations that correspond with the funding. If it's a loan, outline the terms. Contracts can be written in any terms that are appropriate, such as ownership percentages and payment schedules. There are forms online that can be modified for free to specify the terms, but it's always best to have a legal representative or contract lawyer look them over before signing.

Outside financier

There are networks and studios that will fund podcasts, and can even provide the support network of advertisers. Having this kind of backing can be beneficial for logistic support, marketing, and cross-promotion. Larger podcast networks are starting to form around this model. The business side of trying to gather advertisers to fund your project can be a complex and arduous task, and having help to manage this allows you to focus more on the many other aspects of production.

It is important to know that choosing this type of strategy might present creative conflicts, because funding sources and podcast networks can then in essence become the executive producer. Ownership of royalties should be determined ahead of time.

4.2 Contracts

When in doubt, write it out. Many people think that the only purpose of contracts is to protect yourself, the company, and/or the project. Contracts do this, but the more important aspect is that they outline the expectations for someone involved in the production. Every crew member, producer, and actor should have a deal memo, and/or formal contract in place.

It's important to cover specific issues with the contract. For crew members, outline exactly what responsibilities the position has and the timeline required. Crew will often only do what falls into their spectrum of responsibility, thinking they do not want to step on others' responsibilities. If expectations are not outlined in the contract, then there will be opportunity for miscommunication- and there also won't be much legal weight behind telling them to do it. The subject of contracts can often become taboo when dealing with friends who might be helping on the project. Having something in writing conveys the seriousness of the production as well as expectations, and can help prevent friend-crew members from walking away from their responsibilities.

After outlining expectations of work in the contract, a statement is made regarding the person's wage, payment dates, any additional pay with completion of their contract, and lastly, how to pay them. The contract should contain their contact information, address for checks, and social security number. If any person's pay exceeds $599, then they will need to fill out a W9 form, and the production needs that information to file taxes.

When outlining and writing contracts, it's also important to include what someone doesn't receive as well. Is the person or company receiving residuals? Do they receive any intellectual property or publishing rights? If those rights are not included, make sure the exclusion is written in the contract.

Actors' contracts

Crew members are different from actors, and fall under different contractual guidelines. When casting a project, there's a Deal Memo created first, which is a preliminary contract to verify details and specific dates for commitment. This is essential. Following that is another contract to release certain rights and privileges to use that person's voice and/or pictures that were taken on set. If the project is a SAG/AFTRA signatory and filing under "New Media," then there's a specific template that's used for the contract portion. (See Section 5.6 for more specifics on this subject.)

Screenwriter's contracts

Any time one is working with writers, Intellectual Property (IP) needs to be outlined. IP includes anything that comes from the story: the characters, the plot, and even the words themselves. It's important to establish who owns the rights to the IP before anything is written. There are few things more precious and valuable to a story than the IP rights. Someone might want to option the story or characters later. It needs to be established who owns them early on.

Typically there are two scenarios. One is to pay the writer up front, or progressively. Then the materials written would be owned by you as the person paying the fee. The other option is that the writer is part of the production team, and the writer is licensing the story to be created. They would then retain all or partial IP rights. There are variations of both that are possible, but above all, be careful signing any external contracts that jeopardize ownership. Be very clear about everything regarding IP concerns with any contract.

Partners and Creators

There are two aspects of any production that need to be settled before you begin: #1. Ownership of the Intellectual Property and #2. Ownership of the recordings/edited material. Determine ahead of time who will own various aspects of the production, and put it in the contract. Perhaps the idea was from Person A, the writing done by Person B, the production is going to be put together by Person C... you must spell it out in the contract. Outline ahead of time what percentage of the IP is going to be owned by each party after the production, as well as what percentage of the recordings. DO NOT proceed with production until these things are settled and in writing ahead of time. No matter what size production, these aspects need to be determined as soon as possible. It will make things tremendously easier when royalties and profits come into play later on.

Chapter Five

Actors

5. Casting

Casting can start at almost any stage of pre-production, as long as there's enough information to know who the characters are before an actor is assigned. Casting before a script is complete can make things complicated, as certain roles could be cut before production. Also uncertain would be how much time is needed for a specific actor. If possible, have at least the first draft completed. Production is complicated enough as it is, and focusing on re-writes while determining casting against an actor's schedule can easily stall contracts. For bigger name actors, agents want to be able to read the script ahead of time, anyway. If it's in a rough stage, the talent will pass.

With that being said, I do recommend to leave at least one script revision to be completed *after* casting. The reason being so that the writer can change various aspects about the characters depending on who might embody the role. Every time I've casted something, I've ended up with at least one actor who wasn't exactly who I anticipated for the role- be it race, gender, or mannerisms. The actor I cast for Chuck in <u>Lockdown</u>, Kim Estes, did not fit the description written. So I changed the role in the script to an older convict, from one race gang to another, and tweaked the dialogue slightly. Chuck, to me, was almost a perfect character because of casting Kim in that role. Things can change during casting, and the more flexible the casting process, the better the story will flow through the actors.

5.1 Descriptions

When the production is ready to cast, it will require a "casting call." This is a detailed rundown and description of who's being sought for the characters. If you ask actors about their experience with these listings, you will hear that they are often very poorly written, stereotypical, and even sexist at times. The description should convey enough about the character to know who that person is, but not so much detail to close off character development or give away the story. Spend the time to look up good casting descriptions to get an idea on the guidelines.

Here are some examples from our own *Lockdown*:

[MARK DYKSTRA] male, 28-45, any ethnicity. Head Correctional Officer for Transportation Block at Twin Towers Jail. Cynical, defended, and by-the-book. Mark is responsible and headstrong, incapable of trusting inmates or even guards who have less experience than he.

[DANIELLE TYNEKER] female, 23-35, any ethnicity. Assistant Correctional Officer for Transportation Block at Twin Towers Jail. Forgiving, good-natured, idealistic, and unsuspecting. She's strong, but conscious of her own limitations. Ability to roughly read Spanish a plus.

[GAVIN] male, 40-68, any ethnicity. IT administrator for Twin Towers Jail. Once a guard, Gavin brings years of practical experience as both a guard and administrator. He's confident, tough, and doesn't show a hint of aging.

[BOGART HARRIS] male, 20-35, African American. An energetic, fun-loving, and relaxed inmate. Religious, but also modern with his beliefs. Musical, and sometimes freestyle raps. His confidence hides his cowardice.

[JODI LANE] female, 23-35, Hispanic. An inmate who is a former hacker, petite, cocky and selfish (little dog syndrome). Must be able to speak fluent Spanish.

[CHUCK MILLER] male, 30-55, any ethnicity. White collar criminal who's been serving a sentence unequal to the crime committed. Bitter, older, caustic, smart-ass. Ability to speak rough Spanish a plus.

[JEREMY ANDREWS] male, 28-42, any ethnicity. The smooth criminal among the inmates. Mysterious, fearless, atheist. Selfless and headstrong.

[FREDO BRAZORIA] male, 28-42, Hispanic. The beast inmate of cell block eight. Hardened Mexican gang enforcer. Incredibly selfish, strong, rough, and quiet. Massive in size and presence. Must be able to speak fluent Spanish.

[SIMEON EKLAND] male, 18-35, any ethnicity. The slimeball inmate. A liar, thief, swindler. Out for himself. The narrator of the story.

5.2 Casting Notices and Submissions

Nowadays it's pretty easy to find actors if located near major cities. With places like **nowcasting.com, actorsaccess.com,** and other casting sites, it's easy and often free to post notices about the roles needed for a production. Actors typically pay for the website services which entices productions to list there.

After the production information and role breakdown is approved by the website's staff, actors can then choose to submit. You'll generally receive headshot submissions, resumes, and sometimes voice over or video demo reels. Give the casting call a week to receive submissions.

Casting directors can greatly assist in this process. Finding the right actor for a role is crucial, and spending the extra money for someone's casting experience can make the difference between a mediocre production and an amazing one. They can also assist in creating deal memos, and help with some of the union guidelines and paperwork. In the hierarchy of a balanced production, a casting agent is a crucial liaison between the actors and the production.

Once submissions are received, the process of whittling away who isn't right for the project begins. There's a lot of "green" actors who will desperately spam projects, trying to get experience on anything. Those resumes are often short, and include a lot of fluff to make their one-sheet look qualifying. Harsh as it is, the submissions must be judged rigorously to find the person who best fits the role and cut those who aren't a possibility. These are decisions that can not be taken lightly.

On an actor's resume, look for experience that required discipline to achieve. I tend to look for people who are dedicated to their craft, seeking out ways to improve themselves. People who are serious are not too proud to take an acting class, dance, or dialect instruction.

Watch the actor's videos or reels if they post them, and note that this is what they feel is their best work. If there's no demo reel, look at the headshot. The sound of someone's voice can be reflected in their appearance, but not always. Sometimes you just have to look at the person and their resume, and go with your gut as to whether or not that person could be right for the role.

If this is your first production, seek professionals. Don't always hunt for celebrities. Having a celebrity in a role is beneficial for advertising and notoriety, but also adds a level of complexity that would break many projects. Keep it simple, and then grow from there.

5.3 Holding Auditions

Once the selections have been made, create a schedule- one person every fifteen to thirty minutes. Give the actors sides (script segments) in advance for them to read at their audition. A common problem with inexperienced casting sessions is the selection of long sides. All that's necessary is a two-person scene that's 1-2 pages. The shorter the better, allowing the ability to run the scene with the actor multiple times adding changes from the Director. When pulling sides right out of the script, alter them so they include only two people. The scene needs to make sense and also allow the actor to interpret some major aspect of the character, but does not need to include anything not relevant to that scene.

Before the casting date, try to have the recording dates locked down along with any possible table read dates. This will enable the producers to verify an actor's availability at the casting session. Any potential scheduling conflicts will thus be identified and handled at the very beginning. The goal is to be able to record every character that interacts with each other at the same time.

The next step is to find a place to audition. It can be your own office location, or even a rented office. It just needs to be a place that's somewhat quiet and allows the actor to privately read. There are dedicated casting places like Catz in LA, which allow use of their facility as long as the auditions are video-taped with their equipment. This is offered so that the casting location can present pay-for services to review the audition clips and offer coaching for the actor. It's not a bad exchange of services, and the actors and producers at no time are forced to pay anything if they don't want to.

It is essential that the location and atmosphere of where you do your casting is controlled. Actors need privacy to let themselves be vulnerable, especially during casting. Keep the room free of any extra crew members that aren't necessary. I prefer to have a maximum of three people on my side of the table. It's helpful to have another producer or casting director present watching the auditions, giving suggestions, or taking over when the creative director doesn't have anything more to say. After a read or two, someone will say, "Thank you for auditioning with us. We will let you know."

5.4 Casting for Audio

When casting for only vocals, it's not necessary to have a video camera recording, only audio. I prefer to use an external audio recorder and a stand with a microphone similar to what will be used to record all the actors in the studio. There is a list of recommended equipment in the index at the back of this book, so be sure to check there for the individual specs. The recording setup is relatively simple- press Record, have the actors state their names, and then roll into the audition scene.

The reason I recommend recording someone under the same mic conditions as the production is to find out exactly how their voice reacts to being recorded. One's ear is not the same as a microphone and different voices respond differently depending on the hardware setup. Performance is important, but as an audio-only producer I have found that it's essential to observe and determine a variety of technical aspects about a performer at the audition:

1. Does the voice sound too similar to the other actors I'm considering casting? I've had to pass on some amazing actors simply because their vocal patterns were too similar to another cast member. The characters would become indistinguishable for the listener and lead to confusion, potentially breaking the production. Sounding the same is

comparable to looking alike in a movie. If you can't identify a character, you can't understand a character.

2. Is their voice compatible with the production? This one is tricky, and you have to listen closely. When recording the words from an actor, all their inflections and speech patterns are included as well, good or bad. If a performer's mouth clicks all the time, perhaps has constant, harsh "es" sounds, or their voice is too mumbly and slurred, then this should be noted. Sometimes technical problems can be fixed- vocal clicks can be resolved with some apple juice, or some editing software. But other times these unintentional audio distortions are just part of someone's voice. Do not overlook potential vocal complications. Again, and it can't be overstated, the focus of all audio productions is to create the clearest story possible, and speech is the largest component.

5.4a Casting Audio as the Actor or Director*

Casting can be an objectively tricky part of production: it requires you to judge a person based on their talent and abilities to see if they best fit a role. A casting director or producer must look beyond biases or preconceptions about people and the characters themselves to hear what each actor can bring to the production.

Overcoming the first impression and preconception presents the second challenge of performance-based art: **everyone thinks they can act.** While cliche, it's true. A large portion of the acting process comes from skilled scene crafting and an ability to achieve the emotional empathy required to disappear into a role. Some people have a very innate acting ability and can pick up a scene coldly, becoming that person in seconds, yet may not have the required linguistic requirements. For instance, where a language or background is needed for a role, accents and dialects can take years of coaching and training. Short of language exposure, these skills take time to learn and develop enough to sound believable. When all the audience has are words as their guide, loose accents stand out.

Another common misconception is that an actor's talent means they are best suited for any role. Lots of people can act, but that's just the first checkbox. Casting is a balancing act of the talent, the chemistry between actors, and faithfulness to the source material. Each category must be equally weighted as they all come into play for the series' longevity and believability.

How does a director or casting agent choose the best fit? They thoroughly vet the actors, by giving them **all the materials they need to succeed or fail** an audition.

An audition is equal parts an application process and a test. The headshot and bio that actors submit show their prior roles and training. What experiences an actor brings to the role denotes a sense of professionalism and dedication. The more variety in previous characters and mediums, the more flexibility and range an actor typically has. To understand performance differences in various mediums, actors should understand how to move in front of a camera, where to stand on the stage, or how to read into a mic and perform following the restrictions of each. It shows discipline and seriousness to handle different mediums and showcase the same raw talent of convincing audiences you are someone else. However, experience doesn't always mean much compared to acting talent and intuition. This is where the test part comes in.

The "test" casting directors give actors is a side of the material. Often this side is a section of the story, ripped from the pages of the overall script. The actors perform on-camera, and then the performance file is sent in as an audition. This process has become standard practice for most productions now. Afterwards, a review of the materials determines whether the actor is the best fit.

An audio casting agent or production should select a side that embodies the range of the character and tests against natural elements required for the role such as humor, wit, empathy, etc. If the piece is a comedy, there should be jokes in the audition for the actor to play against. If the piece is a drama, give the actors the most profound dramatic moments to see whether they can reach that deeply vulnerable place the character requires. Is the character supposed to be suave, intimidating, or neurotic? Those character traits need to be on the provided side's pages, so an actor can show whether they truthfully embody them. If a character's main trait is their toughness, and the side offers no opportunity to show that, then it becomes more difficult on both sides to demonstrate and evaluate that quality.

Too, sides should have a variety of interactions and dialogue types. Does this character speak a lot of exposition, and serve as a narrator? Then there should be a semblance of that in the side, to test if they can regurgitate facts as their internal truths.

Personally, I like to find a spontaneous moment in the script that tests the actor's instincts. If an actor is not prepared or hasn't considered the materials, it can become apparent at this place of the script. In *Goldrush*, the intuitive line I used to audition Anita's role was, "How long are you going to stay?" The dialogue leading up before the line was all expository, but they are all done with the intention of interacting with a potential love interest, which is the crux of their story. Without that genuine love and caring between the characters, the story would not work. When watching all the self-taped submissions, I would focus on that moment intently. How does the actor switch from Anita's sparse, light banter to the driving question she's been waiting to ask all along? Some actors will naturally understand the meaning and tactics behind the dialogue while others will blow right by it, not thinking about what the character is experiencing or why they are making the choices they make. When watching Brenna Ott's audition performance for Anita, that moment stuck out, and that shift occurred in the dialogue clearly and genuinely. This simple side from *Goldrush* didn't have many actions or characters, but it helped us find the perfect actor for the role.

What else should casting directors look for? Bold choices. I've cast roles that required an over-the-top nature to their personality, and those auditions differ significantly from the dramatic ones. There's a balance between "too cartoony" and no character in audio. If the voice isn't dynamic or naturally alluring in a role that requires energy or excitement, it won't add to the production. However, if there is a choice that draws you in with every line, that voice will most certainly add to the series' audio spectrum: the listener will "want" to hear them speak. I'm not talking about those deep soothing baritone voices that listeners *think* they love, but rather a presence in the audio that makes a person almost *seen* when *heard*.

Side selections for auditions aren't meant to be complete stories, and they don't always make 100% sense when compared to the script. If an actor makes a statement an accusation or interprets something differently, that's great! When in front of a microphone or camera, the editing process loves having options. An actor's range and creativity comes into play with how they interact with the pre-existing script.

I also have a personal list of **DON'Ts** in the audition world, things I — and maybe others — would prefer actors avoid. The first one: **not auditioning through the proper process or channels**. I cast through a website with a robust back-end that sorts all role submissions with their resumes because of the hundreds of submissions for each character that need to be tracked and organized. It's one thing to receive emails from personal friends and professional contacts. Still, I can't tell you how many unsolicited notes or direct-messages I get saying, "This person has a great voice." While I never want to appear rude, I'm never just looking for *good voices*. Good voices are only one tiny piece of a much bigger puzzle.

Next, **don't cast your friends**, or at least don't guarantee a role unless you are certain they are a fit. There might be a better voice compatibility option, and when productions cast roles based on availability or companionship — rather than vocal compatibility — there can be problems. The voice is the face of the character and has to be different enough to distinguish itself from others. Don't trap yourself into not exploring all options and pairings available.

With video submissions, actors can choose to send either a video self-tape or an audio-only audition. From experience, the better test is almost always the video self-tape. When actors submit only audio, their instincts tend to go into a "voice-over" mode rather than truthfully acting and reacting. In my opinion, there is no such thing as "voice-acting", just acting. Sure, there are techniques and such for commercials and advertisements that require particular vocal styles. Still, in audio-theater, actors should disappear into the role and transfigure into a character in the listener's mind. The body is an instrument, and the whole thing should be used when performing for audio.

On the actor's side, there are a few ways to stand out from the crowd. First, look at the script ahead of the audition and figure out the character's motivation. What do they want? How are they going to get it? Every character has a reason they do what they do, and if the actor finds that *WHY* to everything, the scene will make sense. Actors film so many self-taped auditions that they can be a blur sometimes. However, by spending an extra ten minutes to break down the emotional beats will clarify intention when performing. A character always knows what they want, and the actor must center themselves around that desire. Actors should also be mindful of the space in which they record: noisy or echoey rooms with poor lighting will obscure critical aspects of the audition.

After video submissions comes the next stage of casting: call-backs or chemistry reads. Knowing who can perform on video is the first test, and then in-person call-backs allow directors to see who is most compatible. Acting is about reacting to others, not dramatic reading. How does the actor perform and interact with the other people in the scene? If there's no chemistry, your performers are doing little more than saying the lines aloud. When there's fire between everyone and the passion fuels an interaction, it's enjoyable. There are surprises and discoveries between the actors as they play inside the world and scene together. What someone knows and when they do something becomes a part of how well characters respond and, ultimately, determines the energy of the performances. A harmony and balance between the actors can be found and achieved in the audition process long before the first recorded word of dialogue.

5.4b Keys to Success Working with Hollywood Talent*

A common hurdle in audio drama is actually convincing an audience to listen to your podcast or audio program. There must be a hook that drives them to your content, and a notable name or recognizable voice will push an audience over that hurdle to click that "Listen" button. Working with celebrity talent presents a lot of opportunities but also carries its share of restrictions. If you know what to expect, production will run more smoothly and you'll save yourself from plenty of headaches during recording and beyond.

Time is money: time is often the singular aspect that will scare away notable talent from a project at first blush. How much commitment is required on their part is usually the deciding factor, second only to pay. Luckily, audio entertainment doesn't require nearly as much time as a live-action or on-location shoot. A studio environment is usually a relaxing and welcoming space, away from constant holding-for-camera or light adjustments. Also, there's often a recording studio available in proximity to the celebrity's residence. Some notable voices will even have an in-home recording space.

Your first interaction when approaching celebrity talent will likely be with an agent or manager acting as their filter. Rarely will you have the option to personally pitch a project, unless there's some personal connection to the talent.

When pitching to their representation, several things must be clear upfront. First — as stated above — is the anticipated time commitment. How much time will they spend in the recording booth? In multi-cast recording sessions, getting everyone in the same space simultaneously is one of the trickiest aspects. In my experience with audio dramas, celebrity talent loves reading with other actors, especially if their character engages in dialogue with others. Reading blind with readers or stand-ins will often yield dead, emotionless reads. Having the other cast members to interact and "play" with allows talent to open up and produce a more natural performance.

Secondly comes pay. If a celebrity is available, how much will they be compensated for their time? Audio drama budgets rarely can compete with film or TV salaries, but anywhere from $1k to $10k per session is reasonably common. The shorter the commitment, the more likely they are to sign on, but it must also be financially worth it to make the drive.

Third, comes the content and the character. Celebrities love passion projects, characters they don't usually get to play, or covering subject matter that's meaningful to them. If your pitch to the agent or manager makes the celebrity's intended role and importance clear, they are more likely to be interested in the project and sign on. The pitch-deck or proposal package sent to the agent must clearly and concisely explain the project and who the celebrity would portray.

Finally, and not the most important, is the pedigree of your production team. You and your team's previous work gives the agent or talent an understanding of the project's caliber and scope, as well as of your established track record. Celebrity representation will avoid signing their client to something low-budget if they believe the team is incapable of producing an audio drama that will make their client sound good.

The above factors will determine whether a celebrity will come aboard the production, yet, how do you handle them once they've signed on?

First, your project's union status is essential because there cannot be a conflict with their existing work-relationship with SAG-AFTRA, and few celebrities will work non-union.

Next, setting a clear schedule in advance will also help the production and set a predetermined amount of commitment for the recording. When setting up the celebrity's recording schedule, it's essential to try and record the scenes in chronological order to inform their character with their previous scenes and choices. Also, recording every scene back-to-back optimizes their time and makes the artist feel that their time is valued. Allowing talent of their cost and caliber to sit doing nothing between takes does no favors and can cause on-set discord. By maintaining a high level of organization and respect for their time, you ensure everything runs as smoothly as possible.

What do you do when things start to go downhill? Not every talent is easy to work with, and egos can become involved when a celebrity feels "above" the project. While it is easy to get frustrated with negative comments, or a degree of blow-back from taking specific direction, it's best to maintain composure and professionalism at all times.

Keep this in mind, too: there are celebrity voices that are NOT right for your production. If they are difficult during the negotiation phase, that difficulty can pop up on set. It's not worth having a known voice in your audio drama if they'll cause production problems. There are plenty of actors out there who might be better suited for the role, and a positive attitude is more beneficial in the long run than notoriety. Bad attitudes turn into stiff or weak performances and do nothing to elevate the project. Celebrity talent is also not always perfect for the role, and known social media influencers or large follower counts mean nothing if they can't act or blend into the scene. Bad acting, no matter the fame, will stick out like a sore thumb and once the contract is signed, there might be no alternative but to include it and make the performances work.

When all the pieces fall in line, and when celeb talent gets to record with everyone, the results become heightened and elevated. Celebrity actors bring a level of experience that comes with their notoriety. They have often acted in a wide variety of scenes and scenarios that will contribute to others' professionalism and abilities in the recording. In other words, celebrity talent inspires better performances all around. And while there are always exceptions to this rule, especially if they intimidate the rest of the cast, their experience frequently sets a precedent of professionalism. It makes the other actors come to set prepared, ready to engage.

The key to success in working through these factors is confidence. If the creators and producers are confident in their creation and know what they are striving to achieve, that will be evident to anyone who walks onto the recording stage. When we recorded Danny Trejo, who has been in more productions than most artists alive, walked on set to play on our stage with the soldiers in *Goldrush*, it was a dream. The actors played through their scenes with ease, made each other laugh, and ultimately performed at a higher level than the words written on the page. It also created an unforgettable experience for the actors. Rarely would any of our series regulars be cast across such talent, but audio presented both the opportunity and an even playing field.

5.5 Selecting Actors

Technicalities aside, what do you look for when casting? Like any performance medium, it's a search for believability, authenticity, and directability. When an actor is believable, they disappear into the role, and embody who that person is. There have been times when I instantly hear the character come to life in an audition. It's rare, but it does happen. Other times, it takes a few read-throughs to see if the actor can become the role. Callbacks allow the actors to focus and spend more time working with the character, knowing that the director sees something in them that could be what they're looking for. What actor is best for the role, at the end of the day, has to come from your "gut." Who do you believe the most in this role?

More often, in order to get the performance to best fit the role and the story, actors need adjustments. I choose sides/scenes for the actors to read that can be considered "open," or able to be interpreted in a variety of different ways. I might tell them, "Okay, this time, I want you to treat the other person like you're talking to your father," and see how they respond and react. If they take the note, and give a new and different performance, it's a good sign they are open to change- directable. If not, try again, but know that when an actor is inflexible, it's usually easy to tell. Each performance will be similar to the last no matter what new coaching is given. Even the best actors need adjustments, whereas rigid actors don't let a director do their job, which is to maintain the consistency of the performances that best fit the story.

The last consideration of casting a role is authenticity. Does the actor have any relation to the role, in terms of ethnicity, background, or experience? As much as I'd like to say that ethnicity doesn't matter since the audience can't see the actor, I've learned that's not the case. When dealing with language as the primary mode of storytelling, try and stay as authentic as possible when it comes to accents and foreign cultures. The audience knows a fake accent over a real one, and there are no cosmetic advantages or distractions of makeup, costume, or visual environment to sell bad dialects.

These qualities are all things to assess when judging the talents of one actor over another, but there are still other factors to keep in mind.

Is the actor going to be difficult to work with? Are they so unavailable that you won't be able to schedule them or work with them beforehand? Do they bring potential drama to the set? Actors and even crew members can have feuds with each other. There are hundreds of reasons to cast or not cast someone, and the ultimate decision doesn't always come from one person. The larger the production, the more production heads will weigh in. However the decision is made, it should always be for the person who best fits the story (and the production). An actor's fame does not extend into making them a good fit for the role. Choose wisely.

If the selection of the actor comes from the first session, great! If not, and additional time is necessary to work with the performer, then schedule a call-back session with the top choices. Actors are used to lengthy vetting processes to find that optimal cast, but don't overdo it. Performers can appreciate the process of trying to develop the best cast, but more than one call-back for low pay isn't reasonable.

5.6 Deal Memos and Contracts

Once the casting choices have been made, the audio production team then needs to submit a Deal Memo to the actor to accept or deny. That deal memo is a very brief contract that should include the payment offer and outline of all expectations of them as an actor, including recording dates as well as a rough idea of how much time they'll be needed. Include one additional pickup recording session on the deal memo to be done at a later date, with at least 1 hour per finished hour of the final runtime. Billing order is optional to include (where their name appears in the credits), but be sure not to offer the same credit location to two different parties. For some actors just starting out, their intention might be to build up a Voice Over acting portfolio, so be sure to include in the contract or deal memo the free use of clips from the audio production for the talent's reel.

After the deal memo is signed, it is acceptable to let the other actors who auditioned know they didn't get the part. Sometimes not sending out any notification is easier, and actors not hearing back is fairly typical. Then, there are other times when it's not a bad idea to let the actors who came in for callbacks know they weren't selected. Acting is said to be one of the most "vulnerable" professions, and giving a bit of closure with a well-worded rejection letter can go a long way. Don't burn any bridges- it's not uncommon for primary cast picks to fall through. It also must be noted, **do not dismiss any alternate choices for roles**

CAST DEAL MEMO
UNION STATUS

PRODUCTION COMPANY		DATE	
ADDRESS		PHONE #	
PROJECT NAME		FAX #	
CASTING DIRECTOR		EPISODE	
ARTIST		PROD #	
ROLE		SOC. SEC. #	
ADDRESS		PHONE #	
CORP NAME		EMAIL	
ADDRESS		FEDERAL ID #	

SALARY			

	# DAY/WEEKS	DATES	
TRAVEL			
REHEARSAL/FITTINGS			
PRINCIPAL PHOTOGRAPHY			
ADDITIONAL SHOOT DAYS			
POST PRODUCTION DAYS			

PER DIEM/EXPENSES			
TRANSPORTATION/TRAVEL			
ACCOMODATIONS			
OTHER			
BILLING			

Fig. 5-6-1 Sample Deal Memo

before locking in the primary cast and signing the deal memo.

The deal memo should contain the actor's personal information, representation (agent and manager), and if they're being paid as a loan-out from their own company (Many actors will work as a company or corporation for legal reasons). The production will need to safely record and store the social security numbers (SSNs) of the actors for tax reasons and union purposes. An Employer's Identification Number (EIN) will work for tax reporting, but SSNs are typically how the union tracks actors. There are specific security protocols when dealing with SSNs, and I recommend having at least 2-step authentication behind access or encrypted files. Be sure to check your local and state labor codes for exact specifications as to how your state requires handling SSN security.

The last topic to cover about deal memos is to clearly understand that they are NOT full contracts. They don't have the legal status that contracts do. For serialized content, contracts are the only way to require commitment in a legally binding way, and will also allow the release of the actor's recorded performances, as well as any photos or videos shot on set. It's customary to start with a deal memo, and then a contract is worked out closer to the recording date.

Contracts can be scary for certain actors, because they ultimately force an actor to commit to recording and give away the rights therein. That level of assurance is expected when pay is high for large productions. With smaller budgets, lengthy legal documents can be met with hesitation. Communication is key. Discuss the terms with the actor and their agent, and try to maintain flexibility. Contracts need to be finalized before production begins, otherwise there is the risk of possibly losing an actor or not even being able to use their recordings after a production.

5.7 Payment

The most common question I'm asked when hiring actors for audio dramas is, "How much should I offer for the role?" Pay too little, and the job won't be worth it; pay them too much and the budget will break. Audio productions currently tend to run on shoestring budgets compared to their visual storytelling counterparts. The best advice I can give is that the pay amount should be proportional to the overall budget at around 15-25%. For productions with a $50- $100k budget, it comes out to about $150- $350 a day per actor. For extended sessions that rate can add up quickly and take up large portions of the budget. Be sure to crunch the numbers. For example:

7 Actors
5 days of recording
35 day rates to pay. At $350 a day, $12,250 budget for actors.

For *very* low budgets, I wouldn't go below $100 per recording day for actors with experience. A day could be 8 hours of recording +1 hour lunch, which breaks down to almost $9, which is below minimum wage in many states. SAG/AFTRA guidelines won't allow payments less than state and federal minimum wage, so be sure to check local guidelines.

Other options for payments can come from special contracts that offer back-end compensation, giving a certain percentage of residuals from the production itself. These can be in lieu of or in addition to wages. This is essentially giving away future stakes in the project in exchange for involvement, which can be both good and bad. It offers added incentive, but reduces possible financial returns.

Donated time is always an option if the project is low budget and non-union. For union projects, it's not explicitly outlined. SAG/AFTRA New Media Guidelines say: "Initial compensation can be negotiable* under the basic SAG-AFTRA New Media Agreement for productions that do not meet the high budget thresholds; however, local, state and federal minimum wage laws still apply. *SAG-AFTRA reserves the right to negotiate minimum rates, when applicable."

5.8 The Table Read

Soon after the casting process is complete, it's important to bring all the actors in for a table read prior to recording. The more time before the start of production, the better. The director needs an opportunity to work with the actors to round out their characters and voices, before the actors spend a lot of time preparing for the role. It wastes time to jump onto set with an actor who has been running lines with the wrong character in mind. They need some foundation to build off of and to work with before the pressures of being on set begin.

The table read also allows the other actors to hear the other characters for the first time, and may also be the first time the actors themselves are getting a clearer understanding of this medium. One option to help the actors is to record the session, or later read throughs once everyone is relaxed and in character. If sections of the recordings are good scene samples, then send copies to the actors to rehearse against. This will allow them to build expectations in their heads for the other character's reactions and voices when reading through on their own.

Another reason why the table read is an important part of the process, is that the actors can begin to trust those around them, and start to interact with each other. Production wise, it's also critical. This exercise allows the director to see any potential casting issues prior to the recording dates. Is someone not working out, causing issues, or maybe just now it's realized that two people sound alike? It's up to the director and the producer to predict any potential production or story conflicts, and make whatever adjustments are necessary to keep everything moving in the right direction to completion.

Following the table read, don't be afraid to give the actors homework. This is a medium that is new to many actors, so have them listen to other audio productions that mimic the performance style best illustrating the project. They can also learn a sense of timing as well as what sort of sound accompaniment to expect in the final product. By listening to the many VOX components that are captured and implemented- breaths, coughs, struggles, etc., the actor will know what to expect and can start to prepare for what's involved in recording audio theater.

5.9 SAG/AFTRA

Screen Actors Guild/American Federation of Television and Radio Artists, or: SAG/AFTRA. What used to be two unions is now one. If the audio project is to be considered a union production, then the entire project will need to be submitted to SAG/AFTRA under the classification called "New Media," and someone will need to become a signatory. Several years ago, with the rise of the internet, the unions recognized the online streaming and download content market, and decided to create a category that allowed union actors to work for these projects for negotiable pay.

There are different qualifications for each classification, but what sets them apart is in regards to the platform of the initial release. Any project that debuts on the internet such as podcasts, *can* be considered "New Media." If the project is first sold direct-to-disc and only available for purchase, then it would put the production under an entirely different category. For this book we are preparing for internet distribution, so the focus will be solely on "New Media" guidelines.

Using the actor's union is either an all or nothing decision. For union projects: new union guidelines state that every person with a scripted line must be part of the union or else the production can be fined a penalty up to $800 per actor. Non-union actors can be added to the production through what is called a "Taft-Hartley" form with a $100 fee per actor that must be paid by the productions. Those actors are then given an option to join the union. If this is the actor's second "Taft-Hartley," then their status in the union becomes a "MUST-JOIN." This can be a problem in being able to give very small roles to crew, friends, and such. As long as the dialogue is scripted, the actor must be union; even if it's only one line. This can be a major hurdle for audio-only productions. In film, it's easy to have "background actors" that are non-union wandering into the shot, or covering simple actions like dropping off a check at the table. With audio drama, background actors need dialogue in order to appear in the world. The only work-around is that inserted dialogue or walla can be added in Post (which are NOT contained in the script) and would be considered "sound effects." These are not required to be union roles. In the future I hope to petition a change for this rule to contain a certain low-line cutoff for scripted background characters. But for now, it remains in place.

For first-time or for starting productions that are trying to keep things simple and easy, it might be best to follow union standards, but not become a signatory project. There's a lot of paperwork with any union project, which also comes with potential penalties if not turned in at the right time. Hiring non-union doesn't necessarily mean that the actors are any less skilled, but it can be limiting. I'm very pro-union, but also understand that productions are already complicated enough at the learning stage.

What is the process of having SAG/AFTRA actors in your production? The casting process is the same, but include in the casting notice that the project is "Union Only." SAG/AFTRA also has certain guidelines regarding callbacks, such as how many there can be before the actor needs to be paid to audition again. During pre-production, three weeks should be scheduled to become a SAG/AFTRA "signatory". Becoming a signatory is free, but requires an application that needs to be filled out and processed by the union. To start, a signatory is needed for the SAG/AFTRA New Media Agreement, as well as for the Pension and Health Adherence Letter.

Other paperwork that will be needed to become a signatory: Articles of Incorporation (for a Corporation) or LLC (Limited Liability Company); fictitious name statements for DBA or Sole Owner, and lastly if you're doing this solely as an individual, your driver's license or government I.D. If the production has liability insurance, provide a copy to SAG/AFTRA as well. Some recording studios include insurance as part of their package, which will suffice. Even though the project is only audio, the union still requires coverage in case someone is hurt on set.

If the production hits a certain finance level, the SAG/AFTRA signatory representative might require financial assurances against the production, which could be in the form of additional contracts or even a financial deposit. Once all those steps are complete, you are free to start the process of hiring union actors.

We discussed briefly what to pay actors in the previous section, but with SAG/AFTRA, there's an additional cost to add in- 17.1% of the cumulative total of wages that are paid to the actors is owed to the SAG/AFTRA health and pension fund.

As calculated in an earlier chapter, if a production pays an actor $1,000 then $171 would be owed to SAG/AFTRA. The total cost for that actor would be $1,171. This can be a hefty payment depending on the production, so be sure to factor that amount into the budget ahead of time. This percentage also changes over time, so be sure to check the current requirement.

Union performer contracts need to be created and all necessary tax documents obtained and filled out prior to their first date of recording. These contracts should include the release for their performances, and anything previously stated in the actor's deal memo.

After casting is complete and immediately before recording starts, the production will need to process cast clearances. In order to be an active member of SAG, an actor needs to be current on their dues. If they are behind on the payments, the actors will not be allowed to work on the project. There is a grace period for the actor to catch up with paying dues, but <u>the production</u> could be subject to a hefty fine if not taken care of properly and in a timely manner. Performers must be cleared at least 24-48 hours before the start of production.

Call sheets must be submitted to SAG by 11:59pm the day prior to recording. For larger productions, call sheets are typically created and sent by the PA's the day before. During production, Taft-Hartley reports must be filled out, stating any cast members who aren't union. Remember, the production faces penalties if selecting someone who's non-union.

Payment schedule requirements for SAG actors can be very stringent and often come before production has wrapped-up. Day-performers, three-day and weekly performers all have certain payment deadlines. Check the current New Media checklist at signing for details. On recording days, use sign-in sheets that log the actor's in and out-time. Those sheets need to be turned in to SAG/AFTRA by the end of the following week. These rosters (Exhibit G's) are typically handled by the PA's or Line Producer.

Once production completes, you have 30 days to submit a cast report, as well as having Casting Data Reports and the Health and Pension Form with payment completed and sent to SAG/AFTRA. After all those steps are accomplished, the SAG/AFTRA requirements are done.

The union process consists of a large amount of paperwork, so having a line producer or a production assistant dedicated to the process becomes almost a necessity.

5.9a SAG/AFTRA Rates*

There have been some updates to the SAG/AFTRA actor contracts. These are specific rates that apply to productions, based on the overall budget. These numbers are subject to change, and always be sure to check with the union for any updates.

Dramatic Podcast Agreement Rates. Each Performer and Background Actor employed in the Program must be paid no less than the minimums as set forth below:

- For Programs with a budget Less than $25,000
- The minimum session fee for each performer shall be $130.00 Background Actors $96.00
- For Programs with a budget Greater than $25,000 but Less than $75,000
- The minimum session fee for each performer shall be $205.00 Background Actors $105.00
- For Programs with a budget Greater than $75,000 but Less than $150,000
- The minimum session fee for each performer shall be $280.00 Background Actors $115.00
- For Programs with a budget Greater than $150,000 but Less than $300,000
- The minimum session fee for each performer shall be $335.00 Background Actors $125.00
- For Programs with a budget Greater than $300,000 but Less than $800,000
- The minimum session fee for each performer shall be $630.00 Background Actors $170.00

These are the rates required for four (4) hours of work. For each hour afterward, payment due becomes rate + ⅛ of their hourly pay in addition, and the workday caps at eight (8) hours before qualifying for SAG standard overtime rules.

Chapter Six

Scheduling

6. The Fight Against Time

Scheduling is the constant fight against time... First and foremost, scheduling for recording is all about the math- calculating how long it will take to do something against the limited hours of actor availability. The more actors involved in a project, the more complicated it will be to coordinate. Even with an unlimited budget, having performers sitting around all day and not recording is obviously a waste of their time and the production's money. It is the job of the audio production manager or line producer to create a balance between the needs of the artistic process and the integrity of the story, requirements of the actor, and the availability of facilities and personnel- all while not going over budget.

The schedule becomes the backbone of the production, and if it breaks, everything else will soon follow on that path. Creating the schedule is best done AFTER the script is complete, otherwise the number calculations can be thrown way off, and mistakes are then easier to make. Scheduling is difficult, it takes a lot of time, and the only time others will pay attention to the process is when something goes wrong.

In regard to audio theater, there's often loads of content to record in a short amount of time, and countless obstacles will attempt to change things last minute. No matter what hurdle you face when dealing with the schedule, always try to observe the golden rule:

If actors are in the *scene together*, they should *record together*.

How long does audio theater need to record? Usually, a 40-60 page episode per standard 8-hour recording day is a good estimate. In terms of breaking down a script, about 1.2 pages is equal to about 1 minute of produced material. You can sometimes achieve more than one episode in a recording day with a seasoned cast, but it's always good to err on the side of caution. Being ahead of schedule is great, while the contrast of overtime can get costly for studios and also wears on the actors. The formulas, calculations, and spreadsheets contained in this section can greatly assist in figuring out the daily recording schedule. But no matter what, always remember to create a timeline that supports the story content.

6.1 Script Formatting

The foundation of every schedule is the script, and the data reports pulled from it. One of the reasons I highly recommend Final Draft for writing the script is because of its tools that calculates these reports against the written text. In particular, detailed information is exported on the duration of each scene, as well as every character contained in that scene. That may seem like a simple process, but manually checking against a cast list can become daunting, not to mention, inaccurate, as mistakes are bound to be made.

Formatting for the schedule needs to start with the writer. Be sure to brief them early on with the technical requirements on how they need to format the script. The most important formatting note in this section is to make sure sub-scene headings are inserted when changing to different groups of characters. The headings should look something like this:

23B - INT. BAR - NIGHT (CONTINUOUS)
Scene Number - Interior or Exterior (INT. & EXT.) - Location - Time - Scene notation.

The continuous scene numbers are important for tracking reasons. This allows the script to be separated into smaller segments. In a perfect world the script would be recorded in order, but multicast situations rarely allow that, so it's necessary to break down the script into individual scenes in order for certain characters to record out of sequence.

In longer scenes that don't change location, but change characters, a letter after the scene number can help break scenes down even further as in using "23B." In <u>Bronzeville</u>, there was an incredibly long club scene that had to be recorded in sections due to limited actor availability and last minute adjustments. Having it divided at the script level gave us the flexibility to break it apart onto different days, yet still allow the characters to record with everyone they interact with.

If the episode scripts are serialized, make sure that the scene numbers are not repeated, otherwise that will lead to further confusion. My labeling system is that each scene number starts with the episode number: **801 would be Episode 8, Scene 1.**

Annotating the specific location in the scene header is helpful for breakdowns later, and it's recommended that the writer keep these location names consistent throughout the script. If it's called "Warf's Lodge," don't use "The Lodge" or any other title. Keep it consistent so everyone working from the script is familiar with where each scene takes place before it begins. Audio productions need reminders, often. Auto-fills in Final Draft can also help in keeping these names consistent.

Interior/Exterior marks help re-enforce the type of soundscape the voices will be competing against. INT. BAR will be much different then EXT. BAR, in directing with how loud an actor has to be. It is the same with the time of day. The scene notations, such as "continuous," help also for scheduling, to make sure that those scenes are connected for not only recording purposes, but to ensure the energy is consistent between scenes.

Lastly, it is essential for the writer to not sporadically or randomly name side characters. MAN 1 and MAN could be two completely different actors, or the same. If a character is under a disguise, or not revealed, put the real character's name in the script with their disguise as parenthetical. Use TOM (as old man), and **not** OLD MAN (Tom). Not doing this will force an accounting of two different characters in the data reports. The clever hook of hiding one's identity doesn't need to be in the production script. ('Pitching' script on the other hand...)

A clean and organized script will be easier to deal with, and as long as the writer is aware of the above requirements, the next steps will be considerably easier.

6.2 Reports and Breakdowns

This is how to use one of the most beneficial components to Final Draft: Reports. These are generated from a script when specifically written in Final Draft format. The reason these files are different from a script written in Microsoft Word is that the "saves" contain extra meta-data for all the elements contained in the script. It tracks every scene number, break, and even the character name that was misspelled a few times. All essential data, which are needed for the following reports. Be warned! Importing scripts written in other programs can be problematic and require additional steps to reformat the data into the proper categories within Final Draft.

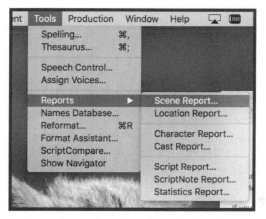

Fig. 6-2-1 Cast Report Options

There are only two reports that we need for scheduling. Cast Report and Scene Report, both in the 'Tools-> Reports' section of Final Draft.

Cast Report
Contains the list of characters, how many lines each one has, and how many scenes they're in. For the sake of calculation, a "line" of dialogue in a script is counted when a character speaks uninterrupted. Some lines can be half a page, or one word, but the general calculations remain the same when they are averaged out.

This cast report also exposes any mistakes or double-characters (MAN vs MAN1; HENCH vs HENCHMAN). Even after removing the identified mistake or have fixed the problem, sometimes the character data is still there. To clean up the list and have a nice, neat cast report, go to the top menu bar and select 'Document -> SmartType.' This will bring up the character list. Select the rebuild option, and the character list will optimize based on the contents of the script.

Fig. 6-2-2 Smart Type Options

If there are still partial character names listed or mistakes shown, then the error is likely still in the script. Use the search function to correct these errors manually, and rebuild again. Don't use the "delete" function to remove the character from the list because the mistake will still be contained in the script.

Before moving on to the next report, make sure that this list is error-free for each and every episode. If the Cast Report is filled with errors, then the Scene Report will be as well. The goal in making sure all these lines are properly assigned to the correct characters is so that dialogue isn't missed or overlooked. It's easy to miss one vital line in a large story.

GOLDRUSH 101 - VER 5.3 -- CAST REPORT

Character	Total Dialogues	Speaking Scenes	Non-Sp. Scenes	Total Scenes
PUCK	154	10	0	10
CARL	72	8	0	8
MULDOON	77	8	0	8
ROBBINS	66	7	0	7
ALEX	108	6	0	6
NICHOLAS	59	5	0	5
VERA	62	5	0	5
VICTOR	10	3	0	3
MICHAEL SWAN	2	2	0	2
HOGGS	20	2	0	2
CJ	9	1	0	1
COLONIST	1	1	0	1
MICHAEL	5	1	0	1
PEGS	4	1	0	1
WEARY STRANGER	14	1	0	1
HUGH	3	1	0	1
VIOLET	2	1	0	1
CHAPTER 1	1	1	0	1
SAUL	6	1	0	1
ROB	0	0	1	1

Fig. 6-2-3 Goldrush Cast Report

Scene Report

These are the reports from which all schedules are made. Every point of data on this sheet will be broken down and used. The only thing that's tricky is that the page length is written in 1/8th increments. When entering data into the Excel spreadsheet (or google doc), it will need to be converted into decimal notation in order to be calculated properly. Since the cleanup work on the script was done in the last step, this scene report is now ready to move on to the initial data entry.

6.3 Creating the Schedule

GOLDRUSH 101 - VER 5.3 -- SCENE REPORT

SCENE #	SCENE HEADING	PAGE #	LENGTH
0	CHAPTER 1 (1)	1	1/8
101	EXT. DESTROYED BUILDING RUBBLE - LOS ANG,Ä¶ CARL (12), MULDOON (18), PUCK (18), ROBBINS (19)	1	5
102	CREDITS SEQUENCE. MICHAEL SWAN (1)	6	3/8
103	INT. EMPTY ROOM MICHAEL SWAN (1)	6	5/8
104	EXT. ARENA - DUSK NICHOLAS (1), VERA (2)	7	3/8
105	INT. PHARMACY - DUSK - CONTINUOUS ALEX (11), NICHOLAS (12), VERA (8)	7	2 5/8
106	EXT. ARENA - CONTINUOUS ALEX (7), NICHOLAS (8), VERA (8)	10	2
107	INT. OFFICE BUILDING - CONTINUOUS ALEX (19), NICHOLAS (16), VERA (26)	12	5 4/8
108	EXT. ARENA STREET - CONTINUOUS ALEX (20), HOGGS (12), NICHOLAS (22), PUCK (6), VERA (18)	17	6 4/8
109	INT. GENERAL PUCK,ÄÔS OFFICE - LATER ALEX (47), CARL (4), CJ (9), COLONIST (1), HOGGS (8), MICHAEL (5), MULDOON (6), PEGS (4), PUCK (72), ROBBINS (8)	24	13 6/8
110	EXT. LOS ANGELES 2010 - EMPTY LOT - AFTE,Ä¶ CARL (20), MULDOON (12), PUCK (14), ROBBINS (14), WEARY STRANGER (14)	38	5 3/8
111	INT. PUCK,ÄÔS OFFICE ALEX (4), PUCK (4)	43	1
112	EXT. LOS ANGELES - EMPTY LOT CARL (23), HUGH (3), MULDOON (25), PUCK (18), ROBBINS (18), VICTOR (2), VIOLET (2)	44	7 6/8
113	INT. HUMMER - CONTINUOUS CARL (4), MULDOON (4), PUCK (5), ROBBINS (3), VICTOR (1)	52	1 4/8
114	INT. HUMMER - LATER CARL (2), MULDOON (2), PUCK (2), ROB (0), ROBBINS (1)	53	5/8

Fig. 6-2-4 Goldrush Scene Report

There are numerous film scheduling programs out there that will take the script file directly and break it down for filming. They are complex and expensive, however, and aren't designed exactly for audio-only productions.

To simplify the process, I developed a simple breakdown system, which can easily be re-created on a spreadsheet with Excel or Google Docs.

Google Docs (Sheets) vs Excel

There have been many advances made in cloud computing over the past few years. Google Sheets, a free online spreadsheet program that comes with every Google account, is able to share one spreadsheet and be edited simultaneously between multiple users. It handles simple functions, which is more than enough for what is needed to contain an entire schedule. With it's offline partner Excel, though, there are some technological advantages. Excel has far more formula functions and advanced features, and does have some online editing options. But I find that less collaborators have access to the program, as it must be purchased through Microsoft. There are options to go back and forth between both places by importing and exporting spreadsheets, but formatting isn't translated perfectly from one platform to another. Personally, I prefer the cloud features of Google Docs, as schedules tend to only need simple form functions. However, some users prefer the offline speed and access of Excel, especially if only one crew member is handling the schedule. For the sake of brevity in this book, I will assume your knowledge about the basics of Excel and how formulas work. What is done here is all very easy to understand and can be learned through Lynda.com or YouTube tutorials on working with spreadsheets.

Step 1: Consolidate the cast lists and associated line count into one spreadsheet.

	A	B	C	D	E	F
1	Chapter 1	Lines	Chapter 2	Lines	Chapter 3	Lines
2	PUCK	154	PUCK	79	PUCK	59
3	CARL	72	CARL	79	MULDOON	68
4	MULDOON	77	MULDOON	75	ROBBINS	85
5	ROBBINS	66	ROBBINS	57	CARL	36
6	ALEX	108	HUGH	12	ALEX	13
7	VERA	62	VICTOR	10	KELLY	22
8	NICHOLAS	59	MICHAEL	14	LIZZY	39
9	MICHAEL SWA	2	VIOLET	9	MAX	17
10	HOGGS	20	ALEX	2	SAUL	32
11	VICTOR	9	DATU	8	HUGH	7
12	SAUL	6	PETE	11	PEGS	2

Fig. 6-3-1 Schedule Step 1

Step 2: Organize the spreadsheet and trim down the character list so that the amount of lines per episode can be clearly calculated for each character.

	A	B	C	D	E	F
1	Character	Ch 1	Ch 2	Ch 3	Ch 4	Ch 5	C
2	PUCK	154	79	59	95	89
3	CARL	72	79	36	74	87
4	MULDOON	77	75	68	64	80

Fig. 6-3-2 Schedule Step 2

Step 3: Transfer the scene report data into a new spreadsheet for each episode or the entire feature. Copy the line count from each character into their respective scene column. This can be a bit arduous depending on the length of the project, so multiple hands will help.

GOLDRUSH 101 - VER 5.3 -- SCENE REPORT

SCENE #	SCENE HEADING	PAGE #	LENGTH
0		1	1/8
	CHAPTER 1 (1)		
101	EXT. DESTROYED BUILDING RUBBLE - LOS ANG,ÄT	1	5
	CARL (12), MULDOON (18), PUCK (18), ROBBINS (19)		

Fig. 6-3-3 Schedule Step 3

The numbers created in Step 2 for Chapter 1 are then transferred to the first column. In the example below, this is column "CL" at the top with the darker shaded numbers. The individual scene line counts are then summed into a single column- in the example below, "CHK". This allows a double-check against two different data reports to make sure there are no lines or characters missing when entering data. This system enabled us to find a mistake in our own data entry. See if you can find it below.

Scene #	CL	CHK	101	102	103	104	105	106	107	108	109	110	111	112	113
Page Start			1	6	6	7	7	10	12	17	24	38	43	44	52
Page count			5	0.38	0.63	0.5	2.63	2	5.5	6.5	13.75	5.38	1	7.75	1.5	0
Character	Ch 1														
PUCK	154	154	18						6	72	14	4	18	5	
CARL	72	71	12							4	20		23	4	
MULDOON	77	77	18							6	12		25	4	
ROBBINS	66	66	19							8	14		18	3	
ALEX	108	108				11	7	19	20	47	4				
NICHOLAS	59	59			1	12	8	16	22						
VERA	62	62			2	8	8	26	18						
MICHAEL SWAN	2	2		1	1										
HOGGS	20	20								12	8				
VICTOR	10	10											2	1	
SAUL	6	6													
WEARY STRANGER	14	14									14				
PEGS	4	4								4					
MICHAEL	5	5								5					
CJ	9	9								9					
COLONIST	1	1								1					
HUGH	3	3											3		

Fig. 6-3-4 Schedule Step 3 Continued

By entering the number of lines one character has in a scene, it's clear to see which scenes each character is in and how much dialogue they have. Adding more episodes, scenes, or scheduling multiple recording days is as simple as grabbing a column and moving it to another recording day. Keeping every recording date on the same spreadsheet can make the file take longer to load, but also makes it easier for adjustments.

Lastly, for the page count rows of the spreadsheet, insert the length of what is listed in the scene report, converted from fractions. The next step involves calculating time, and those equations need to be in decimal notation. Because the length calculation isn't exact, use the following conversion chart for consistency:

1/8 Page = .13
2/8 Page = .25
3/8 Page = .38
4/8 Page = .5
5/8 Page = .63
6/8 Page = .75
7/8 Page = .86

The character list that makes up each row can be arranged in any order that best fits the production. One option for this order would be principle actors first, followed by supporting, alphabetical, or a mix of both.

Scene #		CL	CHK	101	102	103	104	105	106	107	108	109	110	111	11
Record Time (Min)				35	2.66	4.41	3.5	18.41	14	38.5	45.5	96.25	37.66	7	54.
Page Start				1	6	6	7	7	10	12	17	24	38	43	4
Page count				5	0.38	0.63	0.5	2.63	2	5.5	6.5	13.75	5.38	1	7.7
Character		Ch 1													
PUCK		154	154	18							6	72	14	4	
CARL		72	71	12								4	20		
MULDOON		77	77	18								6	12		
ROBBINS		66	66	19								8	14		
ALEX		108	108					11	7	19	20	47		4	
NICHOLAS		59	59				1	12	8	16	22				
VERA		62	62				2	8	8	26	18				
MICHAEL SWAN		2	2		1	1									
HOGGS		20	20									12	8		
VICTOR		10	10												
SAUL		6	6												
WEARY STRANGER		14	14										14		
PEGS		4	4									4			
MICHAEL		5	5									5			
CJ		9	9									9			
COLONIST		1	1									1			
HUGH		3	3												
VIOLET		2	2												

Fig. 6-3-5 Schedule Step 4

Step 4: Calculate the time necessary to record each scene by multiplying the page count by the time needed to record one page. The time needed to record a single page in a studio ranges from 6 minutes per page to 9 minutes. The more experienced the cast, the less time needed. Here's a list of the factors:

- **Experienced cast:** 6 minutes per page.
- **Standard:** 7 minutes per page.
- **Child Actors, new actors, or "green" actors:** 8-9 minutes per page.

Learned from past experience, I average out the time to use 7 minutes per page as a factor for most of my productions. This amount of time will allow at least 2-3 read throughs per page on average. Depending on the content of the scene, this can also vary needing more or less time. Padding can be manually added to the record start time in the next stage, if needed.

The average rate of 7 is factored into each scene and breaks down so that:
[Page Count] x 7 = [Record Time in Minutes]

Scene #	CL	CHK	102	103	104	105	106	107	108	LUNCH	109	111	101	110	112
Record Start			10:00	10:05	10:10	10:15	10:35	10:50	11:30	12:20	1:30	3:10	3:20	3:55	4:35
Record Time (Min)			2.66	4.41	3.5	18.41	14	38.5	45.5	60	96.25	7	35	37.66	54.25
Page Start			6	6	7	7	10	12	17		24	43	1	38	44
Page count			0.38	0.63	0.5	2.63	2	5.5	6.5		13.75	1	5	5.38	7.75
Character	Ch 1														
PUCK	154	154									72	4		18	14	18
CARL	72	71									4		12	20	23
MULDOON	77	77									6		18	12	25
ROBBINS	66	66									8		19	14	18
ALEX	108	108			11	7	19	20			47	4			
NICHOLAS	59	59		1	12	8	16	22							
VERA	62	62		2	8	8	26	18							
MICHAEL SWAN	2	2	1	1											
HOGGS	20	20						12			8				
VICTOR	10	10													2
SAUL	6	6													
WEARY STRANGER	14	14												14	
PEGS	4	4									4				
MICHAEL	5	5									5				
CJ	9	9									9				
COLONIST	1	1									1				
HUGH	3	3													3
VIOLET	2	2													2

Fig. 6-3-6 Schedule Step 5

Step 5: Arrange the recording day. For our example, assuming that Chapter 1 is all that is needed to be recorded, the schedule can be shifted around to maximize the amount of time required from each actor. Start times for each scene can be calculated after that, against the times of the studio and other actor availability. In the middle of the schedule will be other events that need to be added in. Lunch is an obvious one. You can insert additional columns (for lunchtime and such), and block out whatever time is deemed necessary. Other insertions might include a photo session in the middle of the day, an interview, or even a warmup session after a long break. Having the schedule laid out in this way can be helpful for last minute adjustments on the day-of recording as well. If someone is late for a call time, it's easy to see what scenes might be moved up, based on what actors are available, so that studio time isn't wasted.

The notable change in order in our sample was moving scene 1 later in the day, allowing the actors to record that scene out of sequence. This re-arrangement technique is used more in regard to larger projects and multi-day recording blocks. For example, Hugh and Violet only have one scene in Chapter 1, but several in future chapters. Those scenes would be arranged in the schedule so that every instance with Hugh and Violet are recorded back-to-back.

Scene #	CL	CHK	102	103	104	105	106	107	108	LUNCH	PU	109
Record Start			10:00	10:05	10:10	10:15	10:35	10:50	11:30	12:20	1:20	1:30
Record Time (Min)			2.66	4.41	3.5	18.41	14	38.5	45.5	60		96.25
Page Start			6	6	7	7	10	12	17			24
Page count			0.38	0.63	0.5	2.63	2	5.5	6.5			13.75
Character	Ch 1											
PUCK	154	154							6 PU→		6	72
CARL	72	71										4
MULDOON	77	77										6
ROBBINS	66	66										8
ALEX	108	108				11	7	19	20			47
NICHOLAS	59	59			1	12	8	16	22			
VERA	62	62			2	8	8	26	18			
MICHAEL SWAN	2	2	1	1								
HOGGS	20	20							12			8

Fig. 6-3-7 Schedule Step 5 Continued

The most important timeline insertions would be for pickup lines. Puck's lines in scene 108, could be taken care of after lunch, rather than having the call time be two hours earlier for the actor; when it's only six lines. There will be many scenes with just one or two lines from a character which can be shifted to later. Pickups can be inserted into the schedule just about anywhere by inserting a new column. If notes are required, add another row below the scene number for comments.

Single-actor pickups, or small segments that can be recorded by themselves can be easily lost, and need to be annotated and tracked for later recording. For scenes that won't have a certain character present, first highlight that scene number with a color, then put the day number next to the line count to indicate that pickup is rescheduled for another day. This helps track when something is moved to another day, and verifies a record of the move so it's not forgotten.

A missed line can be devastating in Post, especially from high-profile talent.

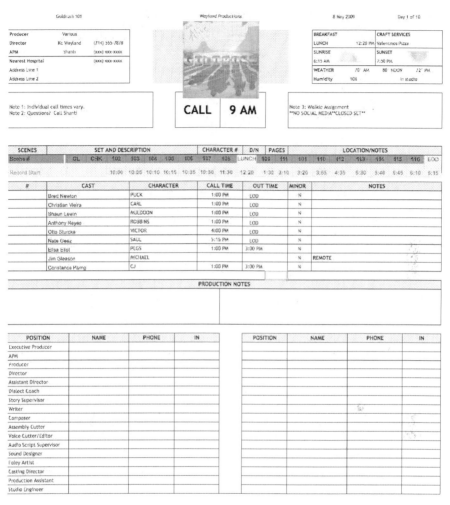

Fig. 6-3-8 Goldrush Modified Call Sheet"

Step 6: Figure out when the stage or recording space is available and create the Call Sheet from the date in the spreadsheet. Ensure there's time annotated for the crew to set up and break down the recording equipment. Setup takes longer, and the more technical the recording, the more time required. Annotate the call times for the cast based on the recording schedule, giving at least 30 minutes to be on set prior to an actor's first scene.

6.4 Further Adjustments and Considerations

There are still many other considerations for scheduling audio theater. Aside from the elements required in preparing the scene sequence, there are countless variables in finding the best times to record. Understanding those details takes planning, forethought, and a comprehension of how actors function.

Here are some of these factors to consider:
- Do the actors have enough time to warm up?
- Is an actor coming later in the day? How much extra time will they need to get into character? (This is a big factor, as it is vital to let an actor who is coming in late warm up to the others who are already in character.)
- After breaks, will the actors slow down and have less energy? Should high energy scenes not be scheduled after lunch when people might be logy?
- An intense scene first thing in the morning is probably not a great idea…
- Don't schedule a funny scene right after a heartbreaking scene.
- Shouting and yelling scenes are best done at the end of the day, if possible. Especially if there are screams that can wear down a person's voice.

As much as one plans and tries stay ahead of everything, there will always be last minute changes: an actor arrives really late, didn't receive the script and doesn't know the material, technical errors in the studio, etc… The nice thing about the spreadsheet schedule layout is that the producers can continue to make adjustments as the recording day progresses. If there are additional recording dates scheduled, scenes can be moved up or moved to later, depending on the situation.

The spreadsheet schedule is used continually throughout the recording process. As scenes are completed, the scene colors can be changed to blue. Scenes that were missed or skipped for any reason can be changed to red to indicate no recording was done, or orange if they were only partially recorded. This help ensures that every scene is recorded before wrap up.

Scheduling is not easy. It's one of the most stressful things about a recording session. Understanding the process and being able to make adjustments is vital to completing a recording session. It further insures that all the pieces are there to successfully complete the production. The key to all scheduling is efficiency. The more projects you produce, the better sense of timing and organization will be developed through the process. Give yourself and your crew ample time to do what needs to be done. Being ahead of schedule is always far better than being behind.

Chapter Seven

Preparing to Record

7. Recording Preparation

How to make contact with the talent: Once all the actors have been cast for the production, it's good to send out a welcome letter (e-mail) explaining the project in more detail. Actors audition for lots of roles, so remind them about the story and what character they are playing. Since this is audio-only, it's also good to give them some tips on how to approach the medium. Feel free to share some of the principles and ideas from this book with them.

This introductory letter includes asking the actor or agent if they have any questions regarding the project, and also if there are any dietary restrictions or allergies to consider. If providing food during work sessions, it's crucial to know exactly what NOT to serve for health and safety concerns.

Actors must be informed, ahead of time, of recording dates that will have any BTS (behind the scenes) photography, and if need be, their agents as well. Any actor who is involved with a publicist, or if the production has one, might need to have approval of photos taken that are associated with the client. These clearances are vital to enable using images of the actors to promote the project later on. This is something the production manager can either address directly with the agent, or you can simply ask the actors. The agreement can either be in writing, or have a copy of an e-mail stating the approval.

I always like to make sure my actors are aware in advance of the days that will specifically have NO photography. This will allow them to dress more casual and comfortable. One of the benefits of being audio-only is having that physical comfort level. On the other hand, sometimes recording studios have booths and studios that run hot because of sound proofing, or else freezing to over-compensate for the sound proofing. Whatever the conditions, it's good to let talent know ahead of time.

No matter what style they wear to the studio, make sure your actors always come in or bring comfortable shoes. Recording has a lot of standing time, and good shoes can make a huge difference at the end of the day. Also remind them to not accessorize in any noisy jewelry. Even though they can take it off, it can get left behind or lost.

Send a copy of the scripts at least two weeks prior to recording to the principle actors. If there's a lot of material to read, make sure there's plenty of time to go through it all. Supporting cast and all other actors need the scripts about a week out. From my experience, more time isn't always better. Actors can forget to review materials if they are sent out too early, or the material can get lost or buried in e-mails.

The principle actors should receive the entire script, and send supporting cast only the scenes or episodes that they're in. Scripts should be considered confidential. Only send a copy to people who need it. You can also include the schedule of the scenes to be recorded on which day. This is helpful to provide to the actors ahead of time, as call sheets usually come late.

The actors should be aware of their committed recording days from the deal memo, but are not given the exact time to be there. Call sheets (covered in 6.3 Creating the Schedule) are created to send out to the actors and/or agents by at least 5pm the day prior, if not earlier. It's also a good idea to ask for confirmation of their receiving the call sheet (or call-time e-mail). The Audio Production Manager should keep track of those who have responded. Don't let actors or agents have the opportunity to say, "I didn't know," when their call-time has passed and no one has shown up.

7.1 Recording Scripts

One of the aspects that's absolutely necessary to audio-only recording is paper script management. There are so many pages of dialogue that not preparing a hard copy ahead of time can be disastrous. As much as I'd love to say there was a green way to handle the scripts, such as with iPads or digital displays, there is still no better way than having the physical pages to work with. Cast and crew need to be able to write notes, highlight, and otherwise prepare with printed pages. Since the script is placed on music stands for the actors, with multiple pages lined up…

SCRIPTS MUST BE PRINTED ONE-SIDED FOR ACTORS!

The obvious reason is that double-sided scripts provide TONS of paper movement during recording, which would be obtrusive, distracting, and impossible to work around with capturing the sound on the mics. Some members of the production team can have double-sided scripts, but actors and script supervisors should have single-sided only. Scripts need to be printed and prepared well ahead of time. The last recording session I worked on had 5,000 pages of scripts to print. That kind of bulk job needs to be handled by a large laser printer or printing service, and cannot be done last minute.

Even the process of preparing PDFs to print for every actor, including smaller roles, is a large task. If you've already followed section 6.1 on formatting the script for scheduling, and also cleaned up excess characters, then the next step is fairly simple.

Principle roles are easy. Print every script or episode they are in. For supporting roles, you can print out only that 'character's sides' by selecting their name in the print page dialogue of Final Draft and saving as a PDF.

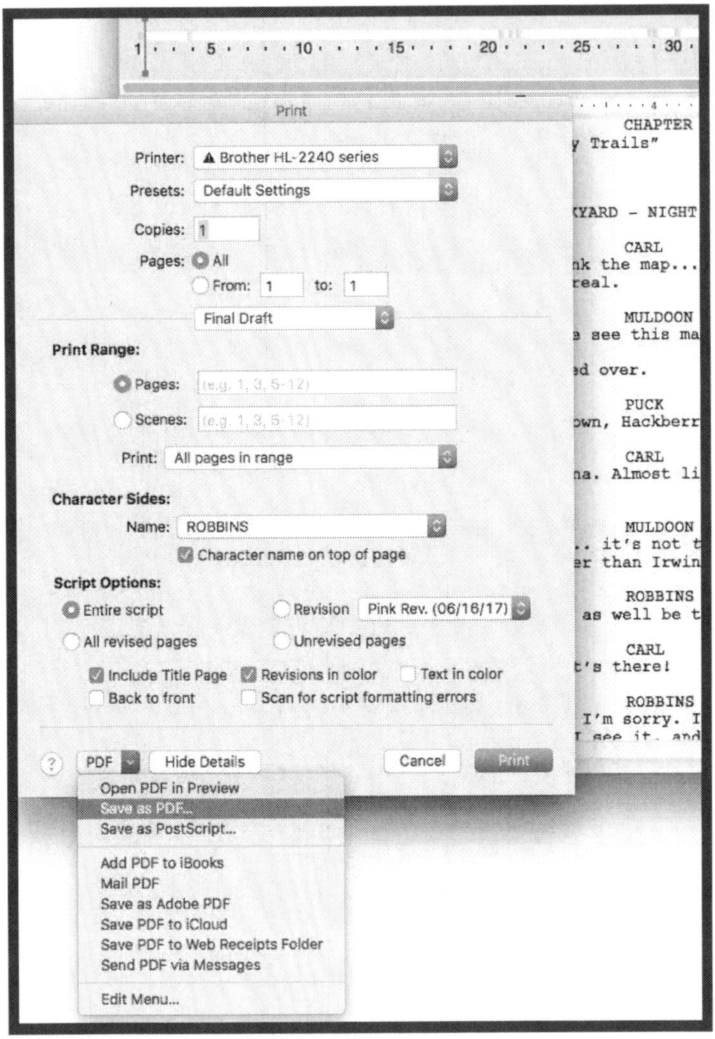

Fig. 7-1-1 Save PDF of Single Actor

By exporting this way, costs will be optimized by only printing the pages that contain specific characters. This method can be somewhat problematic if the character has the first line on the printed page, but that can be easily worked around on set.

Once printing is complete, each principle actor should have their own binder with all of their scripts three-hole punched. That way, when on set, they can easily replace pages throughout the day. Lots of studio time has been wasted searching for misplaced pages.

Organizing pages into binders doesn't just apply to the cast and crew. When I am the Director of a project, I spend extra time the night before recording preparing a special binder that only contains the pages for the next day. This lets me focus on just the material we're recording. I can also instantly see where the next scene takes place, and where we are in relation to the entire recording day.

7.2 Titles and Credits

Titles and credits are read orally in audio-only productions by a narrator. This role potentially needs to be cast, since the voice quality needs to stand out. I recommend narrators who have a strong vocal presence, and not necessarily characters from the story. Keep the "4th wall" standing by only letting the actors speak from their character. If an actor does a VO, it's usually part of the story, not describing the other side of production. Prepare all the narration in writing before recording, and be sure to include any additional verbiage that might be needed to accompany the story for commercial breaks.

The Start of the Program… There are a few specifications regarding billing order that can come from casting and contract negotiation, but other than that, it's really up to the production as to what needs to be said at the beginning and at the end. The intro template I like to follow is this:
- "[Production Company] Presents…"
- "[Title]"
- "Episode [X]" or "Part [X] of [X]" (With a mini-series it's always good to know how long it will be).

Episode intro credits need to be brief, and I don't recommend having any front billing unless it is for a single author or creator. If it's split, with multiple authors, then leave the credits for the end. With film production, credits can play under the action. Audio doesn't have that luxury since everything is spoken. It's best to get the information across quickly, and to move on to the story. There are ways to intercut audio credits with action and sound, but the intro would still become lengthy. Also it would be difficult to be used the same way multiple times for serialized content.

A theme song is appropriate for branding, and would play along with the titles. Hearing specific music allows the audience to transition into the listening experience, easing slowly into the world. The theme becomes familiar to the audience and helps identify the story. It doesn't need to be long and don't bore the audience. A good target is 30-45 seconds for a fully composed intro. If it's simple, then 10-15 seconds.

Introductory Warnings... There's no official rating system in place for audio productions, so the inclusion of a warning being featured in the beginning of the content is entirely up to the production to decide. There are explicit tags in podcast feeds that are required to warn for Language and Content, but an additional warning about loud abrupt sounds is a a good precaution to prepare those who might be listening while driving. Jumping while in your seat at the movie theater- good times and theatrically successful. Jumping in your seat while driving- potentially dangerous. I include a warning about "adult situations" as part of We're Alive, but some listeners prefer more specific trigger warnings.

Commercial breaks... Mid-rolls, or ad spots in the middle of an episode, are starting to become mainstream, and are a key point of profits for advertising. Help the listener transition in and out of the audio story realm with bumpers. There's a sense of nostalgia that comes with, "[Program Name] will return after a brief message from our sponsors." In the golden age of radio, producers used this method to clearly break the content and ads apart. Audio needs assistance: "And now, back to the program!"

Advertisements... Often there is no choice when it comes to ad selection or creation, but if the production does have creative input, try and incorporate as many ideas as possible to make it "fit" into the programming. This is an area in which many producers can be creative when pairing advertisements into their show. Think, "How can I make this ad aurally appealing and organic to the theme of our show?"

The close. The program is over... what now? "To be continued... [when]" or "Join us next week for the continuation of [program name]." Tell the listeners when the next installment is, so they will have a target date to look forward to. Release dates also let fans know that there is more guaranteed content on the way. Building anticipation starts at the end of every episode.

After delivery of the story content, there are specific opportunities to insert other messages to the audience from the production or go right into credits:

"Starring: [Actor billing 1] as [Character 1]"... or simply the actor's name and exclude the character name for time concerns. Don't have narration stretch on forever.

The order and titles of character and crew billing should be predetermined at the contract phase. If their order or placement is guaranteed in a contract, then it must be observed. But know that this is something that isn't always negotiated or even mentioned.

With that being said, credits are in place to thank and honor those who worked hard on the project. Omitting credits is sometimes possible for smaller crew roles, but for any key creative position or SAG actor (non-background), their name should be in the credits. This includes IMDB (Internet Movie Database) credits as well. Being part of an online audio series is included in actor and crew profiles and helps build their online presence.

Working with messages or ads after the credits- the longer the listener has to wait, the less likely they are to stick around. In order to guarantee ad "impressions" (or how many times an ad is heard) and that listeners will continue to the end, include some new content or have a short preview for the next installment. Let the listener know with a slate, "Stay tuned after the credits for a sneak peak from next week's episode." Other things to include in credits are the places where the audience can find more information on the series: website address, social media, upcoming events, etc. This is the space meant to communicate with your audience. Be direct & concise.

Chapter Eight

Recording and Directing

8. Approaching the Material

The "production" starts when you first bring your actors together to rehearse, and ends with the completion of the principle recording. The focus during this period should be to not only capture the highest quality performance, but also the highest possible vocal and verbal clarity. Both of these responsibilities ultimately fall on the director, and can be summed up with two simple questions: "Do I believe what the actors are saying?" and "Is the action clear to someone listening?" More details later on what that exactly means when I cover "the recording space," but let's first break down the responsibilities of a "director" of audio theater.

Directing audio-only productions is similar to directing for film, with a few distinct differences. The amount of overall creative control the director has will vary from project to project. Sometimes the director will focus solely on directing actors, and other times the director will carry the creative decisions across the entire production, which would include focusing on the actors, but also from script to final sound-wave. The focus of this section is to assist in directing actors, and getting those audio-only performances that helps the listener believe we are experiencing the scenes with the characters. This process starts long before the recording session begins.

Approach the material intently. Know the story intimately. Read the script several times. The more you know why a character is doing something, the easier it will be to communicate that motivation with the actor. It's sometimes a good idea to relay to the actors that you expect them to read the script as well, and study up on their character before the recording session. As unnecessary as that may sound, there can be a perception that because it's voice-only, then the prep work can be done on set. There isn't time for that. Often the length of the material of an audio-only production can be intimidating. Ten forty-page scripts may feel like a huge burden to an actor who might be trying to balance multiple projects at once. Poor preparation can result in character traits and dialogue that are skimmed over, rather than focused on. The audio theater format has to say a lot with a few words, and implies more than what's said. There's not a lot of time on set to "figure things out" with such a large amount of pages, so having a firm grasp on the material beforehand keeps the production moving and motivation consistent among the performers.

A good way to assist the actors with preparing for their roles is to have a Table Read ahead of the recording session (as stated in 5.8). Table reads allow the cast to come together and meet one another, and then to read the material or a section of the material prior to any recording session. It's a great way to start familiarizing their relationships with each other as characters, build trust, and also to be able to start "hearing" that person's voice in their head. After one of these sessions, performers can read the script and prepare on their own, recalling the engagement with the other characters. When surveying actors about their recording experience, the table read will often times come up as one of the most valuable exercises, assisting immensely in the preparation for the role. In the modern age of Google Hangouts and Skype, if an in-person session isn't possible, an online video table-read is the next best option.

When recording, the best results come from having your performers interact to each other in the same space, at the same time. It may seem like a simple concept, but recording together can become a battle between conflicting schedules and available facilities. Often I find myself having to come to the defense of the medium, explaining to agents or actors that this process is "not just VO or ADR work." Voice Over (VO) in the film industry is often just narration or other short segments that typically are solo and not reliant on other actors. Active Dialogue Replacement (ADR) has more to do with replacing the audio track for a performance already given and recorded on set. These methods are more about matching to something that already exists in a visual medium, than having to create believable moments using only the vocal performances to create "visuals" for the listener.

Having all the characters in one place when recording a scene offers a few additional advantages, aside from it just sounding more natural. The first is being able to make adjustments. Sometimes the words on the page don't always translate a clear picture, and broken moments can become apparent when read aloud for the first time. Making adjustments with partial casts can become tricky, especially if a character or part of the scene was recorded at a previous time. Another advantage is actor improvisation. There's a lot more room for impromptu changes only if the full cast is present. Those spur-of-the-moment improvements are hard to recreate later, and rely heavily on the casts' chemistry.

When performers *don't* get to record together, a significant problem can appear in post-production. The dialogue between characters won't match energy, speed, or both. Everyone performs differently, and it's incredibly hard to predict how the other actor will interpret their line of dialogue. Since part of the director's job is to make sure performances match, two actors absent from a scene of four people can become difficult to track and match. It can be done with editing the dialogue later, but it does lend itself to sounding "off."

The reason I emphasize the importance of recording in one space together is because the audio-only environment can be unforgiving. When the listener has to understand the scene through only the vocal performances, then all the subtle details and also mistakes come into focus. The exchanges between characters is all about action and reaction, and when one side doesn't match, it stands out. Mistakes made in the dialogue on a television show, or ADR/pickups not matching in movies, aren't always noticed. But in an aural-only environment, an unintentional slur, drop of a word, or mispronunciation is more noticeable and ultimately could make the scene confusing. If the listener stops to think, "What did they say?" then they are focusing on the production. The visual in their head will break down, and take them out of the story. **Remember: "Confusion is the killer of audio dramas."**

"Show us what you're doing, using only your voice." The dialogue is only part of the performance that is captured. When a character says a line during movement or action, it's always best to try and re-create the same physicality in front of the mic. The motion and position of the body affects the vocal cords and cannot be easily imitated. The human voice is essentially an instrument, and just like other musical instruments, the sound can be altered with different manipulations, changing shape and sound depending upon the kind of action. This is the reason for the general rule of the sound engineer to not to let performers sit when doing vocal recording; your diaphragm changes shape, making the frequency of a voice be altered slightly. If a character is crawling on the ground, put the mic near the floor and re-perform part of the action. Scenes that involve characters struggling or fighting often require someone to further assist the vocalization. There have been many times where I'll simply hold a wrist, shoulder, or put an arm around the performer (whatever they feel comfortable with), just enough to give resistance to facilitate and really sell a moment of action.

Don't just capture words. Any sound that emanates from a character's mouth (also referred to as VOX), should be recorded in the scene. If a character is eating, coughing, sneezing, vomiting (best done with the assistance of canned peaches), then all of those things should be done with the original performer, and not added later or by stock sound effects. No one coughs like you do. And out of all the vocalizations that an actor would record, nothing is more important for audio theater than the human breath.

Recording the breath of a performer is essential to frame action when there are no visuals to assist. The rate and intensity of someone inhaling and exhaling is a visualization tool used to understand someone's movement and tempo. It's often at a subtle volume in the final product, but by just hearing it, the audience can relate to what the character is going through. One of the most interesting things I've discovered about using breath sounds, is that some listeners will actually start to mimic and match the rate of the performer's breath. They can become so tuned in and involved in the scene, that they themselves re-create a little bit of the experience. Parental note: This works also for babies... if a little one is having a hard time settling down or falling asleep, match their breathing, then slow yours down... Our connection to sound is biological.

If a performer breathes too often, parts of the recording can always be cut out later in post-production, but trying to duplicate the same stock breaths over and over from one take becomes noticeable. If the breaths are too loud or too soft, that should be addressed during the recording by having the engineer increase or decrease the gain, move the mic, or both. Breaths are also one of the few elements that **should not** be recorded with multiple actors at the same time. They can become impossible to separate in Post, due to their unique frequency patterns. Designate time after intense scenes to record "wild lines" with the individual actors to record clean breaths and motion sounds.

Do not record anything other than sounds from the actor's mouth on set. A little bit of cloth movement creeping into the recording will typically blend into the scene, but footsteps and other movements should be avoided entirely by the voice talent. For running scenes or high intensity moments, it's helpful to remind the actors to keep their feet planted, and not make additional noises aside from their dialogue and breaths. Foley artists will recreate the footsteps and other miscellaneous movements later. The end product will be better if the actors are focused solely on their own voice, and the Foley artists will then focus on re-enforcing those voices through subtle techniques of movements and audible gestures. An experienced audio-only Foley artist can retell the story through the sole of a shoe.

8.1 Warming Up

Warm up the voice and body - and get ready to record. When an actor comes to the stage, they're typically cold. Their voice usually isn't warmed up fully, and it could potentially sound different from a prior recording. Everyone seems to have their own method in preparing their vocal cords. There's the gargler, the green apple eater, the singer, the honey gulper, the bassist, etc… While all those can work, I find that all that really needs to be done is to just do some tonal work with the voice. Here is one easy method that consistently works well for this. Hum, mouth open, let the air flow out. Go from low to mid to high tones a few times and really stretch out those vocal muscles; just like legs needing to stretch before a big run. Doesn't need to be more than thirty seconds to a minute. This is especially important for early morning recordings, when the scripted dialogue might be some of the first words the actors

Fig. 8-1-1 Leslie Lluvet as Jodi, on the set of Lockdown

Just as your voice needs warming up, so too does your "acting body." A common method that directors use is to pick a scene from the day's read to set the tone. This will warm up the actors together by reading the dialogue, focusing on motivation, and getting into the headspace of the characters.

In a lighthearted mood? There's always some improv games such as "Zip-Zap-Zop," "Thunder-Dome," or "Mind Meld." Tongue twisters are a great way to have the actors focus on annunciation and mouth movement. Warmup games like these can add to team cohesion and help get everyone comfortable with each other. For some, coming on set with notable or recognizable voice talent can be intimidating, and a five-minute team builder can start the day's energy level in the right direction. Be warned, though, there are actors who might think these are a waste of time. Everyone's artistic process is different, and directors have to constantly gage and adapt.

Keep the body going... invest in the longevity of the actors' performance. Voice recording days are long. The more comfortable and experienced the actors are, the more ground that can be covered in one session. But any speed this is accomplished in still involves a **lot** of talking, and more than a typical film shoot. Actors and people in general, often forget to drink water because they aren't necessarily thirsty. An occasional reminder during the recording day can make the difference in preventing injuries, like losing one's voice. For sessions that have scenes filled with shouting and conflict, keep a steady pot of tea brewing, with honey to help coat the actor's throat. The most extreme scenes, when performances involve screaming from one's upper registers, **need to be recorded at the end of the day** (or week), and done with a minimal number of takes. Vocal injuries cause delays, and with the right precautions, can be greatly minimized.

8.2 The Recording Space

Optimize the physical setup of the recording stage to maximize the amount of time the actors are able to spend in front of the mic. When every scene is recorded in the same place, the simple plan of having tables for the actors to place their script binders on can save several minutes for every page swap. It may not seem like much, but those moments add up quickly and can cost a lot of time. Disorganization can disrupt the overall flow for the actors. Script management and keeping track of the pages cannot be stressed enough. There can be such a large amount of material covered that sections are often misplaced, as the actors are jumping from scene to scene. Pre-organizing scripts into large three-ring binders let the actors take out only the pages they need, and immediately put them back when finished.

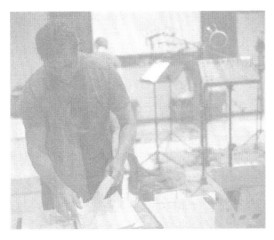

Fig. 8-2-2 James Quattrocchi, on the set of Lockdown, keeping his script organized

I call the process of moving pages from the binder to the stand the "Three Page Switch." A typical music stands only holds 3 script pages at a time when in screenplay format. Instead of each actor holding sheets of paper and making a bunch of added noise when moving them around, everyone swaps at the same time upon completion of those pages. Before the page switch is called by the director, first check with the recording control room for any technical pickups to address if a character went off mic, peaked into distortion at any given point, or misread the script. These mistakes should be caught by the script supervisor. This is almost an equivalent to "check the gate" in the old film days, verifying if anything needs to be re-recorded for technical reasons.

There are music stands that can hold 5+ pages, but if the dialogue and material is complex and involved, that many pages can become exhausting, and the actor can lose focus. If recording an action sequence or a scene with short lines, then performing 5 pages in one take isn't as difficult on the talent. It all depends on the scene.

How are rehearsals run, and how many takes are done when recording?
There's a great deal to benefit from warming up the actors and preparing for that day's scenes before the recording starts. So when the digital spools start rolling, it's not necessary to rehearse before every take. In a large audio-only production, scenes need to be recorded somewhat quickly. It's best for both logistic and creative reasons to have the first delivery of the line be the first recording.

Fig. 8-2-3 Colby (Simeon) and Ed (Gavin) between takes

The way I've approached the first take with actors is to tell them to "give me your interpretation." Often, I am surprised at what I get. The jokes are generally funnier the first time they're performed, the emotional moments sometimes deeper, all of which would have been lost in an unrecorded rehearsal. Something about the actor's first attempt can be magical. And on other occasions, it can also be disastrous.

Another approach for more complex scenes and for actors that might be new to set (borrowed from a very wise Maestro), is to say, "Let's just run through it to get the words in our mouths," and record it anyway. That way the actors get a better idea of what's going on before they start. Either approach works depending on the context of the scene. In the end, having additional recorded dialogue always adds an additional failsafe.

At minimum it's highly recommended, if not required, to **get at least two takes for every line of dialogue**. Even if the first one is perfect, the editor will need options in Post. What sounds "perfect" on set is not always the case later on.

Following the actor's first performance is when I prefer to give adjustments if needed for the second take. Another wise old directing mentor once told me, give only **one direction** to an actor for each take, "Actors can focus on one change much easier than two." This isn't referring to minor adjustments like "a little faster," or "maybe a little more energy," but major ones like "I want you to try to impress her." Then, if the actor didn't hit the performance mark again, give them another single adjustment and go for another take. Always try to build on the last direction given, and if that fails, try something new altogether.

For most second takes during a multi-cast recording, I'll give adjustments to several performers at the same time, and then continue running takes until the scene feels complete. Three or four takes as a group is common for complicated or intense scenes. If there's one performance that continually sticks out, switch to single-actor pickups focusing on one or two lines in particular.

With single-actor pickups, never have more than three takes. In a group setting, some actors can feel frustrated or singled out, and after too many takes, there's a chance the performance will never meet expectations. It's best to move on at that point, and if the director feels like that section still needs to be picked up again, then mark it and work one on one with the actor later.

Fig. 8-2-3 James Quattrocchi performing as Mark for Lockdown

Once an actor has started performing, only interrupt them if absolutely necessary. Constant starting and stopping is jarring to the actor, whose focus is on their character's dialogue. The only time I feel it's appropriate is when the scene has started going in the completely wrong direction. If the energy levels aren't right, there's something notable in the scene the actors aren't understanding, or there are technical errors, stop rolling tape. If, for whatever reason, the recorded material will not be usable, then don't waste anyone's time. Correct the issue and start over.

"Everything good? You like what you heard? Ok, Three Page Switch!"

8.3 Active Listening, Guiding, and Participation

When recording audio-only productions, it's important to be listening closely to what is being said and how it's said. Words become the pillars of the story. They need to be strong and well-defined: verbal clarity is essential for the listener. Mistakes, flubs, and blatant mispronunciations become amplified and are comparable to film's "someone walking in the shot," a bad cut, or flash frame. They break the illusion.

While the director can notice these mistakes, they are more the focus of the "booth team," particularly the audio script supervisor. This frees up the director to focus more on the story and how the material is communicated through the performances. If the words continue to be an issue and the script ends up being a tongue twister, change it. Try to get at least one good take as close to the script as possible, **but if it doesn't sound right, then it's not right.**

Fig. 8-3-1 Kc Wayland on the set of <u>Lockdown</u> listening to both the recording and talent

Actors do make mistakes, and when they stumble on sentences have them return to where they feel comfortable starting again. It often helps to have whoever's line was right before theirs repeat it to "lead them in." After a few mistakes and retakes from everyone, this method of starting over on a line without direction becomes routine. Because sound can be edited so precisely down to the smallest waveform, picking up mid-sentence is possible, as long as it carries on the same inflection and energy before the mistake.

After recording page after page, actors will start to get comfortable, so be careful about them getting ahead of the scene. When actors perform the script, they will sometimes read ahead, become eager, and come in too early over another characters's lines. This feels natural sometimes, but can be a problem when the end of the sentence is a prompt for a response.
"*Did you hear what they said about Mary?*"
"*Of course I did!*"

If the response from the other actor steps on the word "Mary," then that would be an example of *anticipating* rather than *reacting*. If the director notices an actor getting ahead of a line, they can guide them by selecting a word and telling them something like, "Let 'Mary' become your trigger, react to hearing her name."

The precise capability of audio editing gives the director further opportunities to work with actors than what's normally possible on a film set. There's a method that I call "active guiding," that let's me nudge performers in the right direction through immediate repeated takes. This typically happens when the energy of a scene seems to be dropping in what initially started as an amazing recording. I'll interrupt with a direction, trying to match their energy in the scene.

"Take it back to when he enters the room, I want you to **really command him to give you back the key.**" And if the performance weakens, I might jump in and restart them again, "Come in, **kick down that door**, tell him who's boss!" With each push, I raise my intensity with theirs, to guide them to where I want them. "That's great, one more time, keep up that energy." This is a directing style that I've seen used in acting workshops, and find that it's a useful tool to keep in the director's tool belt.

Fig. 8-3-2 Active Participation with Rogelio Ramos (Fredo)

Not all actors respond well to this technique, and it can easily become overbearing if not done in a participatory way. I often finding myself asking the actors what methods work and which don't, in order to help them in the most optimal way. Always try to make sure that the recording environment is stress and worry-free. Comfortable actors respond better to direction.

As a director, the best place to be located during the session is right next to the actors in the recording space. It's faster, more personal, and everyone is more likely to develop a level of trust and participation with the director. When I first started recording audio theater, I always sat in the booth. Listening, and then chiming in over the talkback headphones or speaker, I would often interrupt lines coupled with a click and a hiss. Sure, it works, but when I moved from where I was and started to direct **on** the stage, it was an entirely different experience. I had to be careful making noise in the recording space, but by moving where the actors were, the performances significantly improved. What I was communicating could be understood more (I like to be animated), and we were able to record multiple takes in a shorter amount of time.

8.4 Recording out of Order

To have all the key characters on set at the same time often means the production will need to be able to be to recorded out of order due to scheduling conflicts. This requires moving around scenes to saves time for actors with limited availability. In these scenarios, what becomes difficult for the actors is to know exactly where their character is in the story. On a typical movie shoot, actors have costume changes, makeup, and set design. It's easy to figure out where something takes place in the story. A recording studio doesn't offer any visual references to the material being recorded, providing only the same microphone and music stand throughout. It's easy for the actor to get turned around in the story and confused on where the scene is coming from, or going.

"Catch-up" sheets can be created to assist with jumping around from scene to scene. Once the recording schedule has been made, locate scenes that move into an entirely new time or place. These sheets anticipate that change and provide a small outline of what has happened and where the scene is going. "Okay, moving to scene 39, about two days later. This is after Vinnie robbed the liquor store and he's sneaking into his mom's house."

A director has to focus on a lot, and these sheets are invaluable to remind both the director and actor as to what is the current state of the characters. I don't always to refer to them, but they're a lifesaver when I need them. In addition to the scene info, it's helpful to include the episode, scene number, page numbers, and character list. This is similar to the contents of a call-sheet. Call-sheets are typically so compact that they don't have the space to hold the descriptions for all the scenes recorded that day.

MONDAY July 25th

Catch up sheet - Day 5 Bronzeville:

Randolph - PS 91 - Randolph has "temporarily" taken over the gang again, and giving orders to Willie and Tiny to light a fire under the town.

107 - Episode 5 Page 35
    The fire that Randolph started has subsided. Frank barnes has skipped town, heading home to St. Louis.

113 - Episode 7 Page 2
    Everett is let out of prison. His brothers Zeke and Jesse are there to meet him.

114 - Episode 7 Page 3 - Continuous
    They enter the limo to go home.

116 - Episode 7 - Page 9
    The Royale is celebrating the return of Everett, the party has begun. Randolph meets Everett for the first time after getting out of Prison.

118 - Episode 7 - Page 18
    Everett has the suspicion that Randolph will not relinquish power after his return. He shares his concerns with Jesse.

119 - Episode 7 - Page 21
    Jimmy meets up with Lisa after seeing him talk to Joe Louis, and would like to meet him as well, and of course Lisa's brother, Everett.
*Note, part of this scene was already recorded.

120 - Episode 7 - page 22
    Jimmy gets to meet Everett and Joe Lewis. Everett expresses concern over Lisa's new beau.

122 - Episode 7 - page 28
    Everett expresses his concern about Jimmy to his brother, Jesse, and wonders if they can truly trust him.

82 - Jimmy returns Lisa to Jesse and Zeke. They are very grateful for her return.

Jimmy - PS 4 (1 line)
    Jimmy says "Hey nathan" to another factory worker. That's it.
PHOTOS
LUNCH

Fig. 8-4 Catchup Sheet

8.5 Generics

"Generics" will save you time, money, and a lot of headaches you may not anticipate. Every principle actor should record "generics" when time allows. These refer to a list of short simple lines that can be easily inserted later in Post if needed. These become a safety net for editors who are trying to make the location, entrances, and exits of characters clear throughout the story. There will be occasions when the audience needs to be reminded that the character is still in the scene. In audio, a mute character becomes invisible to the world.

Some examples of generics are: "Alright," "Coming," "Fine," "Later," "Come on," "Yeah." These lines should be recorded with several different versions and intensities, so they can work in a variety of situations. Honestly, the actors have fun performing these. After all, how many different ways can one say "later?"

Other generics include character's names, entrances and exits, questions like, "Why?" and "What?" But the most important generics for Post-Production are sighs, grunts, moans, breaths (running, walking, scared), coughs, and struggles (for fights). These become vital pieces to the audio puzzle that can inserted later into scenes that lack clarity and help provide a clear aural picture in the listener's mind.

Chapter Nine

The Tech Side of Recording

9. Suspension of Disbelief

How does one record the talent? Seemingly this is the simplest of concepts, and often the most difficult in execution. The purpose is to capture the most accurate depiction of a performer's voice in a near silent environment. The result is a voice, clean and clear, without extra noise around it. When voices are like this, they become "audio neutral," and have the ability to be placed in any other environment.

Worlds can be created around neutral voices. The technology is such that there is an overabundance of post-production techniques that ensure incredibly accurate aural depictions and recreations of action and environments. But, if the talent is recorded in a space that has reverb (audio reflection/echo), then it won't be neutral. It will sound like the character is always in the room in which the actor was recorded. There are some pretty advanced pieces of software that can clean things up, but audio can't always be painted over with special effects. The human ear can easily detect audio flaws.

Audio theater dances on the edge of the blade that is "suspension of disbelief." This term is used in films when describing moments the audience fully believes the movie is taking place and are swept away into the story. Lacking visuals, the ability to hold the audience's attention and have them believe the aural world is real can be a very tricky process. The illusion needs to be kept intact, and as the creator, your job is to prevent anything from breaking that suspension of disbelief.

In my experience, the breaking of the illusion comes first from *the script*. And since that's already been covered, the next place is *the microphone*. Where and how the voices are captured greatly influences the potential impact of the story, and thus I firmly believe that all audio dramas need to be recorded in a neutral environment like a studio.

Before I address my preferred method of recording, let me first cover the alternatives. Some people I know record their performances in the field, as in the environments and spaces similar to the location in the story. A great example of how that works well is from people like Fred Greenhalgh. The recording experience can be a purely inspiring atmosphere for actors. Imagine telling stories by a real campfire in the middle of the woods, with all the actors able to feed off their environment.

The major hurdle in this method is that it's inherently restrictive on the process of capturing clean audio. Each actor would need to be individually mic'd, because sharing mics reduces clarity. Lavalier mics work great in the field, but don't sound nearly as good as a studio mic. Shotgun mics are used often for movies and work great in the field, but they too will pick up a lot of extraneous sounds. Think of the fire crackling noise drowning out an actor's lines, possible body movements that step on another's performance, not to mention the noise interference of planes, cars, or even the distant rumble of the city. Unwanted noise awaits 'round every corner and in the many pages of dialogue. While it can be an incredibly pure artistic impression, recording sound on location is honestly a pain in the ass.

The largest consequence of field recording will come more from the difficulty in scheduling actors, and especially if the cast involves bigger name actors. It's the honest truth that no agent would want that experience for their client. Having to drive remotely to a location that is quiet enough to record only audio… well, you get the idea. They probably won't feel it's worth their time.

While all those hindrances might make it seem impossible, there are still scenarios where field recording is a viable option. The largest factor is CONTROL. If the environment and conditions can be controlled enough for clean recording, then field recording might be an option to capture the authenticity of the real world.

For someone just starting out, however, on-location recording can be more accessible than a studio. In fact, I encourage new audio dramatists to explore aural environments and work with eager actors who would love to try something new and slightly experimentational. It's a far easier way to start out and record on location, than to try and make a voice recorded in a room not sound like a voice in a room.

One method to explore physical spaces and not have the restriction of wires is to have each actor individually mic'd and recorded on their own body. This can be achieved inexpensively with cellphones and voice memo apps, or slightly more expensive with individual audio recorders like the Zoom H4N and individual lavalier mics.

9.1 Choosing the Recording Space

The "studio" environment is the optimal place to record audio theater. A studio is really only defined as a dedicated space that is designed for recording audio. A lot of money can be put into designing and sound-proofing these environments to prevent noise and minimize reverb; the quieter and deader the space, the better.

The goal is to find a large enough isolated space to comfortably fit multiple people with minimal reflection. Most recording studios that have spaces this size use them for bands, which isn't the best setup. Music recording studios often contain hard surfaces that add a slight *reverb,* or audio reflection. Finding the right space can be difficult given the parameters, which means it can get costly, but not always. Good engineers can stretch dollars in recording spaces, and decent studios are possible to find or build on the cheap.

How does one check for sound quality? Go into the recording space, and clap. Does it slap back at all? This is how to tell if a space is neutral. Reverb, in strict engineer terms, is the amount of time a sound reflects in a room and is quantified as "reverberation time." The less, the better. A few 10ths of a second is a good target if you have the ability to measure it (which is a tad complex). On the other hand, don't use a space that goes too far and creates a sound vacuum; voices need breathing room. This is a common problem in most VO (Voice Over) booths. They can sometimes be so dead that a voice feels strangled. Mic selection can also be a large factor when testing against recording spaces. Shorter pickup patterns can help reduce the amount of reverb.

On occasion, minor reverb can be worked around. Other times when the actors are loud, the slight echo will bite back too much into the recording.

Reverb can be reduced by adding in more sound absorbers. Sound blankets can be hung on walls, rugs to cover floors, even having couches in the recording space contributes to reverb reduction. It is important to note that reverb cannot be removed easily in post-production. It's better and easier to try and fix the problems at the mic.

There are certain types of noise that are less of an issue. A bit of air conditioning noise isn't the end of the world. Low level amounts can be fixed with noise reduction plugins, but there is also a limit to what they can remove. Depending on the size of your production, there are several more logistics to consider when finding a studio to record in as well.

Accommodate the Actors

Fig. 9-1-1 Recording Stage for Lockdown

Comfort of the actors should be at the forefront when selecting a place to record. Does it have adequate air-conditioning? Lots of people in a space will warm it up quickly. Can it comfortably fit all the bodies recording in that room at the same time? It's a good idea to visit the place you're recording well before booking the time. Other spacial considerations: Is the recording booth (sound monitoring room) big enough to fit several people from the crew? Is the script supervisor able to see the timecode for notes? Is the booth air conditioned as well? Recording days are longer and harder than most realize, and having the right accommodations during that time period reduces stress and anxiety. No one wants to record dripping in sweat.

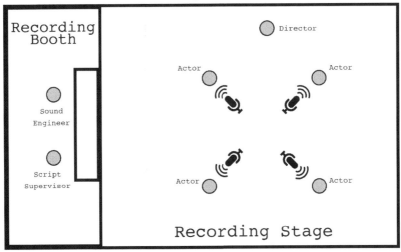

Fig. 9-1-1b Recording Stage Layout

Where do the actors go when they're not recording? Is there a "green room" for them to read over lines or relax when not on set? As a director, it's also good to have an additional space to work in and warm up the actors before entering the recording stage. It's an intimidating process to just walk into the booth having not had a chance warm up.

Accommodate the Equipment

Fig. 9-1-2 Make sure to have room for everything else

Does the recording stage have room for all the mics, scripts, and accessories? Each performing station for an actor should be equipped with a music stand for their pages, headsets to hear themselves and others, a table to hold their script binder, as well as the microphone stand with pop screener (more on these in the next section). These stations should be able to be arranged in a circular pattern so the actors can engage with each other.

Position the stations far enough apart to reduce vocal bleed from one mic onto another. If fewer characters are in the scene, try to position them on opposite sides and not next to each other.

9.1.1 Low-Budget Spaces

I'm an advocate of attaining the highest quality achievable by a studio environment. However, for the guerrilla audio dramatist, there are many ways to achieve similar results with a small budget, some extra space, and a little hard work.

Single voice sessions are easy. One way to set up a mic is using a personal closet as the recording space. Clothes are perfect for sound dampening- just be sure to set the mic inside and speak INTO the clothes, as opposed to away from them. This will absorb a fair amount of vocal reflection.

Multiple voices is where the process gets tricky. Lots of bodies in a small place creates new logistic considerations, such as heat and comfort. An approximate estimate for the personal space needed per actor is about 16 square feet. That's not a lot of space, about 4x4, which is comparable to the size of a VO booth. In order to accommodate larger casts, you'll need to construct a custom recording space.

How to build your own recording space: To create an acoustically dead space is not difficult, given the right conditions. The first consideration of any booth is location. The more closed off the space, the better.

Garages offer an open working space, and are common in most households. The only constraint might be is if there are any attached windows or large metal surfaces (the latter would allow sound reflection). Additional sound proofing can be added to the garage door with kits from local hardware stores, attaching them as such which would still allowing the garage door to open. Heat can become an issue quickly due to low ventilation, requiring airing-out sessions by opening the large doors. Creating the booth inside the garage can become tricky if the rail or automatic door system becomes obstructed. No space is without it's limitations, but these can be worked around.

Fig. 9-1-3 Home recording station set up to Foley Lockdown

Living rooms and bedrooms can offer a large enough space, and also possibly the added bonus of air conditioning. With this also comes lots of extra sound interference: pipes in the walls, fridges, and perhaps uncontrollable ventilation systems. Lower ceilings gives more vocal reflection as well, but unlike the garage, interiors may come with carpeting. Other options include local clubhouses, multipurpose rooms, etc. If a space is available and usable, then the rest can be made portable.

On sound-proofing: One doesn't realize how much sound the world has until you try to remove it all. Now you recognize crickets for the pests they truly are.

Inside of those spaces discussed above, it's ultimately critical to create another *interior* isolated sound space. The walls of the house or garage are meant to provide the first level of sound protection from the exterior. Cars driving by, birds, horns in the distance and such should mostly be minimized by the outer walls. Now the goal is to deadened it further, by creating an additional inner wall.

Using sound or packing blankets, create a square/rectangular recording space in the room. The *room within a room* design leaves a buffer zone in-between that helps reduce even more unwanted noises. Packing blankets can get pricey, but they offer a decent amount of cloth dampening over a large area. Try to find ones that have grommets or holes to hang them so they can be secured. One option is to string the blankets from the ceiling using rope and/or carabiner clips. Attaching anything to the ceiling can be tricky, though, especially if you rent the space where the recording is taking place, or aren't allowed to drill to hang anything. You can also look into mobile sound curtain systems as another option.

Fig. 9-1-4 Ceiling Mounted Curtains and Ceiling Tiles

For argument's sake, let's just say you own the space, have permission, or know how to use spackle to cover the holes later. The hanging of blankets requires drilling into the wood beam structure of the ceiling, and/or using special mounting hardware. Thick material like dense blankets can get heavy, and not securing them properly is a safety concern. A falling blanket onto something like mic can severely damage the equipment, and if it falls onto someone... well, that would most likely just annoy them, but they *could* get hurt.

With most normal home construction, the wood studs in the ceiling can be found using a stud-finder tool. Mark the locations that will be ideal to support the blankets, drill holes, and install eyelet screws. The distance between the grommets on the blanket and the studs in the ceiling won't always line up perfectly, so spend time finding the best configuration. Try to leave a space between the ceiling and the blanket for air to escape out the sides, which can help prevent overheating. Using additional carabiner clips in a chain can allow vertical and horizontal adjustments and provide more space for ceiling ventilation.

This method can be further improved upon by making the recording spaces collapsible and reusable. In my home studio, I installed large PVC pipes at the end of the sound blankets, and hung them from the ceiling. This allowed me to roll them up around the pipe like thread around a spool. Now, when not in use, the blankets are strapped to the ceiling.

Another option, is to mount eyelet screws into the wall, and string rubber coated twisted-strand wire between posts. This creates a sort of curtain rod that allows the sound blankets to be attached with carabiner clips. This then allows the sound curtain to be collapsed to the sides rather than the ceiling.

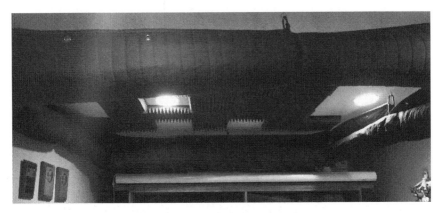

Fig. 9-1-5 Ceiling mounted curtains rolled up when not in use

For the ceiling, I recommend either using foam panels, or yet another blanket to prevent reflection. The more absorbing materials used to further deaden the space, the better results. If using a space with hard floors, additional carpeting might be required. All these extra components could be expensive, so get creative with additional sound dampening. Any sort of thick blanket, quilt, pillow, and even stacks of clothes contribute to noise reduction. Sound proofing materials don't need to be new or look pretty.

Successful spaces that you create in your home can be used not only for vocal recording, but also for Foley work as well. Creating those specific sounds while simultaneously listening to scenes is essential, and having a convenient place for Foley speeds up production significantly.

Cost references:
Sound Blankets = $50 - $200 each (the thicker the more expensive)
Foam Panels = $50 each (order directly from Foam Factory wholesaler)

9.2 Signal Flow & Audio Hardware

Let's talk about the recording setup. This section is going to cover "**signal flow**," where the sound proceeds from beginning to end. Knowing there are many opportunities for noise introduction onto the audio recording, each of the following steps contain ways to minimize unwanted sound to achieve that neutral and clean vocal capture.

Fig. 9-2-1 Signal Flow

The mouth...

Yup, the first piece of hardware is the performer's mouth. It's also a biological system that tends to develop clicking sounds. If this happens, the first step to try is to back the mic away. But if that doesn't work, offer the actor apple juice, or a green apple. The acids work to reduce the clicking by "tightening up the salivary gland," (or at least that's what other sound engineers have told me). It does work often, but regrettably it's not a fix for everyone.

to the pop screener...

The next line of defense against unwanted noise from the actor is a pop screener. Ever see those pictures of pantyhose on a hanger in front of a mic? That's pretty much what these essentially are, except now you can order a better version off Amazon.com for about $20. They scale in cost relative to quality. Metal screens typically last longer than the cloth ones and also hold up better in a studio environment. Cloth or metal mesh both work well, but voices react differently to each material, so having both can provide additional options if the pop-screener is affecting the vocal quality.

So what do they do exactly? The pop screener prevents the performer's breath from causing distortion on the mic. A microphone works by recording the vibrations through internal diaphragm receivers. The movement of air from someone breathing can completely skew the mic's ability to record the voice, especially on the "P's" and any other syllables that push air out ("plosives"). The more sensitive and higher-end the mic, the more distortion can be caused by wind. It's also helpful, if possible, to offset the position of the microphone so that the natural breath goes past the mic, and catches less plosives.

to the mic…

Here's how it works: The sound pressure waves come from the actor's mouth, and go through the pop screener. These vibrations are received at the microphone and then translated into an electrical signal. Without going too "techie," there are a few things you do need to know about mics. There are mainly two different kinds, condenser and dynamic. The condenser mics include the more movie-style mics like "shotguns." While dynamic mics are like the handheld mics you see performers use on stage at a concert. Condenser mics require external power (phantom +48v), are typically more sensitive to sound vibrations, have distinct and sometimes long pickup patterns (directional range), but ultimately are more fragile, and if dropped can break or perform poorly. One can almost hear how many times a condenser mic has been dropped. Dynamic mics don't need external power and are more rugged. Most of these have a much shorter range and pickup pattern, but often don't have the aural fidelity that the other mics offer. If you get the mic types confused (and I do on occasion), think of the "Dynamic Duo," for just as those *dynamic* superheroes didn't need power, neither does a *Dynamic* Mic!

Now, as with everything, there are exceptions. There are high-end dynamic mics that have much better recording quality for voices, so it's impossible to say that one is better than the other. You'd have to analyze the function and design of the mic which best suits your purpose. The range of microphones available on the open market is staggering. It would be impossible to compare them all, so I'll only cover a few that pertain to this medium.

If you're looking to purchase or rent a microphone for a production, I would recommend demo-ing it first, and testing if the quality matches expectations.

If you're not able to handle it in person, read reviews from people who are using that mic for a similar purpose and in a similar space. Mics are designed for their function, so you want to make sure you have a comparable intent. In terms of cost, it is safe to say that "you get what you pay for."

The best condenser mic that I've worked with is the Neumann u87- a classic design that captures a nice, full representation of a person's voice. Studios use them almost exclusively for cartoons and other VO projects. This mic has become an industry standard over the course of many years. The tech world of audio doesn't leap forward with recording improvements like the *video* world does. This mic is here to stay. The downside? Each one is about $3k. Neumann does offer a few other lower cost condensers like the TLM 103, which costs $1k.

There are still great alternatives to Neumann that are a bit more feasible in terms of cost. The next mic down the line, in my opinion, is the Shure SM7B: a dynamic vocal mic that is much more inexpensive at around $400.

For vocal shotguns, I'm a fan of Audio-Technica's 4073 line, and have recorded all of We're Alive and Lockdown with them. They're mid-range as far as shotguns go, have a decent pickup pattern, and can run about $300 for slightly-used models or $600 new. The reason I like this style of "shotgun" microphone is because the tight pickup pattern is ideal for recording multiple-actors, and they have the same warmth and feel as the sound we hear in movies. This is because they are the same style of mic that is primarily used on film shoots.

No matter what mic you choose, remember the quality of the mic is typically the most important factor for overall recording quality. It is the direct translator of an actor's performance into a signal that will be captured by the computer. A production doesn't necessarily need to own their own microphones. It's often more fiscally feasible to rent them (or any equipment for that matter), for only the duration of the recording. Once the session is over, it makes no business sense to have four to six mics sitting around gathering dust. I do, however, recommend at least one microphone be owned, to use for additional pickups and possible Foley work.

For important studio sessions, have an additional backup microphone set up for each actor at their station. Most studios include the mics used during the session as part of the rental fee. During the recording of Bronzeville, I had every station mic'd with both a u87 and a shotgun mic. We ended up using the recordings from both mics at various times depending on the actor and performance. Mics respond to voices differently with each scenario. This choice allowed us the option to choose which was better quality later, and fall back onto another mic if one had any interference or issues. Don't miss a great take because of a technical problem.

to the mic stand…

As long as they hold the microphone in place and don't fall over, mic stands don't need to be super complex. If the mic needs to be moved around a lot, a more durable mic stand will come in handy, such as the Hercules model. These stands have larger and more precise knobs for tightening or loosening the arms for adjusting. For Foley work, I want to easily manipulate the mic stand I use, whereas a voice recording stand doesn't need to be designed to constantly move.

which holds the mic, that's connected to the XLR Cable…

XLRs are those three-pin audio plugs you may have seen before. They are used in practically every music venue and studio setting, and it's hard to find any professional audio equipment that doesn't have balanced input or output jacks. If an audio connection is considered "balanced", it uses 3 wires per channel; an unbalanced connection uses only 2 wires per channel. That headset jack on your phone or the back of your computer? Unbalanced (stereo does not mean balanced). The three pins on the bottom of the mic: balanced. The difference is that *one extra wire connection* per channel. The three signals that go through the XLR, are "HOT," "NOT" and "GROUND." "HOT" being the audio signal, the "NOT" being the *inverse* of the audio signal, and "GROUND" being the noise dump or reference level.

By having the signal and its inverse next to each other, whatever noise was introduced through the cable is then canceled out through phase inversion. That design lets audio cables go for extended lengths without any unwanted interference being added onto the audio signal. The only noise that seems to penetrate the cancelation comes from power cables. Be sure to run audio and AC power cables separate at all times, or else the 60hz of the electricity will ride onto the audio signal.

Balanced cables have two different possible configurations, XLR or TRS (Tip-Ring-Sleeve), which describe not what the cable is, but the ends of the cable. The 1/4" TRS plug is larger than the typical 1/8" headset TRS, but has the option to be used either as balanced or stereo unbalanced.

and the cable is plugged into the audio IO…

The microphone is connected to the XLR which is now connected to possibly a recording device, a computer audio IO (Input/Output), a preamp, etc… There's a lot of potential destinations, so I'll only cover a few that are relevant. In an ideal studio environment, the mic would go first to a pre-amp which provides power to the condenser mics, and boosts the signal while minimizing as much external noise as possible. Pre-amps are built into many different types of consumer recording interfaces, while higher-end studio recorders will have them separated.

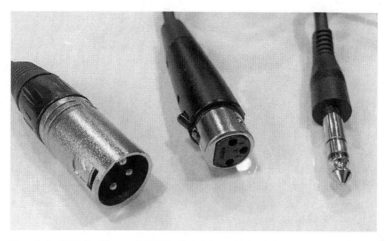

Fig. 9-2-2 XLR (Female), XLR (Male), and TRS (Male)

No matter what audio signal processing workflow the recording studio has, the recording is always going to be done on the computer through some sort of DAC, or Digital-to-Analog Converter. This last DAC component is simply a box that connects the XLRs to the computer typically through a USB connection. The more expensive the box, the more inputs and outputs that can be connected at the same time. The model that I used in my home studio for <u>We're Alive</u> and <u>Lockdown</u> was the Avid Mbox Pro 3, which is a mid-range unit with four mic preamps built in. The standard Mbox 3 has two mic preamps, and the higher-end pro units like the HD Native IO with a 'Pre' system has sixteen. For any recording setup involving audio theater, I would say, at minimum, four mic inputs are necessary. It's feasible to rotate 6-8 actors on four mics in most scenes and make that physical setup work.

the audio IO is then plugged into the computer...

I don't want to spur a Mac vs PC argument, because both systems can run audio capturing and editing software just fine. However, I would not be honest if I didn't say that the audio industry relies more heavily on the Mac platform. And from my experience as an engineer, Macs tend to be more reliable. Audio processing can be resource-heavy on a computer, and the IO interfaces are sensitive to hardware and driver conflicts, along with added speaker noise and grounding issues. The PC market has such a varied amount of manufactures for components that it's not always easy for software developers to test and qualify each possible hardware configuration to work optimally. Fewer models of Apple computers with similar hardware configurations means that audio interface and software makers have to test against fewer systems, and therefore have to deal with less bugs and tweaks to their drivers ahead of launch. I have dealt with major computer manufacturers regarding PC hardware conflicts over basic things like USB ports that introduce pops and static, as well as sound card drivers that don't allow more than one piece of software to use the speakers.

the computer runs the software...

The software is the real brain of the operation. After the performances are captured, every step from then on will be within the program's interface. The only software that I can recommend for this sort of advanced audio production is Avid's Pro Tools. It is THE industry standard and any decent recording studio is going to use it primarily. Pro Tools is considered a DAW (Digital Audio Workstation), and is responsible for organizing all the information and assembling the recorded material into the final export. It's the one-stop shop software, supporting a variety of audio files and IO interfaces. It has a vast amount of plugins available that enhance it even further, automation tools that allow precise tweaking and timing of various effects, and the list goes on and on.

I've have used non-linear editors for both video and audio since they first came to market, but this one continually and consistently grows and gets better with each update. Coming from a video background, I was astonished that I had the ability to edit and listen simultaneously. This is something I couldn't do with video editors, which now saves a lot of time in Post. This would become invaluable as I learned that editing audio takes longer than video, and there's infinitely more ways to change an edit through audio.

That's not to say the program doesn't have flaws. It is expensive. Avid is moving to more of a subscription route in order to establish continuing support of their product, which can add up if using multiple stations. There also are some aspects of the program that are tailored more for music and film sound design, which means it's not very flexible with cutting and extending time like video editing software is designed to do. Even with its limitations, Pro Tools still is the best for this workflow, and will be used as the featured platform for post-production covered in later chapters.

NOTE: This text will cover a large amount of tips and tricks in how to use Pro Tools as the primary editing software, but will not be able to include every aspect of setup and use of the program. There are various YouTube and tutorial programs from publishers like Lynda.com that can provide amazing step by step instruction, enough details to fill many books by themselves.

And that's the end of the chain... but there's still a few more pieces of hardware associated with audio recording. The first being:

the music stand.
These are placed below the microphones, and hold the sheets of dialogue for the actors to read and record. Typically a stand can hold 3 pages, but special ones designed for VO can hold 5, as well as extend higher for taller actors.

Have custom cut pieces of carpet, or sound proofing on the music stand to prevent metal vocal reflection. This also works well to keep the pages from falling off. The placement of the stand is vital as actors tend to move their whole body to read the pages and can go off mic. There's typically a narrow sweet spot for most microphones. Always make sure the actors can read their script comfortably and keep their chin in neutral position, so as to not to crush their vocal cords. You want them to be able to focus on their performance. There are music stands that are designed to have holes through the page-holder as well, to further reduce metal reflection.

Headsets are also a good option to have on hand. There are many actors who prefer to be able to hear their own voice in order to gage their performance and quality. Vocal trainers can teach actors how to use headsets to their advantage, including how their voice responds to the mic and to make their own adjustments for mouth distance or intensity. Other actors view headphones as a distraction, limiting their movement and performance.

An added benefit to having headsets: With the right configuration and setup, you can feed sounds of the environment around a character right into their headsets, or use music to warm them up. But remember to discontinue before recording. Loud headphones bleed onto mics, so never have them louder than necessary and turn them off or disconnect when not in use.

Each recording station should have all the things previously mentioned for each actor. The music stand, a mic (or two if you can have a backup), a chair, water, and a small table to place the script binder.

In a typical recording space, there might be four to six recording stations depending on the size of the cast in scenes. Rarely would more than six people talk at the same time. In the off-chance there is more, it's easy to double up actors on a mic.

9.2.1 Low-Budget Recording

Mics
Recording one person on a computer is easily done with a USB mic.

However, in order to record multiple people at the same time and not need to be right next to the computer, I recommend getting standard XLR-capable mics, and all the same model, for simultaneous recordings. One of the best options for the low-cost market are Sure SM58's. They're typically used for stage and live sound, since they're fairly durable dynamic mics. New, they cost about $100, and that price has stayed the same for a long time. However, positioning these microphones can be tricky in small spaces. There will be audio bleed across the mics, as these are omni-directional. But, as long as the performances are good, having and editing overlapping dialogue is not always an issue in scripted audio-drama material.

The used equipment market such as with Ebay can offer some great deals, but results aren't always consistent or reliable. Different makes and models of mics don't all sound the same, and 'wear and tear' on a mic isn't visible. Voice quality is extremely important and lends to the believability of the actors. If anything's worth spending the money on, it's a good mic.

Buying the mic isn't always the only option either. As stated earlier, I always recommend owning at least one for pickups and additional recording, but for main-cast sessions, renting is always a great low-cost option. The day-rate for high-end mics can be anywhere from $20 - $50 a day on average. This is a great alternative for the guerrilla audio dramatist.

Cabling

We covered the different types in the previous section, but when it comes to low budget considerations, be sure to go with the lower end options for cables. Those gold-plated, titanium re-enforced, 'more plastic than wire' packages next to TVs at the big box stores are not worth it. The cost of the cable goes up with construction, durability, and reliability, and not proportionally with the signal quality. Cheap cables typically sound the same as expensive ones. They just tend to break down quicker with physical use.

Computer & software to record/edit

No way around this, you need a computer. A mid-range laptop or desktop is really all you need. Windows or Mac, there's a lot of cheap options. Reaper, an alternative to Pro Tools, is $60 for the discounted license and will work on both systems, along with a very simple free editing software called Audacity. These tools work great, but can be limited in their functions.

The computer strength needed should be gaged to the amount of work it needs to do. A couple of characters and tracks doesn't require a lot of power. Layers and layers of music, sounds, dialogue effects and real-time processing will require more. As with everything, check the recommended specifications of the software and test out the tech in advance of starting production. Even with smaller productions, though, I encourage looking into discounted versions of Pro Tools. The versatility and expansiveness of the program will increase with your understanding of the inner workings of the software, so you might as well start using it now. There are educational versions available and bundles if currently enrolled.

Analog/Digital IO (DAC)

Figure out how many people it's necessary to record at the same time. The bottleneck for most computer setups are the dedicated mic input channels. To record each voice on a distinct channel, an interface will be required that has a dedicated pre-amp for each attached mic. One I've used in the "prosumer" market price-range is from Focusrite. Take a look at their current USB interface line with 4 mic preamps, which runs about $300 currently. Having one of these Analog/Digital IO's also allows balanced output for monitors.

Be careful with other IO alternatives like mixers with a USB port! These interfaces don't send each individual channel to the computer, but rather only a mix-down, or combination of multiple inputs into a stereo output (2 channels).

Mic stands, mic clip, music stands, and pop screeners

Good recording doesn't require expensive versions of all these items. However, the higher the cost, the more durable and adjustable each of those items tend to be. Again, being cheap/frugal in *this* area doesn't come across on the mic.

Cost References:
Computer $1100 (Lower end iMac ref price)
Mics - 4 x 100 = $400
Cabling = $50
DAC/Analog Digital IO = $300
Studio Headsets = $100 (at least one for sound recordist)
Mic stands (4) = $60 total
Music stands (4) = $100 total
Pop screeners (4) = $50 total

9.2a Hierarchy of Sound Recording*

Sound recording quality is not subjective. The specific harmonics or frequency response of a microphone at high fidelity is subjective. Noise introduced onto a microphone can be quantified and measured, so any amount added other than the voice is unwanted. Neutral vocals that neither carry any noise or environmental artifacts from their recording space are ideal. The only exception to this rule is when recording voices in their native environments, where the accompaniment of additional sound is the desired result.

Noise is bad, period. Each recording session presents a different amount of unwanted noise, so your objective is to mitigate as many of these issues as possible with either environmental controls or specific equipment. High-quality results are achievable at almost any level with the multitude of options in technology, but fundamentally flawed conditions lessen the audio quality. Compromises will always be needed in real-world scenarios, but the elimination of noise should remain an audio recordist's goal at every level of the hierarchy of recording setups.

On-location recording.

When on set, a multitude of noise sources will try to creep into a recording: planes, generators, background traffic, wind machines, etc. As a sound recordist, your job is to isolate the most crucial part: the dialogue. Even if the audio is replaced later, the actors need to have their original on-set voices for reference later. Sound recordists, who operate the recorder and sometimes the boom pole too, must contend with various restrictions. In a moving shot, where the characters are walking, so too must the mic.

The game is simple on set: get the best audio possible without getting the equipment in the shot. The obvious solution to this would be to "just use wireless mics," but this direct option doesn't actually understand how problematic that can be until actually on location. Not to mention the limitations of mic quality with wireless devices. Conditions change from shot to shot — the recordist must know how to adapt and what equipment to use in each scenario. Typically this playbook is the best strategy:

- **1. Shotgun Boom Mic from above.** A classic method, the one seen in movies or TV sets, because it is still the best. Shotgun mics are designed for direct polar pickup so they cleanly pick up audio when directed towards a single spot. The boom mic itself can be swapped out for various lengths, depending on the distance from the subjects. Longer boom mics would be used for further away subjects, but the longer the boom, the more potential for the narrow pickup patterns to overshoot the characters. Because the boom direction comes from above, the overshot is usually the floor, which isn't typically an issue. However, as much as booms focus on sound from the front, they have some pickup and bleed from behind. This is due to the physical construction of the mic. Every boom is different, so it's best to test or view technical reviews beforehand.

2. Shotgun Boom Mic from below. A character might be looking up at the ceiling or the sky in the scene. Therefore, there can't be a boom mic in the shot. The second option is to move it down below the characters, pointed up. The only difference from the last technique is that this tends to pick up the background noise past the characters. Anything above the actors such as planes, AC units, buzzing lights, etc. can be problematic. This style picks up everything in the line-of-sight of the mic.

3. Planted Shotgun Mic. Instead of using a boom operator to hold the mic on a stick, the mic is now planted and hidden in the scene to record what occurs nearby. In a two-person conversation, two planted shotgun mics hidden in a centerpiece will perfectly capture the dialogue without additional crew holding mics in place or unwanted wireless mic appearances.

4. Wired Lavalier Mics. This next step down is a fairly big one. The pea-sized mic attaches to the talent, so close that there's no need for any additional sound team to hold anything in place. The mics must be small just because they must remain hidden on the actors while shooting. As such, the sound quality suffers considerably compared to the shotgun mics. By wiring these lavs directly to the sound system, phantom power will also allow continuous use without battery failure. However, if the actors move a lot, this wired setup can be problematic or even dangerous in the wrong scenario.

5. Wireless Lavalier Mics. What some consider first in convenience is, in fact, last in quality. Nowadays, there are so many wireless devices like cell phones and radios that it's a constant struggle to compete with these noise generating electronics. It's hard enough to get high-fidelity audio with wired equipment competing with cell phone interference, let alone the barrage of the wireless spectrum. Good wireless mics cost a lot, and old ones can be deemed "illegal" by using frequencies reappropriated to other devices. Batteries also become more and more of an eco-issue if not using rechargeables. By having battery-reliant mics, there is a constant need to check and turn off and on equipment, prone to more failures and errors. The quality can also suffer as the heads of the mics are relatively small, and have a reduced frequency response. Wireless mics also can break on talent if used in high impact scenes.

There are a few methods in-between, and some creative others, but the above mostly covers the most ideal to least mic setups.

In-studio recording.

If the subject being recorded is in front of a computer, in a closet, drop-curtain booth, music studio, VO booth, etc., it's all considered "In-studio". The intention with any of these setups is to capture the cleanest audio, no matter any physical or monetary restrictions. None of these options should be considered a limitation in the narrative storytelling process, but each level has compromises in quality. Controlled studio environments will receive less noise interference than most in-home setups but typically come with cost restrictions. There are studios and places that will donate time when asked, or in exchange for services. Home studio setups can be free to use, but so can studios with a few conversations and bartering.

The one significant variable in this equation (a non-issue for the sound team for on-location) is the actor. Off-set, actors now have to do more 'space-work' with their acting. Professional actors can relate this to "acting in front of a green-screen" in that they would need to perform their actions in a blank world or black box set meant to be defined later. Each level of recording also has a relationship with how the conditions respond with the actors.

In terms of ideal conditions for both actors and sound conditions that capture the best neutral sound, this it the priority order:

1. Recording studio with over 300 square feet, zero reverberation, silently air cooled, isolated recordist booth, all actors in recording space, director present in the room, and the sound monitored in a separate isolated area.

Most multi-actor scenes will have three to five people on average. The above amount of space will allow all the actors to record together with enough isolation in terms of square footage between the mics. The performers could be isolated separately into booths, but there is lost intimacy when the actors are separated. Being able to interact within the space will give the actors the ability to react with each other, and build an essential character relationship. Small voice-over rooms do offer desired neutral isolation, but can make the vocals feel constrained, almost bottling the vocals.

It's easy to think of assembling an audio-drama as if it's just pieces of audio performances strung together to make a story, but it is so much more. What should be strived for above all else is believability. Does a listener believe that these people are having these conversations with each other? Frequently, the listener can hear mismatches when speakers are disconnected. The human ear is able to detect the smallest of subtle variations and inflections, especially when audio is the only anchor for the audience. The fabric of the illusion can be shattered quickly if the energy of the actors doesn't match, their conversation rhythm is off, or even if something indescribable deceives the reality of the story.

For the actors, being with each other makes it easier to perform. The logistics of getting a studio might be challenging, but actors feed off each other's energy and will deliver a better performance naturally reacting to each other. In addition, last-minute changes to the script can be made, improvisation is done in real-time, and the fidelity of all the voices match because they are recorded under the same room and mic conditions. Recording environments make up a large portion of the quality of the sound captured by a microphone, and the amount of work to make everything match is significantly reduced.

Avoid rooms that add any sort of reflection or echo in the recording space, as these will bind to voices captured in the environment in which they were recorded. A studio with a variety of flat surfaces — typically useful for musical recording — can interfere with the clarity and neutral quality of the vocals. Thus, recording a voice inside, while wanting it to sound like it originates outside, becomes very difficult.

And of course, the room should be silently cooled in a way so that the vibrations of the air movement or cooling systems don't add additional noise on the mics. Actors perform better when comfortable. Ideally, the sound monitoring booth is also attached to the performance stage, so that audio fidelity can be judged in isolation from the recording space.

2. Home studio with dedicated sound walls and ceiling with isolated recording equipment, all actors in the space, director present.

There are various steps between the two, but the next major iteration is something comparable to the home studio setup. By creating four sound-absorbing walls and a ceiling, the home audioist can record high fidelity in cost-effective noise-reducing conditions.

The thicker the walls, the better, as material density dramatically affects how much noise can be reduced. Tighter-woven sound-blankets will provide more reduction, but packing blankets and comforters are great for temporary setups. Mounting to the walls and ceilings can be done with a few eye-hole hooks into the wall studs as anchors, or if you're in an office space, ceiling tile grids can usually support blankets with a few zip ties. Just be careful not to damage the tiles.

Wood-framed and insulated walls are low-cost booths that can be assembled and disassembled with screws, for more permanent options.

Depending on the ceiling conditions, these can often be the most significant sources of additional noise, especially with in-home and office-built recording spaces. A roof-based AC unit, pipes, house vents, or air traffic can all bleed into the sound space. Tethering an additional blanket to the ceiling over the space will help reduce extra noise, but will also reduce ventilation. If creating a wood-framed environment, an extra roof with insulation is a great option, especially if air-ducting options can connect to the recording space.

The sound recording equipment should be outside of the enclosed space so that the computer fan or the engineer (the person sitting and monitoring the session) will have some sound cover to move around and not get picked up on the microphones.

3. Remote session from home booths/closets simultaneous recording with all actors at the same time, director participating.

This method is the next step in the hierarchy of audio recording spaces and actor availability. All the actors in this scenario would have a personal recording setup. Many regular VO talents already may have something like this assembled, with either a custom-made isolation booth, a closet filled with clothes, or (at the lowest end) a way to record under a blanket.

The isolation booth should cut down on the interferences that bleed into the audio, but there will be worldly noises on every recorded character that will cut in. Sometimes those can be distracting and hard to miss. Interruptions lengthen the recording process considerably, and can be hard to fix later, depending on the severity. Give yourself extra time to account for these sorts of unexpected noises and multiple takes for coverage.

Closets are usually readily available and act as effective sound absorbers, but remember to put the mic in the clothes and then speak into it. Provide room for script handling, but the audio should be good because the vocals shouldn't reflect back into the room and give unwanted reverb. If in sync, this presents a challenge in seeing the other actors, but the audio fidelity increases through this method.

Being able to record at the same time is crucial for any of these scenarios. It will allow the interoperability of the actors in real-time and help them perform with the same energy, as well as respond to feedback from the director commenting on the session. There will be slight delays and hiccups with live-conferencing buffering, but this method will at least allow for cast cohesion.

The director should be part of the conversation to hear the performances, and then give notes back to the actors to make any adjustments that would better fit the scene. Actors can't effectively listen to themselves while performing, at least not in the way that's needed to understand if it meets the context of the scene or story. They need guidance and another ear to tell them how a performance sounded, give them coaching, and even provide words of encouragement.

Recording setups should be as consistent as possible across every actor. The more the mic types match, the more they will sound like they are with each other physically. If everyone has a completely different microphone, it will be challenging to adjust the fidelity for cohesion. Each voice contains unique room noise as it is, which must be cleaned up individually. Mics recorded in the same space typically have the same noise patterns, making it easier to clean up in post. Each mic should be recorded locally and not over the internet as the amount of compression that occurs when talking online destroys valuable information and fidelity from the voice. A Zoom H4N recorder and an attached XLR Condenser mic is an excellent minimal setup. Snowball and other USB mics can work, but are typically of lower quality than XLR dedicated mics. There are software options such as Zencastr.com that will record multiple streams simultaneously and upload higher quality audio.

To keep performances in sync, have everyone count to three and then clap at the same time after pressing record locally. This will allow the editors to match the pacing of the actors, making it easy to edit later. Headphone bleed can be a problem, so be sure that the talent only has them as loud as necessary. Directors should wait until actor performance is over before speaking.

4. Sending scripts/lines with directing notes and asking for performances.

This is the easiest way for those who have competing time schedules and can't record with everyone else. The least desirable option available is to send along a script and let the actor be responsible for recording the dialogue remotely and sending it back. Even if the other actors aren't available, the director could be present while recording and provide notes and feedback in real-time, rather than not being able to make changes once the talent stops. Without direction, this method requires a lot of back-and-forth communication, and often requires pickups later on. Some lines will just not work, mismatching the intention of the other characters and must go back for a re-record. If the director has heard the other performances, and this is just one character to swap out in the scene, they can send along samples to match previous sessions. Requiring actors to read against an already recorded performance can be problematic, though, especially if they are continually getting ahead or behind the other character's material.

9.3 Recording Formats

Mono vs. Stereo vs. 5.1 vs. Binaural- which one is better for audio theater? This topic comes up a lot, and many people have different opinions on which is more favorable than another. There doesn't seem to be a more polarizing topic- [cough]. As stated throughout this book, the primary objective of any audio-only entertainment is to find a way that best communicates the story through sound.

I tend to stay in the Mono/Stereo range for my productions. Most of the voices are mono, and I only do minor stereo effects when it really matters, or with a specific moment. Panning (e.g., the process of shifting the audio from the left channel to right or vice-versa) and stereo effects are distracting, often calling attention to the technology or editing rather than the story. In real life, when someone walks in front of a person from left to right, there isn't a huge shift in their perception of volume from ear to ear. Most likely, if the focus was on a person, the listener would be turning their head to follow. To make it sound correct in editing, panning amounts would need to be controlled, subtle, and precise. The amount of added effort that goes into tweaking perfect panning isn't worth it. There is already an extensive amount of work required to sell this created world and actions with only *audio* at your disposal.

Similar to 5.1 surround sound, which is the decimal notation for soundscapes involving five distinct channels of audio and a sub, or any version of surround sound, the post-production process is very complex and costly to do correctly. Most of the online audiences would not be able to experience it in the intended format anyway. A controlled environment is needed, as in a theater where listeners have a contained experience. Just focus on making a great sounding story in mono/stereo. It can always be re-mixed and re-mastered in 5.1 later.

Binaural is a little different. True binaural means to record the audio exactly as a human would hear it, and mimic the sound location over a pair of headsets, or speakers close to your ears. The experience of "Moments with Mr. Lincoln" in Disneyland, where they mimic cutting hair with sound- that's binaural. Check out some examples of this on YouTube to experience what true stereophonic sounds like on headsets, searching the keyword "binaural samples."

The end experience can be amazing, but the production aspect for storytelling is difficult. There are mic crossing methods, and even specially designed foam "heads" that act as microphones trying to mimic the human ear. The catch is, every sound effect needs to be recorded under the same mic conditions, which can get incredibly tricky to do correctly and maintain consistency. Actors performing around a stationary binaural mic is one method I've seen used, but that also gets tricky with blocking the performer's position. Be sure to test out any binaural workflow from end to end to make sure that this is the right choice for the production.

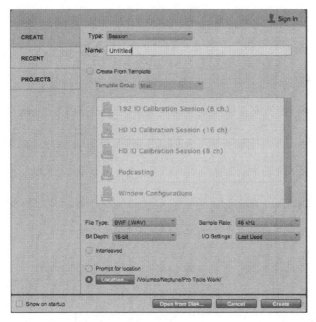

Fig. 9-3-1 Pro Tools New Session"

16 bit & 24 bit - 44.1/48/96khz?! What does it all mean?

I'm gonna get a little techie here, but will keep it relatively simple. Bit depth: 16bit vs 24 bit. The more bit depth, the more amount of information that can be captured from the original audio. The sample rate, such as 44.1khz, 48khz, 96khz, is how many times that information is captured per second. Put them together and that's the measure of how much information is captured from the audio.

It may seem like a simple choice, "More is better, so let's put it to the highest setting!" But the reality is that even with modern computers, there can be an information bottleneck that slows down the workflow. If recording a single voice, then the highest setting makes sense. Recording music, same thing. A single voice won't take up much space on the computer, and even though music has a lot of tracks and instruments, it's typically pretty short. Audio theater becomes a beast for data.

Show me the numbers: If you're recording 5 characters for 5 min, how much space will that take up? Here are the results from Pro Tools recording "pink noise" (a type of generated signal).
- Bit Depth: 16 - Sample Rate: 44.1khz - (Listed at 5 MB per minute per channel) **Test Results:** 5.7 MB - or 142 MB for 5Char/5Min
- Bit Depth: 16 - Sample Rate: 48khz - (Listed at 6 MB per minute per channel) **Test Results:** 6.2 MB - or 155 MB for 5Char/5Min
- Bit Depth: 24 - Sample Rate: 96khz - (Listed at 17 MB per minute per channel) **Test Results:** 18.6 MB - or 462.5 MB for 5Char/5Min

The time can add up quickly. Using Lockdown as an example, we chose to record at 16/48 to reduce our overall workflow size. Large hour-long sessions at 24/96 would have increased our file sizes by three-fold. To show you the math based on the numbers above, with an estimate of 6 people on mic per scene on average:

- 29 Hours of recorded material. At 16/48: 37.2 MB per min, 2.2 GB per hour, 64 GB total.
- 29 Hours of recorded material. At 24/96: 111.6 MB per min, 6.7 GB per hour, 200 GB total.

That size may not seem huge, but that's JUST the voices. All the extra Foley work, music, sound effects, mix-downs and offline processing will add more to the session size. Smaller audio file sizes can often give you the freedom of having remote sessions and online transfers with editors. At 24/96, the file size transfers of entire sessions can get excessive. Upload speeds in many areas, especially in homes, can be far more limited than download speed.

My advice: test it out. Listen for the difference between the two. Can you hear it? Another factor is the project's length. More than 4 hours produced material? Stick with 16/48 for now. Technology will increase in time, so I imagine this statement will become a relic soon. That being said, there are so many existing limits to the human ear that the further advances in audio definition may be completely worthless and the quality increase undetectable.

9.4 Session Setup

Once the recording format has been selected, and all the other logistics are taken care of, then it's time to move into the recording space. One of the most important roles in that environment and the position that's responsible for handling the tech-side of things is the Studio Engineer. Most recording facilities will have one on staff or assigned to the session. The engineer is responsible for making sure everything is recorded properly: the mics are correctly placed, there's no interference on the mics or cables, and the computer hardware is functioning optimally in capturing the voices at the right bit depth and sampling rate. The output of everything is most likely going to be into a Pro Tools session, and part of the job of the engineer and Post team is to make sure that session is set up properly. Post-production has to deal with a large amount of recorded voices, and if everything is left with default values, it can make the digital workflow messy and cause unnecessary delays.

Since this book focuses on a Pro Tools workflow, here's a few extra tips specific to that program that will help later on in post-production.

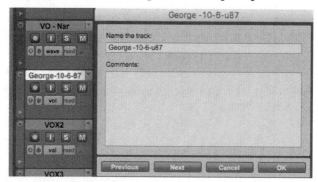

Fig. 9-4-1 Rename tracks before recording to them

Name every track with the character name, date, and mic type. **Example: George -10-6-u87**

It doesn't need to be complicated, just unique to the character. Don't use the actor's name since everything is referenced from the script. The date creates a unique signature that is embedded into the file name, and the type of mic helps identify the source from backup or alternate mics. Pro Tools writes the files based on the track name, which is why the tracks should be renamed when new characters record using the same mic. It's possible to rename the files later, but DO NOT leave it as the standard naming. Pro Tools can relink files most of the time, but it can become confusing if many files on a system have the name "Audio_01." Renaming the tracks before recording will make things much easier in the end.

Another task for the sound engineer is to make sure that the timecode references don't overlap from day to day or repeat if working with new Pro Tools sessions. For example, if the start of the session from Day 1 goes until hour 8:34:00:00, then start the next day at hour 9:00:00:00. This sort of consistency will help editors later on when trying to locate different sources. If each daily session starts at the same timecode of 1:00:00:00, it can become confusing if not impossible to track by the script supervisor.

The engineer will spend a lot of time moving mics, checking cables, headsets, etc…, so it's good to have the Script Sup shadow the engineer, and assist with computer management. After recording, the engineer will give a copy of the files to the post-production supervisor, and the post-process can begin.

9.5 Script Supervising

The only way to effectively track the performances, especially when recording out of order, is to have a script supervisor on set to monitor and log exactly where each take is on the script in relation to the computer's timeline. This role is **not the same** as its film counterpart. The normal duties of a script supervisor on a film set is all about keeping continuity and accuracy when recording out of order. While that's true for both roles, the Audio Script Supervisor's importance is much more significant.

The Audio Script Supervisor, which is referred to as the "script sup," and not the a-s-s acronym for obvious reasons, is responsible for every line of dialogue recorded. This is a tremendous amount of pressure, because without them, content would become lost in the editing process. When recording audio theater, there can be days of material. Each actor has their own mic (or two), and each line of dialogue is recorded at least two to three times from over several hundreds of pages. Lockdown was only 5 hours long when finished, but there was over 29 hours of recordings that spanned about 370 pages. To find and edit that much dialogue, a production needs a clear "road map" to be created on set.

The best place for the script sup is usually next to the engineer in the control booth. This will allow them to coordinate and make sure that the timecode specifications are being followed throughout. "Timecode," for those who haven't used it before, is a digital clock that runs alongside the recorded time. In visual mediums it's used to help keep the audio and video recorded on separate devices in sync with each other. Both are then brought back together in Post. SMTPE (Society of Motion Picture and Television Engineers) Timecode looks about how you would expect it, with one exception: 08:34:55:12-(hour:minute:second:frame)

The last placeholder might be a surprise, but because SMTPE Timecode was developed in the film world, it goes by frames as the smallest unit of measurement. The reason why film timecode is used in audio production is because all of the Post facilities are equipped for it. There are options for timecode with milliseconds, but those standards aren't always supported universally. In terms of the audio recording quality, timecode doesn't make a difference. Timecode is simply a reference (or map) of the recorded material in the session, and the script sup is the cartographer.

Attached is a sample of a recording script with markings. Forgive me as this book might be in black and white, and there are lots of colors corresponding on this sheet. The specific colors are chosen by the script sup, typically from what pen or marker colors are available. The most important thing to note are the marks to the right of the dialogue. Those timecode lines run from top to bottom, with the timecode annotated when the dialogue started to record, all the way till the end of the take. It's not necessary to write down the timecode of the end, just the start.

Each time the actors records a take, a new line is created to the right of the line before, with the corresponding timecode. If an actor was not present for that scene, there is no mark made next to their dialogue. In the sample, Datu's line was recorded later, and annotated later. This way it's easy to track which lines are recorded, and which aren't. Each take is color-coded so it's easy to see on continuing pages which is which. Individual pickups are typically noted to the left of the script, or where there is space. These are done last and sometimes only have smaller sections of the script.

Since this was a multi-day recording session, there was also a "Day Color Code" that highlights the timecode. A specific color identifies "Day 1," and then used to signify which sections were recorded on which day. Additional marks on the page could be noting an important word that was missed or mispronounced in the last take. In Carl's line at the bottom, "shouldn't" was misread for a few takes, and picked up later by itself when Carl finally recorded it properly [9:26:10]. For insurance and assurance, it's best to have at least one good take of each dialogue where all the words are recorded exactly as they are in the script. If there's a loud noise in the take, the actor hit the mic stand, someone went off mic, or the take is bad in some way, mark an X on the line, signifying there's a problem and possibly explaining it briefly. If the director verbally remarks about a specific take working well, mark that take also, as the primary choice. The editors will, of course, listen and decide later, but it's good to know ahead of time what energy level is the target for the scene. The choices made on set are not always the best choices in the editing bay.

What's included or not included in the script sup's notes is really up to the individual production. Once the recording is over, the assets move on into post-production. Make sure all the notes are scanned and handed over to the Audio Production Manager or Assembly Cutters. While the production team might be exhausted from long sessions, the post-production group is just getting started!

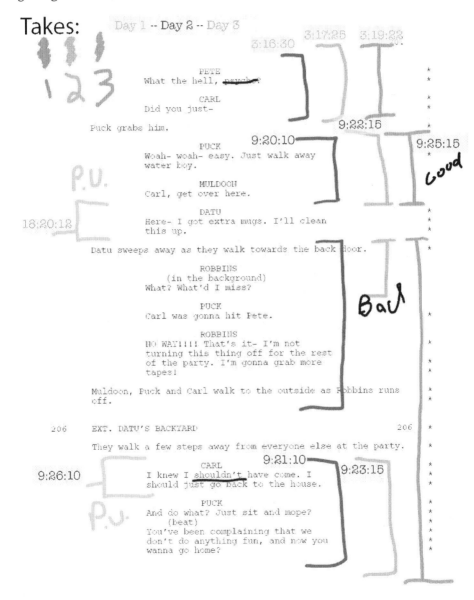

Fig. 9-5-1 Script Sup Demo

Chapter Ten

Post-Production

10. The Story Comes to Life

All the voices are "in the can" and the script is recorded in its entirety. Time to move onto post-production, or just "Post." A large portion of the production time will be spent in Post, as there are many stages to creating a unique aural image. Each step along the way requires a dedicated crew, as there will be many hours in front of the computer, and countless e-mails with updates and cut versions. It's important to be in clear communication with each other at all times, and continually strive to maintain the workflow while receiving notes and making adjustments. It's an arduous, and often thankless part of the production, but this is also the stage when the story first comes to life!

10.1 Post Workflow

A clear workflow

Establish the production's digital workflow early, interviewing and hiring Post positions before heading into production. If timed correctly, the post-production crew can start working right after completion of the first day of recording. It's also incredibly hard to find personnel that meet the qualifications for this medium, having the understanding and knowledge of how to construct things aurally. Give ample time to fill these positions, as they are responsible for putting the project together. The better the Post team, the clearer the picture they'll be able to build with the audio. Responsibility for each stage of post-production is tied to different crew members, where workflow and personnel are coupled together.

This section only discusses the mechanics of the workflow and roles. The artistic side of Post will be covered later on. And with that, the first stage of post-production is:

RAW - The recorded material that has no edits, but contains only the session from the recording. These sessions should be kept safe like the raw negatives of the old film days. Whenever something becomes lost, the Post team can always refer back to them.

The "**Assembly cut**," made by the Assembly Cutters (AC), takes all the raw information from the recording session, removes the breaks between takes, and assembles everything in script-order on a new timeline. The assembly cutters will refer to the script sup's timecode notes CONSTANTLY.

The new timeline will consist of multiple tracks dedicated to the same character instead of being labeled "VOX": Ben 1, Ben 2, Ben 3, etc. The order in which the takes should be arranged is in fact REVERSE order. Ben 1, the primary track, should have the **last take** as usually the last take is when the director is pleased and moves on. The best take isn't always last, but the assembly cutters don't focus on performance, just the recording order. AC's can annotate the take order as well by adding in "Take X" to each filename. If this workflow is preferable, have the AC rename the takes FIRST, before splitting the clips up. There will be fewer files to rename.

The AC is also responsible for removing the empty spaces in the recording when the characters are not talking. When 5 characters record, 4 aren't talking, and the recording tracks still receive the mic perspective from across the room. All of the dead space needs to be removed in order to isolate the dialogue as best as possible. Often times there's vocal overlaps, and on those occasions, it's best to leave them as is for the next stage of post-production.

The "**Voice Cut**," is made by the Voice Cutter (VC)/Editor. The AC delivers the assembly cut, which contains all the "takes," to the VC. The VC then (1) goes through each scene and (2) selects the performances that best fit the story, (3) starts to time out the dialogue, and (4) leave empty spaces for action. The VC job is one of the positions that requires the most experience in the medium. The ability to provide adequate pacing to the dialogue and being able to choose the best performance is a skill that can only be honed by time.

This position is about half-way between a sound designer and film editor. Timing experience comes from working with and manipulating the dialogue in regard to a character's action and reactions. There are many new dimensions to consider with sound, and individual skills like timing out empty spaces for action develops while working with editing dialogue for pacing. As the voice cutter makes selections, the other unused takes are not thrown away, but simply muted in place. Other choices might work better, later on in Post, when adding in elements like music and ambience, so it's always good to keep options.

The composer can receive the completed voice cuts when available, to begin creating the background music necessary for each scene. As the sound effects and timing are honed, so too, is the music. At this stage, the rest of the Pro Tools session should be set up for post-production which will be covered in a later section.

The **"Pacing Cut,"** is the best dialogue performances and complex sound effects to set master time. Vocal cuts only contain lines of dialogue that can lack pacing without major effects such as entrances and exits, gunshots and explosions, even vehicle motion and characterizations. In order to get an idea of the timing of the overall production, big aural pieces often need to be in place.

The **"Rough Cut,"** is made by the sound designer or team. At this stage, sound effects are chosen and arranged on the timeline, and Foleyed effects (footsteps, etc…) are recorded and timed out. The time to complete this stage varies, depending on the level of complication with the action and any special additional sounds. Timing of the overall piece can be adjusted with each stage, and updated cuts are given to the composer, moving towards the final mix. Additional voices or pickups are also made during this stage, replacing or adding necessary dialogue. Barring any complications, the composer should be able to come close to completing the score based on the timing of this cut.

The **"Fine Cut,"** is also created by the sound designer or team. The musical elements are combined with all the sounds from the rough cut, and any last minute adjustments or tweaks are made. As with every stage, additional tweaking and sound design will be added in and the layers are mixed and leveled.

The **"Final Cut,"** is the last cut. The sound designer has finished off all elements, the intro and outro segments contain the title tracks, credits, and any other additional slates for the beginning and the ending. The export is made, and the program is complete.

10.2 Post Hardware

Computer hardware configurations for recording and editing are not always the same. There's no need for multiple simultaneous inputs or pre-amps for the Post process, but the computer specs are relatively the same for both scenarios. The computer needs to be strong enough to run the software at the minimum recommended specs of the Pro Tools version. For more complex real-time processing, there are add-on cards that can extend the capabilities of the software, like HDX cards, but most projects will not need that sort of power. The computer should have at least some sort of analog IO, that offers balanced speaker outputs and a headset jack.

Monitors, Speakers, or headsets?

Studio-quality speakers are called monitors, and can cost on average about $150 - $300 for a nice pair from manufacturers like KRK or JBL. Studio-quality headphones cost about $100. There are ways to find cheaper alternatives for both items, but in order to edit accurately, one needs to be able to listen accurately. Quality sound reproduction costs what it costs. Poor quality speakers will mask artifacts and mistakes in the audio.

Which will you work with?

Headsets are great, but I can't use them for long without getting a headache from the sound pressure and the head-strain. They're nice for privacy and to not drive the people around you crazy by playing the same recordings over and over, but I prefer using speakers in terms of comfort and quality. Speakers are designed to reproduce a more fuller sound tone, and can also give a better indication of clarity and bass. There are some advantages, though, for vocal editing using headphones, as speakers can sometimes hide flaws like plosives or pops in the bass levels.

Data Storage

Don't go cheap, and don't store everything in the same location. Stay away from consumer versions of external hard drives that are "energy saving" or "green." From my engineering days I have dealt with all different kinds of storage solutions, in numerous atmospheres and conditions. No matter what manufacturer, they can all fail. The more professional and higher cost, the better components are typically used. Many hardware developers are starting to catch on and are rating their drives according to usage, enterprise vs "green." Consumer-rated drives are possible to use for audio, but know that most are designed for low usage (like backups) and not the constant data flow which is typical of audio-post. Having an industry-rated drive to do editing work and a consumer-rated drive to back up data is a viable option.

When considering **HDD (Hard Disk Drive) options**, here's what to look for in terms of minimum specifications:
- 7200 RPM - This spec is often hidden, but refers to how fast the drive spins.
- 1 TB (Terabyte) or larger storage space - Most hard drives have far more than this.
- External power supply - So that it does not rely on the computer to give enough power to the drive. Be sure also to label this power supply with the exact drive that it belongs to. Almost every external drive has a different voltage requirement and incorrectly supplied power can damage the internal components beyond recovery.
- USB 3.0 - Most computers are compatible with this connection type. Thunderbolt works as well, but fewer computers have those ports.

Personally, I only use G-raid drives for HDDs, especially for handling large amounts of files. After dealing with countless other manufactures, I find these drives to be the most reliable.

SSD(s), or Solid State Drives, are large storage "chips" that don't have moving parts or platters inside like HDDs. These are more like high speed flash drives, and generally cost more than their platter-based counterparts. While solid state drives are generally more reliable, I have seen a handful fail in the past, making data recovery nearly impossible.

Solid state drives *do* actually wear down, as each file is written to the storage chips. Many audio and video Post facilities choose not to record and edit off of SSD's for this perceived flaw. However, TheTechReport.com ran a long-term "write test" to see how long data could be written on various 250GB SSD drives until failure. The results demonstrated that it ranged from 300TB to 2.4PB of data. So, after 18 months of rigorous benchmarking, the results determined that the data was able to be written to the drive a thousand times over, at minimum, without issue. In general, the failure rate in terms of operating hours on SSD drives is less than HDD by about 25%.

Another benefit for using SSD drives is that they are low-voltage, meaning they do not require external power, and are durable for portability. The cost is typically high for SSD, with low storage capacity, but those trends always change as the technology grows.

Backup, Backup, Backup: Buy drives in pairs, and copy the data to the second one on a weekly basis and store it somewhere else. There's always other ways to lose data permanently like through theft and fire. There are raid options for multiple storage devices working together, like Drobo drives, which have a built-in smart-raid system. This way the physical drives have internal built-in data redundancy, with minimal headache.

Cloud backups are growing as well and offer many off-site storage options for syncing. Whenever data is transmitted online, there is always a chance of someone else duplicating the data, so be sure to always enable two-step authentication with all online servers. 1 TB of backup space is fairly inexpensive on Google Drive and will hold a sizable amount of projects.

10.2.1 Low Budget Options

There aren't very many alternative low budget considerations when looking at editing hardware. The analog IO for the editing station can be reduced to hardware that only has one mic preamp (for Foley), and two balanced outputs for speakers. There are lower cost speakers and headsets on the market, but can also bring with them lower quality reproductions of the sound. This should not be a low budget item to cut corners on. Hard drives are the same way. Data dependability should be priority, and dealing with risky or defective drives can cost far more than what was ever saved. However, instead of the cost of a second drive, I recommend using cloud backup.

Cost Reference:
DAC/Analog Digital IO = $99
Speakers: $150-$300
Headsets: $100
Hard Drive: $200
Online Storage: $5 per month

10.2.a Post Software*

The editing software chosen to put together audio-only programming is the canvas on which all the audio paint of recordings is applied. The DAW, or Digital Audio Workstation, is where everything is layered together to create that perfect aural image. If the canvas is small and limited, the artist loses the ability to edit the intricate details. An oversimplification, sure, but the programs in which an artist can manipulate audio vary significantly in capabilities.

The most expensive software isn't always the best, but often it has the greatest development dollars behind it that boosts the program with additional production timesaving features. A talented editor can make things sound fantastic with almost any audio editing software, given enough time, care and attention. Still, the speed and flexibility of creating good work differs from software to software.

Before we even get into the software breakdown, there is one qualifier that I would require of any audio-editing software, and that's the ability to edit and listen at the same time. If I cannot listen and cut simultaneously, my workflow time is instantly doubled. Editing audio is all done in real time. Video editors can jog and shuttle over sections to see whether a cut works, but sound must be previewed as it is naturally heard. Fast playback is available for audio, but you'll miss all the details at that unnatural speed. If an editor can listen and adjust timing and trim clips simultaneously, it's a significant boost in productivity.

Noise reduction is another area where it's worth the cash spent on high-quality plugins to increase productivity time. What would take hours of painstaking EQ'ing out noise can be accomplished in seconds with a few button presses, but only with the right software.

These sorts of time saving measures allow the editor to spend less time on monotonous repair tasks and more on audio enhancement. As with any plugin that costs money but saves time, a simple cost-benefit analysis is in order. How much is your time worth? If you spend over 40 hours editing a project that could be done in 20 hours with different production tools, the math changes very quickly. When I show professionals new audio tools, the reaction often is, "Do you know how much time this would have saved me?!" While audio is infinite, your time is not.

Learning vs Business: Those who are enrolled in education programs can often take advantage of software discounts. These are great ways to learn and use powerful tools at a lower cost. Students enrolled in courses that use the software, too, will learn far more if they put it to practical use outside of class. However, there are limits to what can be produced with education software, so be sure to read the fine print before purchasing.

Pro Tools

The word "industry standard" gets tossed a lot around for Avid's Pro Tools. From an engineer's perspective, it is far and away the most prominent software used in high-end film/video production. From ADR to music, it's one of the best. Editing and listening can be done simultaneously, and it works with many hardware options along with a multitude of plugins developed over its years of industry prominence. Pro Tools has some of the most robust and versatile capabilities in automation, or changing audio parameters in real-time. Pro Tools costs a chunk of change, but its low-level subscriptions include their default plugin pack, which features TONs of extra plugins, including Spaces, with its super-powerful sample-pack.

In terms of cons, Pro Tools' IO routing gets confusing if not set correctly, which can be very frustrating to new editors. Disabling and muting things can happen with the slip of the keyboard. And the keyboard shortcuts only work if the correct window is selected. Things can happen without notice, and even advanced editors sometimes scratch their heads trying to problem-solve some issues in the DAW.

Many dismiss Pro Tools due to these complications, but I find its value lies in how it's used and taught to be used. It may be complicated in some ways (like bussing and routing), but overall it's a robust and reliable tool. I will say that it's far more stable on a Mac with a dedicated ASIO compliant-card, but any professional who wants to get a balanced audio output will want to have one of those regardless.

One of the common complaints from users concerns file management, it will allow files from any drive path/location as long as it's the correct sample rate for the project but can be corrected by changing default preferences. Other benefits include the user interface for RTAS plugin automation is much cleaner and clearer to see and edit in Pro Tools. The "smart tool" allows a variety of editing methods that I found lacking in other editors. VST plugins are not supported. iLoks — online or physical — are required, as the program licensing is very restrictive for antipiracy.

Logic Pro

This powerful software is heavily used in the MacOS world because it's often bundled with Final Cut or Apple's hardware options. There are few limitations on track counts and it offers similar features as Pro Tools. However, dialogue workflows are particular, and it seems as though this software was created to facilitate music creation and editing. Even Logic's documentation highlights its musical MIDI and sample features. I've seen various narrative projects edited on it, but I don't see many of the automation and control features that come with Pro Tools. Editing cannot be done on the fly while listening, which to me, limits what's possible. The software is also Mac only, which limits options for users.

Reaper

Reaper is an up and coming audio editor, favored among editors who wish to have more advanced features without a hefty price tag. Although the program has many capabilities and can edit and playback at the same time, the interface is clunky and over-filled with confusing elements for beginning users. The speed of usability with Reaper felt much slower even when using the default keyboard shortcut placements. Those who like to customize their tools and cut corners on cost will love Reaper. VST plugins are supported. Overall I was not too fond of the interface: with too many options and tweaks in weird places, there's a high learning curve. Plugin FX location and layout are hard to manage, and the flow of the interface felt jarring and lifeless.

Garageband

This is a decent simple audio editor that is usually included with most Macs but it seems to be more tailored for music and simple audio edits than complex, multi-track audio dramas. Editing can be done while listening, but not easily. Many fade and automation options have limited control, and while the interface is easy to use, it seems better suited for simple projects and music composition.

Audacity

This program can't listen and edit at the same time, overloads easily, and has simple tools for clip editing, not ideal for large projects. It gets easily frustrating when attempting anything more advanced. This is a bare minimum audio editor. The edits are also destructive, meaning they are hard to undo. The software is free but highly limited for advanced workflows.

10.3 The Art and Tech of Editing Sound

When I first approached writing this section about the art and technology of sound editing, I tried to separate the two. As I explored the various aspects of each, they continually crossed over to one another, and were notably inseparable. The computer becomes the conduit for the art, making it impossible to have one without the other. A painting is to the brush as audio theater is to the technology.

Sound is both infinite and finite. The depth and layers can theoretically go on forever, but our ears and human perception cannot. When there are no visuals as a guide for an audio production, there are no constraints, and the amount of sound to include becomes a choice for the individual sound designer. A balance must be created where there is enough sound details to paint a clear picture, but not too much that it starts to distort and distract. As with every step along the way in audio theater, clarity is key.

As I sit here typing this, I am filled with the sounds of the world. The ceiling fan above me, the pull-string on the blinds rapping against the wall, the fridge humming away while gardeners in the distance mow a neighbor's lawn. This aural image is the perception of **ambience** from where I sit in the kitchen. It doesn't change much as I continue to sit here. **Audio Ambience is like a "bed" of sound that shares the setting with the characters.**

My movement, my typing, the occasional adjustment of my chair, the glass of water I move and set back down— are all accompaniments of **sound effects: the aural action of the scene.**

If I talk to my wife as she comes into the kitchen, cough, laugh, etc... **any noise involving the human mouth is considered "VOX."**

A radio playing in the background would still be considered a sound effect since it's diegetic, or the source comes from *inside* the environment. If I imagined there to be a score under the scene, an accompaniment that is not present with the characters, it would be classified as **music**. For the sake of logistical grouping, even synthesized tones are still considered **music**.

Broken down, all sounds can then be categorized into several distinct groups, all of which help the organization and flow of audio-only post-production:

- **VOX**
- **Sound FX**
- **Ambience**
- **Music**

How those elements and groups interact with each other can paint a picture of what the audience is meant to "see." Before we cover each area of editing, I want to give a general piece of advice to all aural editors and designers: *go with your gut*. The way that something sounds is already known to you. Sound has been something that has surrounded you all your entire life. Focus on listening. You already know how a voice sounds in a car, in a bathroom, or the rhythm of a natural conversation. If something feels *off*, then it is... find a way to make it feel right.

10.3a Noise Reduction*

Noise reduction plugins are available from many different 3rd party-developers and do not come standard in Pro Tools. These are add-ons from companies like Izotope and Waves. For general background noise reduction, most follow a single principle: listen to a sample of what is considered noise, and then remove anything that fits that sample's parameters. Most noise reduction plugins are filters that remove unwanted elements like room tone, air conditioning hums, and other exterior ambient interferences from the audio recordings. Other filters focus on removing vocal clicks, plosives, reverb, esses, and crackles. These focus more so on dialogue cleanup and are used when those instances arise in the recording. When applying a general reduction over the entire recording of a singular — or multiple — tracks, there are methods to employ early in the process that will lighten the necessity and amount of time spent with cleanup in post-production.

As a typical recording setup, it's best to record five to ten seconds of clean "blank" recording before or after every take, especially if the sound profile has changed. If the microphones are ever moved or adjusted in any way, the profile for background noise will change. While it is possible to use a quiet section between dialogue, the sampling works best if it's free of any breaths or vocal elements.

When applying noise reduction, it's best to apply these filters BEFORE any additional editing takes place. When recorded elements or dialogue are cut into smaller pieces, it takes MUCH longer to apply the noise reduction filter profile to multiple clips. In terms of workflow, editing should go as follows:

[Individual track of recorded Dialogue] -> [Noise Reduction sampling and rendering] -> [Editing Assembly Cut]

Each microphone will have its own unique noise profile, so a noise sample and reduction should be performed on an individual channel. Even when recording in the same space, every mic points in a different direction and one could capture more noise from a remote AC unit, while another might pick up a particular hum or fan from a computer. Modern noise reduction software can remove many unwanted artifacts as long as the proper procedures are followed for recording and processing.

When removing unwanted noise from tracks, it's also best to "render" or process the audio, which will create new audio files. To continually calculate the filtration process — determining what is noise or not moment to moment — will overload the processing power of the computer if done in real time. Always save the original raw recordings separately from any edited session, in case there is ever a need to return to the unfiltered masters.

In Pro Tools, this process is done by using noise reduction plugins via the "Audio Suite" menu and clicking the "Learn" function for the areas of the clip left "blank" for the room noise profile. After the plugin samples the profile, select the entire clip to preview and adjust the amount of reduction to the noise threshold. Then, use the "Render" function to save the resulting clean clips. Each plugin has individual controls for the amount of reduction and noise threshold to adjust artifact removal against the desired sounds in the recording. If the reduction is too strong, the reduction plugin will eat into the wanted audio, creating artifacts and artificial sounding waveforms that will sound robotic or resemble recording in a tin can.

Izotope RX reduction software, in particular, offers two different types of general noise reduction: vocal or spectral. Vocal emphasizes preserving the spectrum of audio typically occupied by the frequency ranges of the human voice. Spectral noise reduction is used for everything else, including footsteps and various other elements of foley.

10.3b Advanced Audio Editing Samples*

Instead of the visual materials on a television or movie screen that are quickly processed by the eye, sound must travel an indirect route of being received by the ear, translated into information, and then interpreted. There is a higher level of comprehension required by the audience. If an audience hears a cat's meow or sees an on-screen image of a cat, it doesn't take much to understand to identify the thing as "cat." If presented with a scene where the cat jumps on a surface and knocks something off the table, that's visually easy, yet aurally complex. The communication of these aural images and the story's intentions must intertwine and work together with the audience at a rate they can handle and still comprehend.

Post-production is the technical process of limiting the aural bandwidth the listener receives to enable an understanding of the story. Drawing out the pacing of events and dialogue has both a dramatic effect and affects interpretation in audio. As more post techniques are discovered, each should contribute to the medium's singular goal: Does the audience understand what's happening?

With each audio project I produce, new challenges and opportunities emerge in post-production to experiment creatively and technically. The more time I spend editing, the more techniques reveal themselves through practical exercises. These advances and experiments all revolve around how an audience receives an aural story.

Because these instances are often one of a kind, it isn't easy to document or verbally illustrate with audio what everything sounds like. For the enhanced 2nd edition of Bombs Always Beep, I have included clips demonstrating the techniques learned and applied. To reference these clips, be sure to not include advertisements as that changes the timecode location.

Editing Dialogue

Editing dialogue in audio presents a multitude of options when splicing two or three performances together. Sometimes, one take of recorded dialogue will have the proper inflection and diction, but portions might have a mistake or missed word. By cutting on the start or end of a common merge point like a word or syllable, it's possible to assemble multiple takes into one. Here's a sample of making two takes into one from Goldrush:
Example: 16:04 Goldrush Chapter 1 - Nicholas Two lines

Some final performances can end up being "Franken-dialogue," several performances at various sections spliced at common merge points to create an entirely new performance.
Example: 33:09 Goldrush Chapter 8

Interrupting dialogue at the right moments allows a natural exit for a scene: fading in or out a scene is less engaging than sudden changes.
Example: 20:40 Goldrush Chapter 1

Too, performances sometimes can have stutters in the middle of a dialogue that can add confusion. By finding the common merge point within the same take, that mistake can be corrected easily in post, saving an otherwise perfect performance.
Example: 23:12 Goldrush Chapter 6 - Anita Stutter

Seldomly can dialogue be sped up or slowed down without noticeable results, but then some lines are delivered slowly enough that a slight speed increase isn't noticeable and helps the performance match the scene's context. This is a rare instance from Goldrush.
Example: 31:05 Goldrush Chapter 8

Pickups

Pickups happen when, for whatever reason, a line of dialogue doesn't match. Sometimes a missed inflection, mispronunciation, or dialogue change requires the insertion of newly recorded material seamlessly into previous sessions: a pickup. However, the replacement dialogue sometimes can be awkward to even out against the original. When inserting new replacements, one technique is to let portions of the original syllables to partially overlap the replacement to make it sound natural. Two lines of dialogue become one.

This technique will often trick the ear into thinking there's no difference. The "seam" or common merge point that transitions from one line of dialogue to another can be the very start of a consonant, the beginning or end of a breath, or practically anywhere the two lines have a point of convergence where both sound similar. That matching portion of line or word acts as a junction between two different points.
Example: 1:53 Goldrush Chapter 1 - Fish line

Shaping a scene with editing

The intentions of a scene are shaped with sound effects after recorded. In many ways, sound effects can interact and accent the emotion of the existing dialogue. In *Goldrush*, I created a scene entirely in the kitchen, which included a significant amount of action through breakfast preparation. Nothing in the conversation references what they are doing in what is an "open scene". The intentions through the actions were created after the recording, adapted and timed for the story's needs:
Example: 15:38 Goldrush Chapter 6

Sound and Silence

Sound and action play a hefty part in the actualization of the scene. Sometimes it's not a matter of what sound effects are selected, but rather their timing and execution. Constant sound is noise, so finding the spaces between the active waveforms help illustrate the physical space. In this clip, it's meant to visualize aurally an infected body falling downstairs. Knowing that a constant washboard of sound would paint little imagery, I chose to create a looping space to denote the doubling over of the fall, letting the space between the crunches sound like a spiraling figure, with a slinky's momentum.
Example: 2:03 Goldrush Chapter 2 - Infected fall downstairs

EQ

EQ or equalization is all about adjusting the various frequencies of existing audio. It can bring out high frequencies that might have been overpowered or lost at the microphone. These corrections are made to make the spectrum of sounds match in fidelity. This makes all the vocal recordings feel like they are equal, and no dialogue is lost off-mic. Often, an actor will turn away from the mic in the booth, or add some motion to the mic that's out of place in the scene, and the voice needs to be fine-tuned to match. If voices are too muffled, an increase in the highs or

mids will add balance and ensure the vocals are all present.
Example: 10:50 Goldrush Chapter 2 - Voice EQ Sample.

Music

Music can often rise above the scene in a non-diegetic way but still allow for further interaction. Changing the tempo of the music or having it match a particular action can assist the definition of a scene's time and space. An example of this is the tram ride near the end of Chapter 5 of Goldrush. By speeding up and slowing down the tunnel's length, the audience can experience the feeling of being an aural passenger on the tram with them.
Example: 23:18 Goldrush Chapter 5 - Tram Ride

Using music in a scene can accent and reinforce emotions to the audience, punctuating what's meant to be felt at that point in the story. But sometimes, the start of music in the scene can be a bit jarring or feel slightly awkward. Sound edits are meant to be mostly invisible, and music rides the 4th wall, breaking the suspension of disbelief of a scene with a few misplaced notes. In this scene in Goldrush, going from a quiet atmosphere to music was very noticeable. By having dialogue overlap the first note of the song's start, the intro blended into the previous lack of music.
Example: 20:10 Goldrush Chapter 7

On Foley

There are certain areas of action in which a performance requires Foley to be intricately timed to match. When recording dialogue, the additional sound effects are always done separately for more flexibility later in post. However, simultaneously recording the Foley action while listening to the voice track is the most effective for impact and timing. Much of a voice performance convinces the ear thanks to the actions' corresponding sound effects.
Example: 4:11 Goldrush Chapter 2 - Kicking the Zombie on the ground

When recording practical footsteps in sync against an audio track, some individual steps come across louder than others. This is simply the randomness of walking meant to be achieved in Foley. Adjusting the individual gains in post for those outlier steps maintains a consistency of volume while walking. If the footsteps' perspective changes unintentionally, the listener might get confused as to who stays in focus of the SPOV.
Example: 4:51 Goldrush Chapter 2 footsteps consistency.

Footsteps

Footsteps are one of the most underutilized elements of audio dramas. It's often easier for minimal sound design to ignore all footsteps, but then the voices float throughout the world without being grounded in any spatial reality. Footsteps denote the speed in which an action takes place, the state of the character, and function outside of the characters in the narrative structure. One of the biggest parts of storytelling is entering and exiting scenes -- footsteps can be a carrier through those transitions.

In this clip, the cadence of one character's footsteps in the present matches and fades to the same rhythm of the steps of a figure from the past. By moving from one scene to another, mimicking the same pattern, the footsteps become the common element that helps cushion the transitions of environments while using a human constant.

Example: 2:14 Goldrush Chapter 6

Breathing

Breaths are part of VOX and are an equally powerful expression of what the character is experiencing. By hearing a character experience something, the audience shares in the action and emotion. Sometimes, when breaths are missing from a recorded performance, it feels unnatural. A breath then needs to be borrowed or lifted from other lines of dialogue. The following example is one of those instances where something felt unbalanced without that inflection.

Example: 9:46 Goldrush Chapter 6

10.4 Post-Session Setup

Like the previous sections, the following will be tailored for Pro Tools. And as stated, the basic functions of Pro Tools will not be covered, but more specifically how to tailor and use the program to create audio theater. For those who might be using other programs, the principles are still the same, but there might be some software limitations. Pro Tool is not perfect, either. There are some areas open to improvement pertaining to the functions and use for this medium, but also some workarounds.

The more streamlined and organized the session, the easier it will be to manage assets. Audio Track organization and optimization becomes essential for faster editing. The more scrolling and searching, the less time to edit. Since audio has to be previewed in real time, any ways to cut corners or speed things up should be considered. It's all about optimization and efficiency. I've also included the color codes I use to correspond with certain track categories, as it's a helpful method to visually differentiate between them.

Track Order

Signal flow is the term which describes the order in which sound travels from the mic to the speakers. This is a linear path that can be followed through various forms of equipment from beginning to end. The same rules apply for the *virtual* signal flow. Audio travels through multiple tracks and is modified and manipulated in what's called DSP or Digital Signal Processing. Understanding and keeping the signal path clear will be important when dealing with a large amount of tracks.

The following breakdown contains the track grouping and order that has been refined over years of audio theater production. The images included in this section are from the final edit for <u>Lockdown</u>, which might have some extra parameters that are unique to our project. Keep in mind, as with every session that's continually worked on day in and day out, they can become a bit "untidy" in regard to clip naming. With that being said, let's dive in.

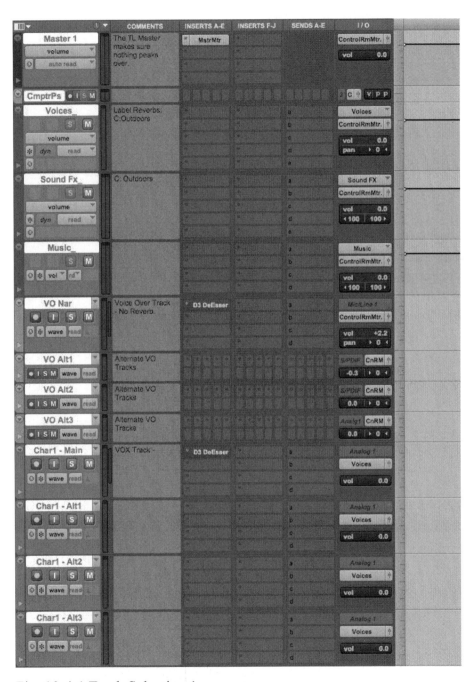

Fig. 10-4-1 Track Selection 1

1. Master - The top tracks handle where the audio leaves the system, the master being the last stop before the final output. The track type, is in fact, "Master," if created in a new session. All audio leaving the speakers will pass through this one point, so if there's any last step processing or "Inserts", they would be added here. The inserts used on our Master are a compressor/limiter and an audio meter.

2. Passthrough Track [optional] (Type: Normal Track, Stereo) - This track lets the computer system audio pass through into Pro Tools. The sound fx search program, Soundminer, cannot directly share the sound output with Pro Tools (there are other methods using ReWire). This requires the signal to be routed through one of the aux inputs on the Mbox interface used in our studio. Notice the IO panel on the left side of the track. Analog 3-4 is an input, and toggling the "Track Input Monitor" button shown in green, the audio can stream through to the speakers without having to be in a record mode. This kind of track can also be useful for talent talkback (where you are talking to the actor during recording), using a mic as the input and passing the signal to the performer's headsets in a recording booth. The green "I" can be toggled on and off to enable and disable the track pass-through.

3. Aux Bus(s) (Type: Aux) - These tracks are like sub-masters, where all the outputs of like-tracks cumulate into one point. Instead of going directly out to the speakers, the audio output from similar tracks come together into a common Bus, which acts as the input to the Aux Track.

Pro Tools allows for many different Aux/Bus combinations, but the template we use is set up with three in mind: Voices, Sound FX, and Music. The reason the tracks are grouped this way is to give the ability to apply effects over a broad category of tracks, rather than having to apply everything individually. For instance, when environmental effects are added, it's more efficient to have the tracks grouped by the amount of reverb needed. This way the amount of reflection for sound effects is different than what is used for the talent- echoey footsteps with the not-as-echoey voices.

The Music Bus combines the music and the atmospherics/environments. Since those two categories are rarely processed, it made sense to group them together. One of the reasons the signal is routed together like this is to reduce the amount of work and real-time processing the computer has to do. If all the effects were applied individually to each track, then the computer would have to compute each separately. Generally, the result is the same but the amount of processing power difference is staggering. With the addition of more and more tracks, the computer may start bogging down, and session optimization like this helps.

Other effects that might be included on the Aux Busses could be things like compressors. Putting a compressor on the SFX Aux Track can prevent peaking.

4. VO Narration and Vox Tracks (Type: Normal, Mono) - ORANGE - Voices belong at the top because the vocals guide the session. They're the first asset, and the foundation for what follows. Each vocal group should consist of one main track and several alternates. These alternate tracks act as a bin for the other takes, while the main track contains the primary selection of that character's vocal performances. Editors who come from a film background normally have alternate takes organized in bins and folders. Since this is an audio-only environment, relying heavily on sync, a more efficient way to have the alternates stored is in the tracks below the main selections. This method makes it more convenient and faster to swap out, or to take portions from multiple performances of dialogue and splice them together. If there's a wording issue or something in a line that doesn't work, the alternates are a button away. Alternate lines can be dropped in all the way up to the last cut, especially when adding in additional elements of sound design and environment. A word of warning: the alternate tracks cannot be hidden when making any timing adjustments, which happens often in an AD session. In order to keep things in sync, minimize the alternate track to the smallest size when not in use, and mute each track by the individual clips.

Other additional VOX track options are ones dedicated to "Clean" or "Explicit" lines. It might be necessary to create two different versions of a product, one more audience friendly and language-free, and the other with the original uncensored intention. This method allows the editor to easily switch between the two and make sure that even though the lines may change slightly, the experience doesn't.

Depending on the size of the cast, some workflows benefit from the use of generic "VOX#" naming, instead of specific cast names. Creating a new track for each character with a big cast creates an unnecessary amount of scrolling. If recorded to the standards in this book, the individual clips should have the names of the characters already, making the clips easy to discern. To further differentiate the tracks, there's an option to assign alternate colors or include text comments on which characters share those tracks: e.g., Burt/Mark. These specific instances work when characters are never in the same scene.

5. Foley Record Track(s) (Type: Normal, Mono) - PURPLE - This is where the input for the mic resides for all the Foley work. When I Foley, I want to be able to see the timing for the dialogue so that I can anticipate the action, and also move these tracks around. In this group, it's common to have one record track and a minimum of five Foley FX "dump" tracks. After one

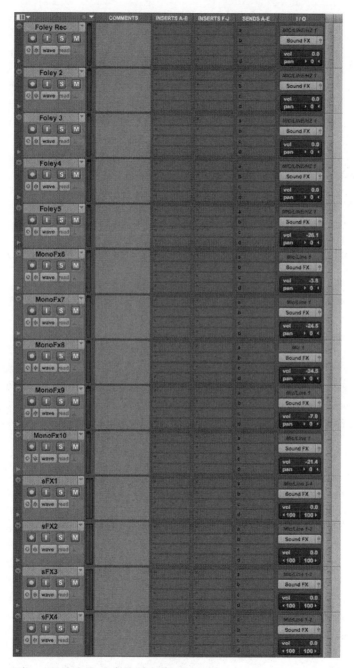

Fig. 10-4-2 Track Selection 2

performance of Foley, the clip is then moved down into the other Foley dump tracks while still maintaining sync. The Foley Record Track should be renamed to whatever clip is being captured to ensure the labeling is consistent.

It's good practice to keep the Foleyed effects in the same area of the session, so if there's any mistakes or extra unwanted sounds on the recording, they're easier to find. Sound effects from libraries typically won't have artifacts like breaths, bumps, or other mistakes that are common with large Foley clips. The record track should not go through any other Bus, but directly to the speakers/headsets. While recording Foley, it is important to listen to what's being captured without any reverb or modifications.

6. The Mono FX Tracks (Type: Normal, Mono) - RED - These tracks are where most of the mono sound FX will go and typically this is where I arrange the most sounds. Mono tracks will put the action in front of the listener, and has become my go-to area of focus for the sound of character action.

7. The Stereo FX Tracks (Type: Normal, Stereo) - DARK BLUE - These tracks are for the stereo effects. I mostly work in mono, but there are sounds that have a better feel when presented in stereo. Vehicles tend to be one of those. By having two channels for an individual sound, the vehicles can blend a bit better at lower volumes and not overload a scene. Every sound is different in how they interact with each other within an aural space.

The last track of this group is informally called "SFX Unclip." This is intended as a bypass to the SFX Aux Bus, going around any compressors that might be on that Bus or any other type of processing that might distort the sound effect. There have been occasions where reverb or compression has rendered a clip inaudible, like gunshots.

8. Ambience Tracks (Type: Normal, Stereo) - LIGHT BLUE - These tracks are used for all of the background sounds of the scene. Room tones, wind blowing, outside crickets, etc. This is where to build in the details of the atmosphere.

9. Music Tracks (Type: Normal, Stereo) - GREEN - These tracks are for the individual stems or mixdowns from music compositions. Often times a fade or transition is needed between pieces, so having multiple tracks is essential. Music composition is typically done in another session as it requires a vastly different setup and arrangement.

10. The Announcer Track (Type: Normal, Mono) - DARK YELLOW - Having a key announcer or credit track at the bottom rather than near the VO tracks at the top is beneficial because the timing is usually done against

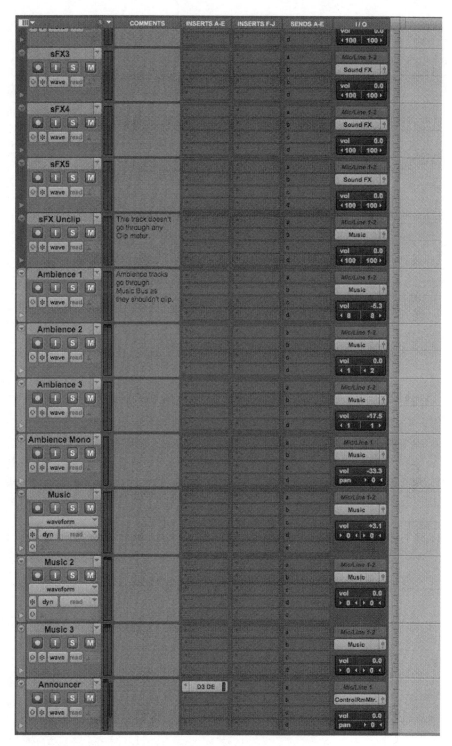

Fig. 10-4-3 Track Selection 3

the music, which is crucial for credits and slates. Scrolling back and forth from the other voice tracks is less efficient, and this makes it easier to keep character vocals separate.

11. Marker Track (Type: Normal, Mono) - When there's a marker tone, those sounds are stored here. Having a 1k tone marker to indicate where commercial breaks are at the pre/mid/post rolls makes it easier to find in the session later on, especially as that information is needed by advertising partners. (Not Shown)

10.5 Assembly Cut

The start of the Assembly Cut comes directly from the audio script supervisor's notes. The scanned PDF of the script with all the timecodes and notes are passed along to the assembly cutter, along with all the recorded material on a hard drive. There could be multiple sessions to deal with, but the script sup's notes should function as the road-map to the timecode locations of every line, making sure nothing is lost or missing.

The primary goal of the assembly cutter is to arrange all the good takes and stack them together sequentially following the script-order onto one timeline. This way all the options are there for the next stage of post-production. Selecting which takes are the "best" is not necessary for this stage. The focus should be to include everything from a specific episode in one place. By individualizing this task, it is easier to break up the workload.

Combine recording days using the "Import Session Data" option and then select the session file from other days. If the timecode instructions were followed, there shouldn't be any overlap to deal with and the added takes should be inserted at the end. As new cuts are created, continually use "Save As," and keep a sequential file name appended with the date, version number, and the initials of who last worked on it.

FILE NAME SAMPLE:[Lockdown_ep101_1Jan-V3-Kc.ptx]

Session files are relatively small, and saving a new version every few hours can prevent work loss. By creating unique file names, there's also no concern about over-writing an older session because the session names are always different. Do not rely on auto-saves, although there are those as well in the "Session File Backups" in the project folder.

One additional tip is that before starting to cut up the large clips from the recording session into sub-clips, rename them by adding the take number from the script sup's notes. As clips are broken down further into smaller pieces, the take number continues with it. This method reduces the amount of renaming required later on. **IMPORTANT: Do not select the 'rename file' button** when adding the take number, only change the clip name. That way if Post crews are working on multiple sessions at different stations, the file references don't change, only the clip name within the session.

Breaking up the raw recording clips into smaller sub-clips is a process of carving out the dead spaces and unusable portions, and saving the dialogue and any usable recorded VOX. The best way to start the process is to take out the large sections of silence between each character's dialogue. When characters record only for a few lines in a scene, the system continues to record what is considered dead air. Using the selector tool, you can clear large chunks of unusable clips from multiple tracks by hitting the delete key. In Pro Tools, this doesn't "delete" the clip, it only removes the link to the audio files of the session.

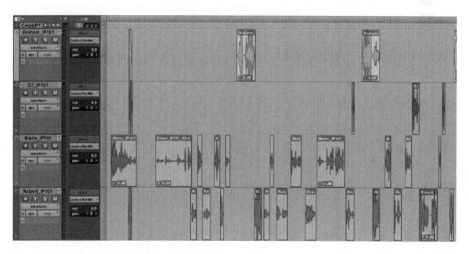

Fig. 10-5-1 Assembly Cut in the early stage

After cutting out the spaces, start compressing or extending the timeline. Moving small groups of clips is fairly easy, but moving large sections can become tricky and disastrous if done wrong at later stages of production. One of the drawbacks of Pro Tools is that there is no easy way to add or remove time. It's not designed like a non-linear video editing program, which DOES have that feature. Timelines retaining sync is typically how the program functions for Music. So, instead of inserting or removing time/space, the contents have to be shifted to sooner or later spots on the existing timeline. Moving large amounts of content across a timeline needs to be done carefully. Follow these steps, and after a while it will become a familiar technique.

1. **Do not hide tracks.**
   If the track is hidden, then the content won't move with rest of the selected material.
2. **Leave automation expanded.**
   If there is keyed automation, like reverb on the aux tracks, then leave those visible, don't collapse them. Otherwise, if a scene is extended out, that key won't move and any reverb automation will become out of sync.
3. **Create a marker (enter on number-pad)**
   where the timeline will be spliced and extended. This will create a reference point to use later on when relocating other existing markers. Label this "BREAK."
4. **Select everything.**
   By selecting the top bar of the timeline, a line appears down the entire session. Hit the "b" key to insert a break through the entire timeline at that point, and then Alt+Shift+Return to select everything to the right of that line that needs to be moved. This method makes sure that nothing goes out of sync, with the only exception being that any markers will need to move afterwards.
5. **Move the markers.** [Not super-easy, I know] To move the markers after the clips, select the marker track (thin horizontal strip where markers usually live above the tracks) where the marker "BREAK" is, created in step 3. This should still be at the original break location. Using the CUT (CTRL+X/Command+X) command while still in the marker track, PASTE (CTRL+V/Command+V) the markers to the new correct location on the timeline. Make sure to align the original "BREAK" marker with the new location of the break on the timeline.

Keeping the timeline in sync requires a bit of practice, but is incredibly important at all stages. Fixing sync errors take a lot more time than verifying that the content was moved properly.

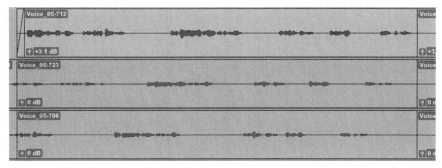

Fig. 10-5-2 Primary track and alternate lines below

As the assembly cutter starts to piece together and organize the timeline, **the take order should reflect the reverse recording order.** The main VOX track should contain the last take from the recording, unless the script sup contains notes from the set on which is considered the "Best Take." The second to last take should be ALT1, the third is ALT2, and so on. Typically the director will move on once they hear the performance they want, which, as stated before, is most often the last one.

If performances have a lot of overlap, reactions, or breaths that bleed into each other's recording, then the assembly cutter should leave those as is, and not attempt to cut them down or separate them. At the next stage of Post, the voice cutter can listen to the options and cut around the best take. It's not the best use of time to cut apart dense dialogue if it won't or can't be used. Occasionally there will be sections that were not in the script, but are still recorded on the timeline, like wild breaths or "action grunts." Include those in the assembly for the voice cutter to work with, otherwise they can get lost between Post stages.

Listen *WHILE* cutting.

The last tip for the assembly cutter, and frankly for all stages of post-productions, is to listen while cutting. Pro Tools allows the option to play and edit at the same time. It might take a little getting used to at first, but after a while it becomes second nature. At later stages of editing, adjusting audio levels and cuts become like laying railroad in front of a locomotive, staying just ahead of the scroll bar. Since audio must be previewed in real time, being able to listen and edit simultaneously saves an extraordinary amount of Post time. This technique is something that's not possible with most video editing.

10.6 Voice Cut

Approaching the voice cut.

The first stage in shaping the sound of the story starts at the vocal cut. The assembly cut doesn't involve as many creative decisions and is more about getting all the pieces in place so that the editor/voice cutter can easily make selections. Choosing which performance is best can be one of the most subjective parts to the editing process. There are many instances where part of one take may work better than the rest, requiring the voice cutter to piece together the performances.

How do you know which take is the best performance? Listen for the four C's: **Character, Cohesion, Cadence, and Clarity.**

Character - Do I believe that this dialogue comes from the person in the story? Does it sound like they are reading?

Cohesion - Does the line sound out of place with the other characters? Do the performances blend together?

Cadence - Does the performance match the energy and pace of the rest of the characters?

Clarity* - Is what the character saying comprehensible? Does the listener have all the key lines to understand the story and what's going on in the scene?

*Mistakes aren't always a bad thing. If a word is repeated, or fumbled in a natural and believing way, it's up to the editor to keep it. A crackle in a voice, a clearing of the throat, an oddly-timed breath can all contribute to the realism of the scene, depending on the story and character.

The other component of the voice cut, aside from take selection, is timing. The speed of a scene is variable, allowing full control by the editor to adjust the distance between the lines. Being able to understand the specifics to rhythm and cadence of dialogue comes from experience. The more one edits and listens, the better developed their sense of timing. The context of a scene can completely be changed by extending or compressing the space between the lines. Sometimes a shorter space feels more natural, and the longer pauses become more dramatic. An editor's job is to feel out those moments, and find what best fits for the scene.

There are limitations. If dialogue runs too rapid, the pace can be become faster than what's natural or possible, which I call "fore-talking." I mentioned this briefly before, when talking about directing, but it is prevalent in the editing process as well. Fore-talking is most often observed when a response to a question precedes the natural timing required to hear and react. The difference may be only a fraction of a second, but when it happens, it is noticeable. When performing with scripts, this is very common for actors to do, and also for editors not to catch. The actor is caught up in a moment, reads ahead, and responds to a question with unnatural timing. **An example:**

- Adam: Did you go to mall?
- Beth: I did! I got this amazing dress!

If Beth starts her response on top of, or unnaturally close to the word "mall," then it's considered fore-talking. Without "mall," Beth couldn't possibly have a point of reference to answer. She needs to hear the word, and respond in a natural amount of time. On set, directors can make an adjustment by telling the actor "react to the word 'mall,'" but sometimes it's easy to miss. In Post, it can accidentally happen when cutting down scenes, and can be fixed by adding more space. If the dialogue overlaps in the recording, then the actor might have to re-do the line.

Timing dialogue at this stage of post-production also involves leaving blank spaces for effects. Is a character opening a door, or getting in a car and driving away? In a rushed Post environment, often the composers are having to work against the clock and create music to the voice cuts. By leaving a general amount of space for the sound effect elements to be added in, the composer will be able to have a better sense of timing to work with when trying to match with music.

There's the story that's written, then there's the story that's recorded.

The voice cutter has to work closely with the script, but also have the freedom to make changes. Sections of dialogue might not work in Post and may need to be re-arranged. The script at this point becomes merely a guide through post-production. The audience won't hear the words on the paper, so changes must be made throughout all stages to translate the story as clearly as possible. When there are scenes that still need extra clarification, additional dialogue from the primary cast may be necessary to record. If those moments are identified during the voice cut stage, then it's easier to schedule and arrange pickups.

Other necessary dialogue may not come from the cast, but the environments, requiring a specific walla to be inserted. Walla is the term used that refers to background characters' dialogue. Usually in film, it's barely audible, but in the case of Audio Theater, everything is heard. An editor needs to be careful not to break the illusion, and creating background dialogue can be tricky. For specific instances of walla, writers may need to supply additional lines to record so they match the environment.

Franken-Dialogue

When doing voice cuts, sometimes fragments of lines from one performance can be combined with another, ultimately editing together pieces from multiple takes. This technique can save a performance that otherwise might be unusable due to a stumble or missed word. For smooth dialogue editing, when combining sections of lines, the transition point is often between the very end of a breath or the start of a new word. Swap the performances on that mark, and the breath will fuse both clips together naturally.

The splices can be divided all the way down to individual words and fractions of words by swapping or combining them to create the desired performance. When editing *fragments* of words, the transition point should be at a place that has the same consonant sound or vowel. Finding the common tone between the source words will make for a more seamless edit. After the edit has been made, group together the fragmented word or lines of dialogue so that the carefully timed edits are preserved.

The last technical suggestion during the voice cut, for more advanced editors, is to apply a reverb track that matches the anticipated setting while cutting together the vocal tracks. e.g., two characters whispering in a church. How a voice reacts to the environment it will be placed in, can greatly affect the selection. A **forceful line** choice can fill a room and bounce off the walls. In the example above, selecting which dialogue *remains a whisper in the church* setting might be essential for the Voice Cut process.

10.6a Performance Selection and the Editor*

One of the most subjective parts about post production is the dialogue selection process. In other words, what is the best read (or take) of dialogue? Using the 4 Cs established earlier —Character, Cohesion, Cadence, and Clarity— the matter is still very subjective. Using "Character" as an example, if the performance comes across as too aggressive for that character, but another producer feels that it's a natural progression of anger, it becomes a weighted selection process. Which fits best?

In the end, the selection typically comes down to producer or editor experience. After numerous productions that require sorting through countless auditions of the same material, or pouring over multiple takes from the same actor trying to find that perfect inflection, the "ear" becomes more trained for "good vs bad" material. Regardless, even the most experienced editors still have difficulty identifying "truth" in a performance.

When approaching aural entertainment, there is a tendency to think that film sound designers make the best editors for audio drama. This is not always the case. When designing sound for a movie or TV show, there's usually a picture lock already set by the film editor. This picture editor determined the pacing of the scene based on the available footage. As such, the audio editing process is limited to what media coverage is available through different camera angles and takes, allowing for the flexibility for pickups and ADR.

Editing audio dramas is all about selecting the performances and setting the pace of the entire world. There is infinite space in audio editing, so much so that it can often become daunting with the number of available choices. How does an editor selectively choose dialogues to present a scene? With so many variables, it can overwhelm. Frequently, editors are merely trying to make the performances match and don't have the freedom or time to explore all options. By breaking down the process into the following steps, it becomes easier to approach pre-recorded takes and make the best edits.

1. Listen to every performance from last to first take. The final take is often the best, but not always. On occasion, actors are better timed and more relaxed on the first attempt or their jokes land with better pacing on initial delivery.

2. Find the general take that is the best and make those sections of dialogue the primary selection. If following the three-page-at-once method, this would be the general best take of those blocks. That take becomes the basis for all selections and swap-outs.

3. Find the weakest links in that general take. Is there a line that's flubbed or stumbled? Is there a line where the inflection just doesn't hit right, or the line's drama doesn't match the intention of the scene? A technical error on a line that makes it unusable?

4. Replace the lines that don't work with ones that do from other takes. Go line by line to preview and search for that one dialogue that works best for the scene and swap it out. Is it a partial line or only an inflection in a word? Audio can be replaced in tiny pieces or large chunks, depending on what is required. Sometimes the end of a cut-off word is all that's needed to change its inflection of the line and better interpret the events in the scene.

5. Find the spaces that need to be cut or added. The pacing of the recording from the booth is NOT the pace of the audio drama. On the stage, spaces for action are cut and need to be readded, along with any additional dramatic timing. The spacing before someone walks up and speaks their dialogue says something in itself.

6. Listen to the scene all-together. Does it flow? Is there enough space to add the actions and sound effects later? Do the characters react honestly to each other, and feel like they are in the same space and time? Is there any dialogue that holds up the action or changes the tone enough to be cut? Not all lines in a script are necessary, and it's better to lose out-of-place pieces that slow down the intentions of the story.

7. Is anyone missing? Scenes can bury a character, invisible unless they speak up. An occasional cough or chuckle reaction to the scene reminds the audience who is present. Generic recordings come in handy here to bring back characters that go missing in the scene. A simple "I'll be right back" or "Alright" wildly recorded and manually inserted keeps characters present.

8. Move on and return later. Occasionally, dramatic scenes work with just the voices, but others will need additional sound elements to understand them fully. It helps to include big elements like doors opening or closing in early reviews, as these clues inform where entrances and exits take place and allow them a broader sense of the overall pacing and flow. If a line of dialogue still sticks out even with sound effects added, then a pickup or re-recording should be done.

9. Compile a list of pickups over the entire production to be recorded all at once. This saves time and money by bringing the talent in for a single day and not multiple times. There usually are places in scenes where a pickup replacement could save hours of editing time. If an actor is coming in for pickups, a few more lines usually won't take long. It's not always easy for the actors to match inflections or intentions in pickup recording, so reference takes of the original performances will help the actors.

The subjectivity of performance selection is often unique to each editor. If they understand the nuances of human performances, they can listen carefully for certain inflections and reactions. "Is that genuine surprise?" "Is that character reacting how they should to that line?" More often than not, it's a chemistry of performances and whether they all flow together. If a director is actively listening on the recording stage and coaxing variety in the takes, then the editor will be able to work more effectively, selecting what works from what doesn't. The more complex scenes often require more takes, as do heavily emotional scenes. Sometimes, though, there are few options, no pickups available, and what's recorded is what's recorded. If all else fails, an editor has to work with what they have.

10.6b The Pacing Cut*

There is a new iteration of a production stage called the "Pacing Cut". Vocal cuts only contain lines of dialogue that can lack pacing without major effects such as entrances and exits, gunshots and explosions, even vehicle motion and characterizations. In order to get an idea of the timing of the overall production, big aural pieces often need to be in place. When someone enters the room correlates to how soon they would be greeted, effectively changing the timing of the lines and delivery. The goal of a Pacing Cut is to have most of the elements that will set the timing and atmosphere in place. Producers will be able to give more effective notes at this stage, along with a much more complete cut in terms of timing for the musicians to begin composing. Essentially this would become a "picture lock" in the visual world, where the timing is set to build everything else around. If no adjustments are made to pacing after this point, it makes it easier for foley as well.

Once the pacing cut is locked, the minor sound effects can be filled in and flushed out through the various rough cut-stages.

10.7 Rough Cut

The rough cut is essentially where all the sound design begins. Any additional aural elements are created or inserted during this stage. A variety of sources can be used to enhance the clarity of the image… a recording of the performer grunting or struggling to handle a heavy object, the rattle of a chain (obtained from a sound effect library), the Foley of footsteps kicking the ground, using the reverb of the room to shape the environment, or even the on-location ambience recorded in the surroundings… all utilized for the perfect presence.

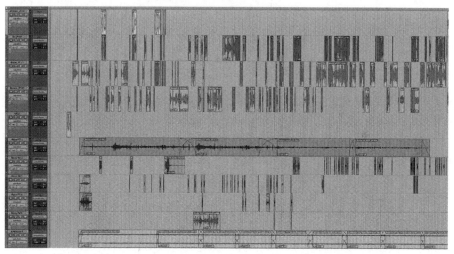

Fig. 10-7-1 Rough Cut

At this point in the workflow, it's best to determine how much of the intended final program is necessary for each Pro Tools session. Is each episode 10 minutes? 30? 60? Sometimes it makes more sense in the workflow to have multiple episodes on the same timeline to be able to easily drag elements and effects between them. On other projects, with multiple Post-crew members working on the same series, it's best to break out individual episodes for multi-tasking purposes.

10.8 Sound Effect Libraries

Every audio drama will need some sort of Hard Sound Effects (meaning they are already set and recorded). Whether they're bought in bulk from companies like Sound Ideas (whom I have worked with a lot, thank you Ron!), or individually through websites like sounddogs.com, a production will need lots of additional sound FX. The amount of time saved trying to cleanly record specific sounds will be well worth the investment. Not everything a sound design needs can be found in a library, but with the ever expanding catalogues, it's pretty close. Background environments, gunshots, vehicles, and such are all relatively difficult to locate and record in real life (IRL).

I recommend not using anything from SFX libraries when the sound is to originate from the characters in the scene. These include actions such as footsteps, cloth motion, writing, chair movements, etc… (more on this in Foley 10.10). Other times are when a sound source is used consistently, or is a recurring element that's unique, like a certain classic car engine like a Chevy Camero. Finding something authentic IRL and doing some field recording can be much easier than trying to find specific sounds in a library. Animals and pets that are recurring characters don't often fit into the molds of what's available either.

Fig. 10-8-1 SoundMiner Sound Effect Searching

To speed up the process of searching sound effects, there are programs designed to index and categorize libraries of audio clips. One such program that I use is called SoundMiner. It allows our editors to quickly find, preview, and insert sounds quickly and efficiently. The faster the sound designers are able to work with these hard effects, the quicker the aural scenes are built.

Through the process of creating episodes, your own production will start developing its own original SFX library. Having an organized sound catalogue dedicated to the show can also improve efficiency and sound-cohesion between multiple editors, as everything isn't having to be constantly re-created or developed through Foley.

10.8a Foley vs SFX*

It's impossible to clap the same way three times.

When working with various sound editors, a question tends to emerge: "When do you use Foley or canned effects?" Each has its merits, but the choice of one over the other in different situations is worthy of discussion.

Let's define the different types of sound effects that can be applied:

- **Foley:** Sounds recorded in real life in front of a mic to recreate/match the action.
- **Canned Sound Effects:** Sounds that are already pre-recorded and cataloged for use
- **Digital Foley:** Canned and pre-sampled recordings played in response to a human interface like a keyboard.

Digital Foley is fairly new in usage but has existed for ages. Sound Designer legends like Ben Burtt incorporated these techniques in Wall-E, which required a fair amount of synthesized sounds. Digital Foley integrates the human input of timing, pressure and sensitivity with the sounds corresponding output. It's Foley but under a slightly different classification.

In the case of most human interfaces, the samples are all pre-recorded. In the case of Digital Foley footsteps, such as those generated by the Walker plugin, the sourced footsteps originate from pre-recorded sound. The interface responds to variance from human controls to simulate the imperfections of walking. Today, the technology is advanced enough to provide realistic results, but specific characterization textures are lost.

Back to the first sentence. It wasn't a joke, it's an experiment. Try it! Clap three times and listen to the variations in each. I'll wait.

This experiment harkens back to the scene in *Jurassic Park*, where Ian Malcolm drops the water on Ellie's hand to describe the variations with vastly different outcomes. That's the unpredictability in human action. Each clap differs subtly depending on where the hands collide, differences in the motion's pressure, speed, muscle fluctuations, etc. Physics plays a role in the mechanics of any organic movement.

That all may sound overtly technical, but I discuss these elements because characters should have those subtle dynamics of human variation. Their emotions are expressed through the actions. Genuine Foley is needed to catch those specificities, nearly undetectable by the ear yet meaningful to the mind's eye. In short, there's nothing better than the real thing when it comes to footsteps.

In some cases, canned and pre-recorded sound effects — like footsteps — work perfectly well in a scene. When there are few variations in action or emotion, it's easy to sell a canned sound with some subtle editing techniques. As the scene grows in complexity and suspense, then it becomes more difficult. The speed and intensity of the way an action is completed varies greatly with the person and the infinite variables surrounding their character. Subtleties disappear in samples, such as the slight shuffle or misstep that alludes to something mysterious in the scene's background. Random movements and alterations thrown at various times can feel awkward. Not every scene may need to be Foleyed in real-time against the audio playback, but a noticeable difference occurs when it's done.

I experienced this in an early cut of *Goldrush*. I was working on the scene in Chapter 8 when Robbins is running through a field after their vehicle died. I used countless versions of pre-recorded footsteps in dirt to try and match what worked for his character, and then reactively slowed down when he got tired. Even after hours of trying to find and edit pieces into cohesive action, it didn't sound genuine. The performance and the footsteps felt off, and eventually I had to go back and re-record both the voice and Foleyed feet in the scene. The result sounded totally believable, and the emotion of the actor matched the footsteps perfectly, giving the scene the pacing and intensity needed for that part of the story.

There's a good rule to follow: **if a character in the scene handles something, it should be Foleyed.** This includes interaction with a pen, paper, book, cell phone, door handle, steering wheel, chair, etc. The way that character interacts with any object expresses their emotion through that action's sound. If someone is angry at their smartphone and tapping at it furiously, that sound makes sense to the listener: the density of the phone, the shape, the grip of one hand adjusting as the other slams into the plastic but solid, buttonless screen. No other object I know can replicate that specific sound other than the reality of repeating the phone action in front of a microphone in cadence with the character's voice. Creating these true moments of interaction between the aural world and vocals ties them together in a believable way, making each moment more genuine.

Foley can save performances. Adding a level of action over the character's voice accentuates dialogue: the listener hears more of *what* they're saying through the actions of *how* they are saying it. There are times when I will listen to every take of a performance and not believe it, but by placing a subtle movement underneath the voice, the intention of the line changes. Sometimes those specially timed creaks and shifts in a chair can make a line more menacing or direct.

Foley is one of those areas where sound becomes infinitely editable in audio. Additional elements can combine and be stacked to the point where the characters can be heard no more. However, the art of editing audio-only entertainment lies in understanding the balance and timing of where and how to include particular sounds. High level audio editing requires an understanding of the human ear's limitations and the ability to hear and frame a line of dialogue where it rings most faithful to the story and character.

10.9 Sound Design

There are many different approaches when designing sound. For me, I like to lay down some simple ambience first. Filling the spaces with what would be diegetic to the environment, such as an air conditioner, nearby construction, or in the case of We're Alive, crippling silences, wind, and sprinkles of synthetic tones. "Diegetic" is often used to describe sound in film that's visible or implied that the source of the sound is in the scene. Non-Diegetic sound would be things like the musical score, or synthesized tones riding in the background. By creating the environment first, I construct a sense of place.

10.9.1 Establish Location

Tell the audience where the SPOV is at the start. Establishing where the characters are at the beginning is important when a listener is trying to understand the location. Even if there's an audio slate from a narrator telling where the scene is taking place, sound is still needed to fill in the details. Does the scene describe what time of day it is through the audio? Night might contain subtle **[AND I MEAN SUBTLE!]** crickets, distant dogs barking, a light breeze with other *minimal* "exterior" sources like cars and people. Mid-Day would be much different than the night. The streets would be busier, lots of traffic and commotion. Even in a small town, people are awake and active. Or even more specific, such as morning time around my house: lots and lots of leaf-blowers, lawn mowers, people starting up motorcycles and airplanes flying overhead.

Introducing location at the start of each new scene is pivotal. The audience is immediately trying to figure out where "we" are when a new scene begins. To continually be wondering is distracting. If possible, establish the scene with sound before the start of dialogue. At a train station, we hear the whistle of a locomotive. At a bar, the pool balls break in the background, while the aural hint of the opening of beer bottles repeats behind the bar, and a person in the background gives a drink order. Scenes can be specified further with custom footsteps that give the exact location of who we are hearing in the aural world. A polished hard marble surface would denote a place of wealth and elegance, in contrast to the gritty and rocky asphalt at the side of a highway road.

The beginning of the scene is often the most dense in sound effects to first articulate the location. Then, reduce and blend this into the background as the scene continues. Don't have sound FX compete unnecessarily in the aural space with the dialogue. This is another reason to establish location before anyone starts talking. Even if the writing is lacking scene establishment, build the aural environment out of whatever might be available. Background noises like a copy machine, pencil sharpener, and/or stapler can help establish that a scene is taking place in an office.

There are other scenes where the focus is on the action or the characters, and knowing the exact environment right away isn't as necessary. Every situation in a story has to be approached differently. There are times when not revealing the environment plays into the mystery, and compels the audience to wonder, "Where are we?"

After the scene has been established, then start inserting sounds from one cue to another. Hit the big action moments first, and work your way down to quieter details. Doors are a great first addition to help shape the timing and circumstances of when certain characters come and go. Explosions, cars, any sort of sound that's going to dominate the scene- place first and build around them. This is the stage when large sound FX libraries come in handy, and whatever is missing in the libraries must now be created.

10.9.2 Sample Scene

Let's run through a scene, breaking down the details of the sound design, and how I would approach creating all the sound elements that would compliment that scene.

A man runs into the room and shuts the door behind him. A distant truck is heard approaching outside, muffled by the walls. The man takes deep breaths as he takes out and checks his revolver, before closing and spinning it. The men outside shoot through the windows as the man scrambles across the floor, just as a molotov enters the room and sets it ablaze. The man knocks over shelves to get to the back door and checks the handle. It's locked.

10.9.3 The Sound of the Scene

Here's a complex scene. No voices at all, just sound. The great thing about scenes like these- they're blank canvases, and sound represents all the possible colors of paint...brushes ready?

The first step I would complete in order to start editing this scene, is to record all the voices. It's important to get multiple takes of breaths and vocal expressions (VOX) to be able to illustrate the energy and emotion of the characters. I would run through the scene several times with a male actor playing the man inside the room. I would instruct him to re-create *the action* in front of the mic, exaggerating every action with his breath. I want to hear him run into the room, stop, catch his breath, check his gun, react to the car approaching, quiet himself, then give me *the vocal* performance of the man running across the room, give me a few grunts of movement as he pushes away the debris, and shakes the back door ferociously. Lastly, a quick breath in...ending in silence.

The breaths and movements of the character would be blocked out and staged first, creating a paper map of the action. Cutting and adjusting the recorded performance for the general time needed for each movement would then occur. Afterwards, I would start to build around the VOX. The door opening in the beginning could be a library SFX, with fast movement. Because the action is so specific, though, I might even record my own front door to get the right speed and intensity for the entrance. Every footstep would need to be Foleyed to fully depict the action, including the movement of the man putting his back against the wood door. This action against the door was not in the prompt, but something that I feel would better aurally illustrate the scene. The rattle of the hinges would give placement to the man, and the listener would know exactly what's going on at that moment with the single door impact.

For the distant truck coming into the scene, I would need to use a SFX library. Cars and trucks are common elements. The difficult part is finding that right energy and perspective of the engine noise. For this scene I'd use a muscle car, an old mustang [or 67' Chevy Camaro as suggested by my editor ;)]. The rattle of the engine cooling down and the subtle pings of the engine popping would add to the tension. The car is parked, and not going anywhere. The choice of having the car shut off means something in the story, as if whoever just showed up is going to stay for a while. These people are not interested in a quick getaway. I would adjust the EQ of the sound of the car's engine, dropping the gain on most of the high frequencies, since it's being heard from the building interior and this would make it more muffled.

The inside of the room would have a reverb profile of a mid-sized room, 300-400 square feet. The floor would be hard tile. That would provide an atmosphere with enough echo to hear the footsteps reflect back, along with bouncing around the bass of the engine from outside. There could be a small window AC in the corner that kicks on every so often, just to be annoying or for added suspense, with the loud start and continuing rattle. The time that the man inside is waiting by the door... is a long while now. About 20-30 seconds in he might check his gun, slowly. He empties out the shell casings, and we can picture the action as we hear him nervously shaking out the old shells. A solitary empty brass casing drops to the floor. Thankfully, it seems that no one heard. The motion of this moment would have to be Foleyed, and re-enacted with a real bullet shell. Many of these motions are too specific to be in a sound effects library. On the other hand, Foley movement can sometimes capture too much motion, requiring it to be cut down to only the needed moments of action.

The sound of *inserting the bullets and spinning of the gun cylinder* would be from a SFX library. Many libraries have gun movement and handling sounds. Guns movements IRL aren't actually that loud, but in our aural world, they're enhanced to clarify and specify the action. There's the *reality* of sound and then there's the *spirit* of sound.

Footsteps from the men are heard outside the room. These could come from SFX libraries because they're muffled and distant, which means they can be generic and not stand out. Add some additional car doors opening and closing, while the footsteps grow in volume and clarity against the concrete. Suddenly, the action of several shots ring out from multiple 9mm pistols, followed by the splintering of the wood reacting as the bullets pass through, and finally striking something metal and glass inside. The shots are immediately followed by shell casings faintly clinking against the ground outside, all these sound-actions and reactions occurring within barely a second. Almost every sound event, in this case a gunshot, consists of an action with multiple sound reactions- any less and something will feel missing.

The man scrambling across the floor would need to be Foleyed. The sound of his hands slapping against the concrete as he moves is clearly heard. The audience will know these are real impacts on the ground, and it will feel intense. Human skin is a distinct conductor of sound. The gentle touch, slap, or impact against the palm and fingers is an identifiable and relatable sound. With the Foley session, I would scramble on the floor myself, and then pick the most "visual" take, combining the most useful sections. The Molotov cocktail flying through the glass would be pieced together from SFX libraries. I've smashed a full bottle of wine before, to find that it sounds deflated. The water squelches the high pitched shatter of the glass, almost making it sound phony. "Fake" glass shatter, combined "fireball" SFX, would be layered with several additional impacts of the Molotov as it comes into the room. The first impact is at the entry point through the window, lightly forcing glass shards to the floor on the way in. The action is subtle and quick, but compliments the dimensions of the space. The second impact, when the Molotov hits the ground, would have additional layers of *water spray sounds* included as the fuel explodes out initially, followed by the whoosh of a fireball as the flames push into the room.

As the fire spreads, the man continues his anguished retreat, knocking over the various shelves and debris in the way. Most of these impacts can be found in libraries, but they would also be combined with specific Foleyed footsteps, stumbling from place to place. When I Foley a specifically intense scene, I try to "let my feet illustrate my heart," as I play the panic through the sound of my motion. As the flames build up in the scene, I Foley the last bit of my hand grasping at a door handle, putting every bit of strength into pushing it open… but it won't budge. A few more added impacts from human hands, clawing at the wood door, the fingertips sliding down the door. Re-enacting, through Foley, the man turning and putting his back against a wood panel, the scene is closed out with SFX libraries as the flames engulf the room. The man breathes in, but no exhale is heard, leaving the audience uneasy.

10.9.4 Aural Design Techniques

What sounds wrong, is wrong. What sounds right, is simply, and recognizably, right. The real water-filled wine bottle didn't have the same impact as the more glamorous glass explosion of an empty bottle. An important concept to repeat: There's the reality of sound and the spirit of sound. Cheat it appropriately and make it sound correct. The same goes for a lot of signature effects: weapon suppressors never sound like real silencers, guns aren't very noisy when handled, and footsteps aren't always so apparent. In our world, doors *always* creak, switches are loud, and bombs *always* beep... otherwise how would anyone know what and where they are?

Adding more and more sounds doesn't always enhance a scene. Heavy amounts of footsteps throughout the scene, constant crickets chirping, the motor loudly running constantly, the air conditioner rattling on and on... All of it can contribute to dissonant sounds for the ear and are processed as just harsh noise. There's a fine line between the entertaining audio accents, and incredibly annoying noise. Let a loud siren or alarm run for over a minute in a scene, and an audience might just stop listening. For consistent loud elements, try to choose the least irritating tone. In addition to annoying the listener, they distort the aural image. Things become less clear when competing with other sounds. Sometimes there are ways through the story to creatively cut them short. *The alarm is only set to go for so long, or the alarm shorts out and fails due to damage or decay.* **Find ways around hitting your audience with too many "earitants."** [Dad genes kicking in...]

Choose moments of audio that best help define the scene. The audio cue for when the man hit his back against the door was a good example. These become instances when the character connects to the world intimately. The more times the characters interact with the environment, the more enhanced and visual the image will be.

Clarity is king, confusion is death. If the action or intention of a scene can't be followed, it fails to communicate. Test this out having others listen and ask their thoughts on the action, "What happened in the scene?" At the same time, it's helpful to know that not everyone who listens can easily interpret and understand action in audio. Quality control sampling with several listeners will be helpful to test whether the scene works or not.

Performances can be sold through editing and additional Foley. I use the term "sold" here to refer to the listener "buying into" what they're hearing. The addition of proper sound design and a little editing can enhance mediocre performances into something amazing. Setting down a glass of water in the middle of a line adds a new sense of purpose to the dialogue. Sound Designers become almost like puppeteers, making performances do what they want using sound. Every action that takes place around the dialogue can change what it means. *A boss is talking to an employee in an office, takes a pause in the conversation and leans back in his creaky chair.* That creaking sound now means something. This delayed response becomes a response in itself.

Editing audio controls both time and space. *That extended moment, when the man was waiting against the door...* that "moment" didn't exist in the script, but was created in Post. These newer additions of sound were used to create almost a new scene and better defined the relationship between the characters. Giving a scene like this a little more time to breathe can increase tension, and build suspense. No other medium lets the editor control exactly when and where something takes place within a few button clicks. In the previous scene, the men who were waiting outside can be shifted from being distant to only inches away, from moving slow and methodical to fast and hurried, all with a few sound effect changes. The editor has to choose what aural moments are best to focus on, which to speed through, what locations to fill with sound, and which suspended incidents to let hover in silence. Some of the most powerful aural moments consist of total "darkness."

Never forget the power of human touch. The sound of human contact is a shared human experience, is easily identifiable, but is also not always noticed. Emphasizing the subtle touching of skin against a surface rarely occurs on film, but in the audio world it can bring a sense of frailty and connection that's often missed. The tapping of fingers, the stroke of the binding on a book, a touch of the wall, the scratching of a head, or rubbing of hands- all are ways we interact and live in our world. It can be incredibly subtle. *A scene takes place where a plane is taking off, separating two lovers. One looks out the window and presses their hands against the thin second layer of the hollow plastic window.* Fingers makes contact, the touch is heard, and a connection is made between the emotion and the environment.

Create your own unique sound. As Editor or Sound Designer, construct the spaces using your own internal aural instrument. The more scenes created, the more advanced an editor becomes, and with that comes developing the methodology for creating their own sound. This can come in a practical format, like combining multiple fragments of sound effects into a new one, to recording effects in the real world and manipulating them for what is needed. Take the time to tweak and play with sound in ways that aren't expected, and experience the reaction. After all, creative sound engineering is what turned birds into dinosaurs in Jurassic Park.

10.9.4a Audience Digestion, Limitations, Lufs, and Levels*

The rate in which an audience can receive and process new information is often very low, particularly in audio. With film and television, visuals serve as reinforcements for the story. In books, the words provide all details and can be read and re-read at the speed that fits the reader. For audio, the lasting memory of sound is all that remains. It requires slightly different pacing, the slow introduction of characters, and sculpting ideas within a scene to allow for easy interpretation. Audiences first hear, then process, and — once that's complete — wait for the next bit of material. Spreading out information between characters and throughout various scenes, and using audio sound effects to reinforce dialogue will often give an audience ample time and knowledge to keep up with the story.

In audio, where there are infinite variables, it's easy to attempt reinventing the wheel to try to over-do a scene, exerting every option available.. The ease of manipulating the audio is tempting for first-time editors, able to pile effects, pitch modulation, sound effect stacking, or sped-up dialogue to the point of incomprehensibility. Just because an edit can be made doesn't mean that it *should* be made. The primary focus of the creator should be the audience's engagement. If an edit is distracting, it should receive immediate attention.

Audiences have a sensitivity to sound that should be respected, too. Pop-out sound effects -- sound effects that play much louder than the average previous sections -- should be within tolerance and not peak past a point where it would be painful for a listener. Meters are essential for this reason, but not all editors know how to use them properly. Today's standard measurements of audio are decibels (dB) and Loudness Units Full Spectrum (LUFS). dB is a measure of air pressure displacement at one time, while LUFS is more an average scale over time. They both measure loudness, but LUFS measures over an extended period, allowing for more consistent volume.

Various types of shows will mix at different levels: the LESS the negative value, the higher the average level. The closer to 0, the louder it is.

Rock Music: -11.4 LUFS
Youtube: -13 LUFS
Regular talky podcasts: -16 LUFS
WWW: -18 LUFS
Broadcast TV: -23 LUFS
We're Alive: -24 LUFS
DVD/BluRay: -27 LUFS
Theatrical Releases: -31 LUFS

Why so many different levels? Most of the time, the volume is determined by two things: where the audio is being played back and what the content is. With a rock album, listeners should be able to rock out without hitting the max limit on their volume level on their phone or adjusting it constantly. If something plays back and it's still quiet, its LUFS need to be higher.

With something like a talkshow, an editor would ensure that speaking levels are consistent, and the audience doesn't have to adjust the volume to understand the conversation. Since the content doesn't change much over time, the LUFS of a talk show can sit at -16.

However, in the case of suspense shows where the story varies from quiet scenes to larger action-packed moments, the dynamic range of the audio needs to be far greater. A lower number like -23/-24/-27 allows for scenes of closeness and subtle sound, while still having big segments of action and many layers of audio. The same rules apply to Blu-Ray and theatrical releases, as they have audio systems that typically support a broader range.

10.9.4b Dissonant Sound*

Dissonant sound is something that all editors should respect. Dissonance occurs when a sound effect plays that contains a specific frequency or range that causes discomfort in the listener. Tolerance for these types of sounds are about 3 seconds, and that's it. Any longer, and the pitch or tone is unfair to the audience. Most often, a listener would then shut off the program and move on, but some will suffer through it. Others may not even hear it, depending on their speakers or playback system. Remember: when a scene in a film is unpleasant, the viewer can always shut their eyes. Humans cannot shut off their hearing.

The editor/sound design team needs to be able to hear everything the audience will to manage the sound output. In the days of the FCC, they restricted certain tones and levels from being broadcast to maintain equipment and protect the consumer. If something was transmitted outside of that standard, fees and fines would be levied. Podcasts can't afford that kind of monitoring yet. There will most likely be automated checks that verify the intensity of the file published in the future. Even then, it would be nearly impossible to automate the checking of certain dissonant sounds like ultra-high frequencies. Editors should monitor to keep spectrums from 20hz to 20khz clear. Sometimes headsets won't produce those high frequencies and even the lower frequencies that could rattle and blow out particular bass and LFE equipment. Professional audio monitoring setups separate the frequency reproduction to individual speakers so that an editor might hear those instances of intense highs or low rumble.

In short, ask whether the sound is annoying to hear for a long time. Or so intense that it is awkward? A super-close mic of someone's vocal clicking can be almost as unbearable as an ongoing screaming alarm. There are always methods to work around these sound annoyances. I make my characters break or shut off alarms in the scenes to allow for realism while preventing overexposure. An uneasy listener isn't necessarily a bad thing when a scene calls for it, but the listener must WANT to listen at all times unless intended.

10.9.4c Mixing to the Voice*

No matter the medium, an audio mix should prioritize the volume and gain of the voices and mix around that. Set the vocals to the proper level and mix all elements around them without making further adjustments to the voices. Too often, an audio editor will chase levels higher by adjusting the music gain and then push the vocals higher to match, and then later adjusting the music again to those new levels, and so on. Minor adjustments and tweaks are always welcome, but as long as the vocals are averaging into the area or -12db to -18db, then adjust no further.

10.10 Foley

Fig. 10-10-1 Feet have no gender in Foley

"Foley artists connect their feet to their hearts."
Foley is the process of connecting the recorded voices to the story through re-creating action. The dialogue becomes fastened to the drama *through the footsteps*, making contact with the ground. Without it, everyone feels like floating heads.

The importance of Foley cannot be understated. In my opinion, it is what typically separates high-end productions from hobbyists. Foley can be hard, and costly. It requires equipment and experience to be done correctly, but when it works, it breathes life into the soundscape.

Foley gets its name from Jack Donovan Foley, who started in the radio business doing live sounds. He brought his skills to the film world for the first time with "The Jazz Singer" in 1927. In this radio transition to film, it had to become a much more subtle art than how it used to sound in the old radio days. The process of Foley (seemingly always capitalized) now has come full circle, back to the audio world in a big way. Today, in the audio-only medium, it has again become more vibrant and active in the scenes. One key to successful Foley in this medium, is that it needs to be slightly exaggerated for better illustration of the action.

Voice actors are not "motion actors."

The best audio Foley artists can paint a picture with just using feet. The way a character moves or grabs something- any interaction with their world can explain a lot about them and what they are experiencing. Every Foleyed SFX has this potential power. The speed in which the cloth is grabbed or metal chains are rattled aurally describes a character's energy & intensity.

There are additional tools IRL that can further manipulate the sound of Foleyed action. A plastic tub deepens the monster's voice, wet cloth on the ground gives the splashes of footsteps, and even VHS tape strips sound *like grass when stepped on*. The reality of sound, is only what the perception of it is.

"Foley is a sound experiment."

Anyone can Foley, but it does take practice to develop an "ear" of knowing when something sounds "right." There are some people who are more gifted in this area naturally. However, most of the ability to create artistic sound comes from experience. A Foley artist learns to tune their ear to the actions. "How do these motions translate into sound on the mic?" The perception of audio through a mic can be very different from one's own ear, and every microphone is different from the next.

The key is to experiment. Find methods, devices, or tools to create a sound. If it works, great! If not, try something else. No matter how experienced the Foley artist, it continues to be a sound experiment in figuring out what, aurally, creates the necessary action. When I was working on a scene where a specific pistol was being smashed into many pieces, I struggled to find something with the right level of metallic strength, yet fragile enough to best mimic the nature of the gun being shattered. I settled on a caulking gun, and took a hammer to it several times. After layering in additional elements of harder metals and then adjusting the pitch of the Foleyed smashing, I was able to achieve my desired result.

One technical variable of this experimentation is the physical distance from the sound source to the microphone that's recording it. Depending upon the distance, the mic can capture completely different properties of the waveform. A great exercise is recording water from varying distances, listening to how vastly different each one sounds. Notice how uncomfortably close the water feels when the mic is within inches of a waterfall. This strength of flow can overwhelm the senses. Water might be one of the most obvious examples, but what about more subtle SFX like footsteps? How far away should the mic be in order to reproduce that aural experience?

The answer is, it's up to the sound designer or Foley artist. Footsteps can be recorded from waist height, to make the more subtleties of the movement stand out. The crunch and sharpness would still be there. Footsteps can also be recorded from a mic at "ear-height," to reduce the perception and impact in the scene, cutting out most of the high frequencies. Each technique has a purpose and application.

In the post-production workflow, Foley (aside from footsteps) should be done fairly late into the rough cut stage. Whatever sounds can come from a sound effects library would be put in place first, and whatever isn't found should have markers left behind to note where the remaining Foley elements need to be added. As each sound is recorded, the markers can be annotated or removed, leaving a session complete with all the necessary sounds for the scenes.

10.10.1 Footsteps

Cloth movements are fairly simple to do. Keep it light, hit the big moments, and don't perform the action too close to the mic. Most of the actions in Foley, like this, are exact re-enactments meant to mimic real actions. The big exception- footsteps.

In order for a Foley artist to record in front of a mic, they need to stay in one spot. To simulate the process of walking, the motion requires a special technique in order to stay in one space.

Walking for Foley is a movement of pressing the heel down first followed by the rest of the foot: heel-toe, heel-toe. The process of walking is actually a form of controlled falling, and the first point of contact is the heel. If you ask someone to walk in place, they typically step with their toes first, making a very different and unnatural one-part sound. It takes practice to keep in step and rhythm with this technique. With a little practice and experience, it'll be easier to adjust and improvise shuffles and slides, altering the cadences of the footsteps. Also, different surfaces can require different coordination, and the same can be said with different types of shoes. (I have yet to figure out how to record flip flops and stay one place!)

In order to properly Foley footsteps, it's necessary to be able to hear to one's own footsteps for timing while listening to the rest of the voices and sound elements. When re-performing the footsteps, Foley artists need to view the audio session timeline in order to see upcoming dialogue clips and anticipate actions for their character. Having a second monitor in the Foley space will help with the timing, and adding a remote mouse and keyboard will facilitate a one-person Foley session.

Keep in mind that these actions are a performance. When "playing the body" of a character, try to become them. Get into their head, and see how they move. Notice the speed of their turns, or the limp in their step. Create a little more action throughout the scene than what's required of the footsteps and then cut back the excess movements later on. This does create more editing work, though, so don't go overboard.

When recording footsteps of multiple characters in the same scene, it's not necessary to Foley everyone individually. The sound of five characters all walking at the same time can becoming a jarring amount of noise. Three or four footstep tracks at the same time is the equivalent of five characters walking.

To further economize efforts, it can help to Foley multiple types of sound effects at the same time. This technique limits what's possible to edit in Post, but cloth, footsteps, and even chair movements, are so connected that it can improve overall cohesion to record them all at the same time. Foley actions are done in real time- which means that a several minute scene of footstep action, multiplied by every character, can't be easily sped up, and adds up to a lot of production time spent on repetition. With so many details needed to be recreated in audio, every method should be geared towards saving time.

When dealing with editing Foleyed footsteps, and making sure they don't overpower the scene, most editors simply lower the volume. This only pushes the footsteps into the "general noise" range, and in essence making the action nothing but background. The better approach is to cut out the footsteps that don't fit the action. Leave the specific steps that help define "the emotion of the motion" in the scene. With enough time dedicated to crafting the sound of footsteps, the editor will be able to mute the dialogue tracks and still communicate what's happening in the physical space.

On the technical side of editing footsteps in Pro Tools, there's an option to add a fade at the end of the clip. Important tip! Don't use this tool to fade out footsteps to simulate someone walking away. Instead, use the automation track to lower the volume slowly. The drop-off range for hearing footsteps is fairly thin, and automation offers better control for fading distance.

Lastly, the raw recording sound of footsteps can compete with dialogue at times. To help blend footsteps and cloth, lower the high frequencies via EQ to better blend them into the scene.

10.10.1a Sampled Foley*

Walker is a new plugin that can significantly assist in creating customized footstep Foley in real-time. By using a midi keyboard a user can press: left foot - left scuff - stop - right scuff - right foot, while listening to the actors' speech. These samples come from various surfaces and shoe types, able to adjust clothing to coincide with the footsteps and even change the profile of the microphone. It's a powerful, convenient, and fast way to create believable sounding footsteps to add depth to the audio.

Where the program falls short is in the customization of footsteps for a scene. The subtleties of a character's movement contain an element of chaos in the weight, flow, and rhythm. Also, the samples lack the grit and grime on the surfaces of footsteps, as no walking space is clean, consistent ground. The other drawback is the limitations when switching out shoe types. If I have three to four characters in the room, the difference in footsteps can be adjusted slightly within the Walker plugin program by adjusting weight parameters, but ultimately they will sound very similar. Nothing yet replaces the aural profile as genuinely changing to a different pair of shoes.

In the end, Walker is a great program and well worth the amount of time it saves in the regular production cycle. It's ideal for background characters, and additional ambient fills to already existing layers of footsteps can be made faster and more customized than searching clips libraries and adjusting speed, tempo, or pitch manually.

10.10.2 Editing at the Mic

Mistakes happen when performing Foley, especially with long takes.

Instead of stopping the take and starting over, keep going and CLAP after the audible mistake so in editing later, it's easy to identify and take out. Clapping sets a visual marker in the waveform, so it becomes clear that something needs to be removed. Talking, sneezes, coughs, or smaller noises are not always caught, and can end up in the final mix if they're low volume. In this way, **editing starts at the mic.**

'Pre-editing' in this way should continue throughout all recording sessions. Capture what's needed for the production and move on. Don't record multiple takes that won't be used. For short actions, repeat them a couple times for safety, but if it sounds close, continue to the next necessary edit. There's plenty of potential adjustments to be done later in Post, as long as the pieces are there.

10.10.3 Equipment

Sync and timing are very important in capturing the natural fluid motion of the scene. Having a recording facility where you can Foley in a sound-neutral environment and also simultaneously see and hear the session, is not easy to find and can be costly. This is an area where the art NEEDS the technology. Isolated audio is necessary to be able to manipulate sound without any extra noise or reverb. Foley requires a lot of studio time, making rental spaces not as economically viable. There are options for building single person Foley spaces, one of which was covered already in the Recording Space 9.1. Additional walking surfaces can be inexpensively constructed for these setups. Low tubs can hold varying amounts of gravel or sand, and even wood surfaces can be cut and nailed together.

The way a mic is setup is a bit different for Foley. Generally, only shotgun mics are used. Their pickup pattern is directional, making it easier to hone in on specific areas. Shotgun mics are either short, medium, or long. The longer the mic, the further it can pick up sound. Short to medium shotguns work best for Foley, and most brands are similar. There are occasions where other types of mics can do specific functions that shotguns can't, so try them out. Test and figure out what sounds best.

10.11 Modifying Audio

There are almost infinite ways to modify audio through Pro Tools, or most any editing program. There are even more ways to expand what these programs are capable of through "Plugins," which add additional ways to process the recordings. This section could go on forever with the variety of public tools available, but we will focus on only the areas that apply to editing audio theater.

10.11.1 Cleaning up Audio

Even when recording in a studio, there will still be some artifacts in the audio that will need to be removed, or some segments requiring enhancements to make the sound clearer. Here's a few scenarios of noisy recordings, and what is necessary to fix them:

Fig. 10-11-1 EQ Plugin (AudioSuite)

Too much bass or too high-pitched - Whenever dealing with modifying audio through equalization (EQ), we are talking about changing the frequencies of the sound. High frequencies consist of anything with a elevated pitch, like a whistle. Low frequencies are what makes the bass thump, like a drum. The EQ plugin (7 or 3 band) will raise or lower the gain for each range of frequencies of a clip. It can be used to enhance vocal clarity, and also be used to make a voice sound distant, such as behind a wall. When a performer's voice mumbles slightly over a certain portion of a line, this segment of dialogue can be improved in clarity by raising the high frequencies through the EQ.

The S's in an actor's dialogue are sharp and piercing - Sometimes when recording a performer, their S's can be so sharp that it can actually hurt the listener's ears. This one is an easy fix, but commonly missed. Using the Pro Tools plugin, "De-ESSER," select the preset for male or female, and you can make minor tweaks to shave off those harsh tones. If the correction is being applied to one or two words, select the harsh S section of the clip and render it out using an Audiosuite Plugin. If the performer continues to have this issue throughout their entire performance, a RTAS Plugin can be applied to the entire track. The De-ESSER plugin affects only the high S sound, so having it over an entire performer's VOX track is relatively safe. But be sure to tweak the default settings should the voice become muffled as each person's voice responds differently.

Fig. 10-11-2 DE-ESSER Plugin (RTAS)

Plugin Technical Note: There are two ways to use plugins in Pro Tools. A clip or section can be modified and rendered appropriately through an Audiosuite Plugin, for specific single instances. An RTAS plugin, however, applies to an entire track. The RTAS way is non-destructive, meaning new files aren't being created for every modification, and so the processing can be done on the fly. The "render" process of Audiosuite Plugins creates a new file, and the previous generation only resides in the clips bin. Whenever doing a render, make a copy of the original clip (hold ALT) onto a new track and mute it (Command+M/Windows+M), so that you can more easily find the original un-modified version. There will be times when it's necessary to tweak the original, and looking for original clips can be time-consuming. Higher-end versions of Pro Tools now allow these Audiosuite Plugins to be used non-destructively per clip, but anything not pre-rendered still puts a strain on the processing and memory of the computer. It can pile up after a while, which is why per-clip plugins are only available on the higher-end Pro Tools HD.

"The P's are a-popping!" - This saying refers to when actors emit a "plosive" syllable, essentially a burst of air directly onto the microphone. This air causes distortion and creates a "puff" on the recording. Depending on how bad it is, the distortion can sometimes be fixed by removing only the low frequencies for that one section using the Audiosuite 7-band EQ. It's only necessary to EQ the part of the clip that has the "plosive." Removing low frequencies on a section causes the clip to sound slightly "tinny," so only use it on as small an area of the sound as possible. When played with the rest of the larger sound, the small section with the cleaned up "puff" goes by so fast, it won't be recognized.

Artifacts, clicks, and hums - These types of noise can be difficult to fix. Clicks might come from certain mouth movements, on-set disruptions, and even equipment noise. Hums generally come from constantly running motors in the environment, like AC units and generators.

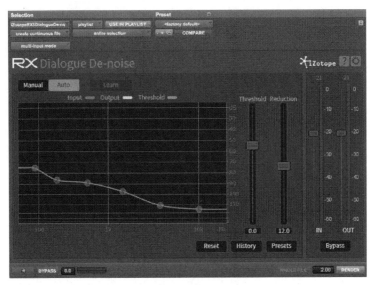

Fig. 10-11-3 iZotope Noise Reduction Plugins

By default, the only noise reduction in Pro Tools comes through the EQ module, which doesn't work very well reducing and removing a large amount (or large quantity) of artifacts. If the project will require a lot of cleanup, I would recommend spending the extra money on third-party plugins. Specialized software that focuses on noise reduction has improved greatly over the last few years. For about $130, iZotope sells noise reduction bundles for pops, hums, and crackles. Most of them can clean up a great deal of unwanted noise. There are other, more expensive options, like the higher-end iZotope packages or the Waves Bundles. Many of these plugins offer limited time-trials and demos, so test them against the problem to see if they can resolve the issue as each program processes and reduce noise differently.

Unwanted reverb - There are some plugins available that try to remove reverb, but *ultimately fail*. The recorded echo is so embedded in the audio that no matter what tweaking is done, the audio will always sound processed. In the future they might be improved, but still the best way to get rid of reverb is to fix it at the mic.

10.11.2 Enhancing Audio

For the times that it is necessary to use plugins for enhancing the audio:

Limit certain frequencies of a sound effect or voice - The EQ module will allow for the adjustment of any frequency or range. It can enhance the bass to force footsteps deeper and more menacing, crush the highs and lows to create the sound of an old fashioned radio, or just pull up the mid-range to give the voice a bit more presence in the room. Treat EQ delicately. When first experiencing the power and control of EQ, editors will oftentimes overuse it.

Pitch/Time Change - There are a few built-in plugin modules in Pro Tools that change the pitch and/or speed of a clip. Quick Tip: Want to change the tone of someone's voice to make it sound like a monster? Lower the pitch. Effects like these can be done with Pitch-Shift and Time-Shift. They have options that can slow the tempo of footsteps or even speed them up to communicate more urgency.

Reverb - This is the big one. This is how voices sound to reflect the specific environment they are in. Some might call it "echo," but the proper term is "reverb," and it can help reproduce the proper sound location to hear a voice. Voices respond to their container. If you listen closely, every room has a certain amount of reverb. Places like bathrooms have a lot because of all the flat hard surfaces that reflect the audio.

There are several plugin options for reverb, like Altiverb and Avid Spaces. These additional pieces of software typically come with a pack of sampled environments, as well as options to order others. Real-life locations are space sampled, meaning that a team of engineers with vibration recording equipment measured the amount of reflection given off by a certain area. That information is then translated back into an algorithm that can be applied to other audio clips that are recorded neutrally.

Reverb plugins are one of the greatest tools for giving the feeling for a space, and the sampling keeps getting more and more accurate. The plugin called "Indoor" from Audioease is so advanced, that it can triangulate the scene in 3D space. A sound designer can thus track the reverb changes right as the characters move, matching the real-world reflection exactly as it would occur IRL. These plugins are sometimes the most important tool because they make the environment more believable for our own ears.

Fig. 10-11-4 "Spaces" Reverb Room Profiles

Radio effects and special processes. In most of the audio theater I write, there's always some sort of communication device in the script, usually a phone or radio. There are plugins dedicated to this sort of special processing, one of them being "SpeakerPhone." It includes a vast selection of different mic and speaker options to modify existing audio, and also adds elements to reproduce the qualities of specific devices. If there's some "old phone" needed to be matched, or a special broken speaker- it has it all. There are other miscellaneous plugin enhancers, like flangers, voice modifiers, and loads of additional filters. Since it's impossible to cover all the options, experiment with the audio. If you are looking to achieve a certain effect, then chances are there's something out there that can help. Download demos and trials, and find what works best.

Plugin and Effect stacking. When using multiple plugins on one clip or section, there is a hierarchy in which the layers of effects need to be applied. Let me explain with an example. While editing Lockdown, I kept hearing an effect over the radio that didn't sound natural. The issue I discovered was that the reverb (echo) applied to the sound effect was done *after* the EQ "radio" effect, instead of before. The radio should have received a certain amount of echo first, and then be rebroadcast over the radio. The room that contained the radio would then have its own reverb.

A little hard to follow, but if it were to look like a flow chart with the original sound on the left, it would be like this: **Villain Character's Footsteps Foley -> Room 1 Reverb -> Radio (EQ) Effect -> Room 2 Reverb**

The end result was hearing the internal echo of the monitored room over the radio, making it sound all the more creepy and isolated.

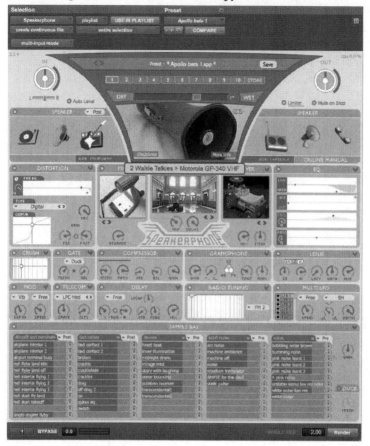

Fig. 10-11-5 Speakerphone Plugin

Audio needs a limit - There are a few situations that might require limiting the intensity of an audio recording, the most common being using a compressor. What a compressor does is act as a crusher of the peaks that go into distortion. When working with a multitude of sound effects, sometimes it's safer to have a compressor on the SFX Aux track to make sure those types of sounds don't overload the output. Compressors also work to change the dynamics of the sound and can completely crush loud sounds like gunshots. This can be good or bad, depending on the situation. The compromise is to have tracks that specifically go around the compressor, and then manually adjust those sounds to make sure they don't peak and distort.

10.11.3 Aux Track Effects

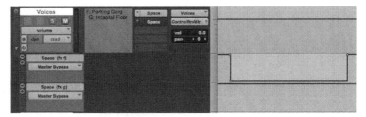

Fig. 10-11-1 RTAS Reverb Automation

To apply an effect to an entire group of tracks, simply click on one of the blank "Inserts" next to the Aux Track that receives the output from the different types of tracks. By default, it will apply reverb to the entire track for the length of the timeline. With a few automation settings, the reverb can be made active or inactive at certain portions of the timeline.

Once the effect is added to the Aux Track, click on the Plug-In Automation button, then select "Master Bypass." This acts as a switch to turn the reverb on or off. When the characters walk into the kitchen, the Kitchen reverb insert activates, and deactivates when they leave.

Fig. 10-11-2 Enable "Bypass" for Plug-in Automation on the Reverb track

To turn the plugin on or off, select the arrow under that specific aux track and select the automation "bypass" to modify. For each reverb plugin insert, the more breakouts will appear under this section as seen in Fig. 10-11-1 with Space (fx f) and (fx g) on their own sub-tracks. Expand only the master bypass for now. Looking at the timeline to the left of Space (fx f), there is a new automation line similar to what 'volume' looks like on the normal tracks. Since this is a simple bypass switch, the automation options are either on or off.

Multiple plugin inserts can be added to one track, up to 10 instances per aux. In short, that means there can be 10 different room options. There's also an expanded section for each track called "Comments," where notes can be inserted. Label each insert space here with the corresponding reverb setting, i.e.:, A: Walt's Bedroom. B: Ruby's Kitchen. and so on.

If the aux tracks need more inserts, there is a more advanced option of creating an additional sub-aux. Have the aux output go to another bus, which then goes into the additional aux track, thus giving an additional 10 spaces for reverb profiles.

10.12 Fine Cut - Adding Music

The fine cut is the last stage for adjustments in post-production. All the sound effects should be in place and adjusted, and now music will be added in for the final mix. The addition of music changes the entire feel for a cut, and might require timing adjustments and leveling of sound effects and vocals. You want to make sure that all elements that need to be heard still rise above the music.

10.12.1 Theme Music

Branding is important in the modern media age. Being able to give a production something iconic help audiences identify with it. For Audio Theater, that would be the theme music. This theme is heard many times over, which adds a lot of pressure to get it right- so start this creation process early. The length of the music shouldn't be longer than 45 seconds. The theme can be used throughout as well, including providing background for the credits, as well as playing under sections of an episode, if appropriate. If the front billing credits are known ahead of time, it can be helpful for the composer to start their work against those elements before receiving audio cuts from the production.

Personally, I feel that any theme song should not be less than 20 seconds. This becomes part of the transition time, bringing the audience into the world. Theme music warms up the audience to something familiar.

There's always the option to change the intro format and do cold opens with themes coming later. Changing the music in a series for special occasions will break up monotony, but the branded signature theme should still be used the most. I also strongly recommend NOT to use any stock music for this. The theme should be unique to YOUR production, and not confused with someone else's.

10.12.2 Composed or Stock Music

There are two options when choosing musical accompaniment. Either someone needs to compose the score or an editor must customize selections from stock music/royalty-free options. Composers cost a lot of money, especially given the characteristic length required for most of the music in audio programming. The intro is just the beginning, as the rest of the program will need moments for musical enhancement.

A contract is necessary to be signed ahead of production which would include a payment schedule and to outline the rights and royalty issues of the final composition(s). The (song-writer or composer) has the option to either license the music made and own the rights (sometimes costing less), or the music is payed for and owned by the production or producing company. If the production owns the music outright, it makes things far easier in the end when selling publishing rights or signing other distribution deals.

The complications and costs can make it seem like having a composer is not worth it, but a custom score makes a huge difference in the production. There will be specific moments that need to be highlighted with certain musical elements, and trying to arrange and manipulate appropriate stock music is difficult and limiting.

There are various companies that offer royalty-free music rights on a per song basis, or as a pack of songs. A simple Google search will bring up hundreds of options for royalty-free music. Each company has their own licensing considerations, so be sure to read the fine print. Hidden details in the license agreement might contain many limitations on how many downloads a production can have before paying more licensing fees. Others don't allow the sale of any production with their music included, and there are some that don't allow download rights, only streaming. Explore the options before starting production, so the costs and restrictions are known ahead of time.

I've worked with both for my productions. Lockdown was all originally composed, and We're Alive - A Story of Survival had a mix of both stock and custom. At the time, I didn't have the money to pay a musician, so I used what elements the company could afford then. Later on, when I had access to better music options, I replaced the instances of music in the first season that were less than flattering. No matter what, you have to start somewhere.

10.12.3 How to use Music

Music needs to have a seat at the table, an equal partner in the scene with the other players, SFX and dialogue. Music for film is easily integrated into the background, but music inside audio theater has to embrace and surround the characters. There are many ways music can be used to tell the story through leitmotifs (themes), giving clues as to what's going on. It has the ability to intensify, and build more *and* **MORE...** adding suspense, but it can also be used to bring feelings of pain and loss to the surface.

Choosing where to put music in can be tricky, and varies depending on the story. The most common place for audio drama, similar to film, is when the emotion or action of the scene is at a peak and the score is needed to push it even further.

Another area unique to audio-only productions is the use of music for bridging scenes. Transitioning between locations can be jarring, and music can blend time and space, bringing a flow to the entire production. Creating music with this complex goal requires a cooperation between the producers and composers, so that all the key moments work together and don't compete with one another. A musical score takes time to create, so be sure to give the composer as much as possible and deliver the audio assets on a set schedule. Once the remaining elements of the sound design are complete and ready to put into place, the composition process can be taken a little further to better tailor to the action in the scene.

The score, indeed, has the ability to tie specific sound elements together and raise the emotional reaction, but only if the right moments to use it are chosen. A constantly-running score will only lessen the overall impact. Music can become tiring for an audience if overused, or looped more times than a single song can support.

In an alternative workflow, if the production is using stock music, bring in the compositions earlier in the cutting stage. The timing of the scene can then be adjusted to the music. The beginning and ending of songs are the most important parts. Does it come in and distract the listener? Does it end in an odd place? Does the accompaniment feels like it fits the story? Stock music comes from such a variety of composers that it can be difficult to keep thematic consistency throughout.

What about using both? What about swapping out stock for an original composition later? "Temp" music can be good or bad. By trying to get the feel for a scene, having a temp score might help, but it's easy to fall in love with temp stuff, and potentially closes off creative options for the composer. Also, in using temp music, there's a tendency to create a less fulfilling sound design because of the early presence of a score. If a scene can support itself with the sounds alone, then the music will only enhance it further.

10.13 Finishing

Productions will go through a variety of stages for the review process, requiring many revisions to be made along the way. With each step, an export is made, changes incorporated, and the process starts all over again until everything is ultimately polished and ready for the final export.

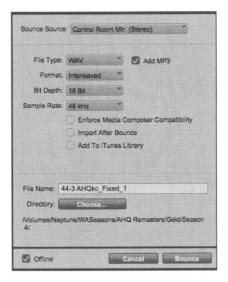

Fig. 10-11-3 Bouncing/Export options

Whether to export the project for review, or for the **final export**, the steps will be the same. If the timeline has multiple segments, highlight only the desired selection on the timeline, and only that section will be exported.

Using the "Bounce to Disk" option in Pro Tools, create both a WAV and an MP3 file. Make sure the settings match your production, which is likely to be "Stereo Interleaved" at 16/48. Also, select "offline," otherwise the audio will be rendered in real-time.

Now that the production is "in the can," either hand it off to the publishing company, or if you're doing this yourself, proceed to the next section.

Chapter Eleven

Publishing

11. Out to the Public

"How do I get people to hear what I made?"

This is the common question among those starting out in the medium. The answer depends upon two things: the quality of the product and the ease that someone has access to it. I have the philosophy, "If you build it, they will come." If what's being created is good, people will catch on and come to the story. The second issue, ease of access, can come with a lot of caveats. Let me explain...

Pay-walls or Podcasts?

There are several options for distributing the content: sell it exclusively through a "pay-wall" (paid website subscription), or offer it free as a podcast. (Note: If "SAG/AFTRA" contracts for New Media are intended to be used, be sure to check the guidelines on how the content must be published first. Podcasts are an acceptable distribution method for New Media, whereas CD sales fall under different union guidelines.)

If the decision is made to sell the content rather than distributing it for free, then I recommend shopping around for a publisher. This route gets complicated when trying to self-distribute or sell your product through someone else. Many audiobook aggregates like Apple Podcasts or Audible require minimum book counts before hosting content for sale.

My opinion on why they do this? Because smaller producers often lack the infrastructure for sales, and ultimately can become a liability for a larger corporation. There are ways to set up personal or professional websites for individual sales, but these also require a highly technical setup and specialized security to create an online store.

Aside from all the logistical limitations of self-publishing, a pay-wall can limit overall growth. By requiring listeners to pay up front, even with a preview for a non-established brand, it still is a hard sell. For so many reasons, if you're a first time producer, I recommend going the podcast route, and then expanding pay-for platforms in the future.

Podcasts

What are podcasts and how do they work? Podcasts are like an internet channel, not a website. They are a special feed hosted on a server that strictly contains audio episodes (and yes, there are video podcasts). They can be hosted on a website server, or a special podcast hosting server dedicated for that specific function. A listener then subscribes to the channel through their podcast app, or listing aggregate like Apple Podcasts to download or stream the feed. The feed typically contains a list of episodes, with images and descriptions for each. Newer podcast indexes now allow the individual classifications of episodes into seasons and other categories.

One of the nice things about podcasts is that anyone can make them, as well as fully control them. It's a direct-to-consumer route that bypasses all other distribution networks. The producer is fully in control of the content. This is one of the reasons that podcasts drew me in. There are some exceptions, though, to content management, such as if the podcast contains explicit material. The only requirement, then, is to label it accordingly, in order to be listed on most aggregates.

Podcast Aggregates

When someone says, "My podcast is on Apple Podcasts," what they're really saying is that their podcast is LISTED on Apple Podcasts. Apple doesn't store the sound files, but allows the feed to be listed in their directory. Google Play, Stitcher, Zune (still around... kinda), are all the same way. To submit a podcast, the episode(s) must first be properly uploaded to a podcast server and then the "feed" url is submitted to these aggregates for verification. If the podcast checks out, then it will be listed on their index. Most of the ways any listener will find the production is through these podcast directories.

Some of these aggregates have their own legal terms concerning podcast submissions, so be sure to read the fine print. Here's an example of some of the rules from Apple Podcasts in regard to content.

- *Podcasts can't use: Third-party trademarks or content without authorization or usage rights.*
    - Explanation: This first rule concerns intellectual property. Is the production allowed to use this content? If you're trying to make fan fiction about Star Wars, there's a chance it might get flagged and removed.
- *Podcasts can't use: Content that could be construed as racist, misogynist, or homophobic.*
    - Explanation: This is here to prevent hate speech channels.
- *Podcasts can't use: Content depicting graphic sex, violence, gore, illegal drugs, or hate themes.*
    - Explanation: The third rule is where things get a little tricky for Audio Theater. Even after my reaching out directly to Apple to get clarification, the rule still needs interpretation. This restriction has more to do with the condoning of the actions, not its inclusion in the story.
- *<explicit> tag must be set to "yes" when explicit language is in the podcast.*

This last rule is a big one: the EXPLICIT tag. This is an important red flag that can be used as a designation for either individual podcast episodes or the entire podcast channel.

There's a lot to consider with this 'little' tag. If the podcast has any episodes flagged as explicit, then specific countries in the world will not be able to access the feed. Also, some apps have child-age locks built in to prevent listening and downloading. For social reasons, a lot of parents use the tag to limit exposure for younger audiences. Either way, having an "Explicit" label will limit reach.

What does "Explicit" mean exactly? Currently, it's subjective. And if labeled improperly, then a podcast could get flagged and removed. Apple Podcasts and other indexes don't police episodes or check against a list, so any incidents of removal is more likely to be a reaction of someone to the podcast and submitting a complaint.

My suggestion for censorship guidance is to follow the FCC guidelines regarding Primetime TV. If something can be said on broadcast television in the United States during normal times of day, then it's not considered explicit.

Since most of the rules about what's "seen" don't apply, audio-only productions need to focus on what's said. For purely academic reasons, the words **that can't be said** according to H.R. 3687; Section 1464 of Title 18, United States Code are:

"shit, piss, fuck, cunt, asshole, cocksucker, motherfucker, and tits."

You won't find these words on the FCC website, and many places shy away from mentioning them. They are listed here specifically because an author needs to know exactly what the restrictions are in order to adhere to them.

11.1 Podcast Hosting and Websites

Podcast hosting

I don't recommend hosting a podcast on a website server. It's most likely ill-equipped for the type of bandwidth and response time required to handle all the incoming data requests. Use a dedicated podcast host like Libsyn or Podbean. These will be more in the consumer range of $5 - $20 per month, depending on the additional services offered. There are other options, but these two are the most common and reliable ones. Choose wisely. Once the hosting decision is made, stick with it. Transferring podcast hosts can be done fairly easily now-a-days, but statistics DO NOT TRANSFER. Before migrating, be sure to download all statistical data for longevity.

For the business side of podcast hosting, there are other industry-level hosting options like Art19. Art19 allows for dynamic ad-insertion on download. With this function, every time someone hits download, a new and current ad can be inserted, allowing "evergreen" content such as audio theater ads to consistently stay fresh.

Website Hosting and Domains

Having a website to accompany a podcast or a production *is essential*. In order for any listener to find out more information, they need a place to go. Also, having a domain that's the same name as the production can be a key component for people being able to find it. A domain refers to the specific web address like www.thetitleofyourproject.com. These addresses costs about $10 a year on average. This is only the location of the website. The next component required needed is 'hosting.'

Hosting is the space on the server that holds the website files: code, images, etc… The more users that are expected to go to the website at the same time, the better the hosting plan that will be needed. Hosting can go for as little as $5 a month, and scales up in cost with the added features. Domains can be bundled with hosting to reduce cost and technical setup.

There are alternatives to website hosting with pay-in programs like Square-Space, which handle all of the website creation.

Wordpress

For companies just starting out that need more web flexibility, I recommend installing Wordpress as the website host platform. Setting up Wordpress can get a little complicated, so if a hosting solution like GoDaddy offers automatic Wordpress setup, it might be worth it for the less technically savvy. Some website hosting places have built-in installers and customization features.

Once the template is installed, I recommend taking a look at different theme websites for customization. There are many themes available online for Wordpress, so it should be fairly simple to find something that fits your production.

Protection of a WordPress site is made easy by a few simple steps. Upon setup of your site, you should have a separate database user to use instead of an "all access" user. A standard user can be given a few low-level privileges to make, update, read and delete basic information on the database. This will help thwart those that want to break in.

When first installing WordPress, you need to choose an administrator name. Most people default to the standard "admin" or "administrator." *Don't do this*. Having "administrator" along with the /wp-admin as your login page gives those pesky robots another advantage. Choose something unique to you or your product. Also, I can't stress this enough, pick a **strong** password. I always go with something at least 15+ characters and never something including a common word.

Another method to protect your site is to rename the admin login page. WordPress at default makes the login page /wp-admin for every install. This makes it easy for those crawling script robots to scour the internet looking for WordPress installs with the defaults. All in one Security by Tips and Tricks HQ, is a great plugin to have and makes protecting your site much easier. With all the built-in options, it's easy to build a strong wall around your website fortress.

When it comes to backing up your website, you can put several strategies into play. The best option may be to contact your hosting provider to make sure there is a running backup in place. If you prefer a more direct and immediately accessible backup, there are ways to connect WordPress to DropBox to have a full backup at your fingertips. WordPress *Backup to Dropbox* provides an easy access option to manage your site.

Stores and Merchandise

There are different options for creating online stores for a production's merchandise. Options like Zazzle, which offer individual custom-branded products sell for relatively higher prices. The financial returns are small for each sale, because everything is made on demand. But there's no additional work for the podcast producer, aside from store setup and maintenance. What is offered on the store site, though, is limited as to what they can create.

There are other online store options such as ones that can be bundled through GoDaddy, which give more advanced choices for a custom web store, but requires someone to handle all the merchandise, shipping, and orders. Additional considerations to this option: the monthly fees are in scale with the store size; there are some limitations on web formats; and the custom store won't match the exact look of your website, as it is hosted on a different system and has its own template.

The top tier for production merchandise is a store plugin like Woocommerce, which is one that creates a completely custom storefront. This option can be costly and complicated to setup, as it's a requirement to have a secure site with a web security certificate, showing that your site is validated (https).

Also know that the merchandise itself for this last option still needs to be handled and created individually. There are bulk printing choices for things like t-shirts and posters that offer a large return with smaller overhead, but merchandise still needs to be created and designed in order to meet manufacturing specifications. Shipping costs also should be factored in, as product weight affects profitability. Even after all these considerations, the bottom line is that merchandise needs to be wanted.

Each tier offers some drawbacks as well as benefits. From the cheaper, but less profit per unit concept to the more profitable, but with equally more work… it's ultimately your decision.

11.2 Marketing and Social Media

Marketing
"How do you get new listeners?"

In person
There's nothing like one-on-one interaction to entice potential new loyal

fans and listeners. This can be done by having a booth at a convention, listening stations at a fair, or just by telling others about the project face to face. All of these interactions contribute to someone new being able to pick up their headsets and listen for the first time. It can be as easy as showing someone how to download and listen on their phone. The simple technological hurdle of knowing *how* to listen or even what exactly a "podcast" is, can be enough to prevent someone from reaching your production.

Custom iOS and Android Apps can help bridge the ease of listening. A simple app dedicated to the show can provide an easy way to attract new people. "Just go to the app store and download We're Alive," is easier than telling someone to download another app like Podcatcher, and then to search for your title.

Podcast hosts sometimes have apps as part of their package deals to assist listeners in being able to tune into their channel. This costs extra, of course (having any app in the App store for iOS is $99 a year, but free on Android). To create a custom app, costs can add up quickly, but then the sky is the limit when considering promotional possibilities. Custom apps can also include links to the production's social media feeds, online store, and even multiple productions- all in one place.

Online Marketing

The production's website is the first place listeners go to get an impression of your show, and decide if they want to listen. Does the production have a logo? Does the layout look professional? Can people easily find where to listen, and is it easy to keep listening to ongoing programming? These are all things to consider for marketing on the web. People leave websites quickly when they can't find what they want. Even a website with long load times are a deterrent. Another consideration: work places often restrict certain access to podcasts. Is there a place on the web to stream as well?

Forums and chats

I like having a place where people can talk openly with each other about the show, and a forum is a great place for that. In off-season, the chatter does get a little quiet as web forums in general tend to age, but it still is a nice place for fans to congregate and communicate. True story: fans have even become engaged and married through communicating with each other, having met through our websites.

With the expansion of social media and interaction hubs like Reddit (www.reddit.com/r/Werealive/ or /www.reddit.com/r/audiodrama/), some online perceptions are that forums won't be used for much longer, but I tend to disagree. With the control and visibility filtration of social media, having a place that's open, free, and completely unfiltered can be beneficial and appreciated by the fans.

Other websites, groups, and forums

There are places online where people already gather to talk about audio theater and podcasts, and perhaps are even including the topic or theme of your story. When the <u>We're Alive</u> podcast first went online, I posted in every forum or group I could find. Anything that was either Survivalist, Zombie, or Horror fans. A lot of places struck it down as spam, but I kept at it where I could. It's best to strategically find places to promote your show without being obtrusive. Sometimes website regulars or social media threads are already talking about, "What's your fav podcast?," or "looking for something for a trip?" which become opportunities for organic promotion. Social media groups for podcasting and audio books can sometimes be great places as well, but watch for rules about self-promotion because some posts can be flagged and removed. Marketing online is all about creative ways to be noticed, but not annoyingly.

Social Media

Social media is a big game, with ever-changing regulations and post-filtration. A social media manager has to stay current in order to be able to keep engaging the audience effectively. For smaller brands, it can become harder and harder to reach an audience with the pay-for-impression restrictions that are expanding from the social media companies. In other words, a production has to pay to boost the message to stay in the game, otherwise the followers or fans of the program may not ever see the post.

Having to pay to reach your fans isn't ideal, but there is another way: **engagement**. No matter where the account is for the show (Facebook, Instagram, Twitter, Tumblr), the only way others will see the posts is if there's someone actively engaging them, and make the posts worth following. The more comments and "likes/hearts/thumbs ups," the more fans will see the post. Social media is all about engaging in a two-way conversation, so it pays off to interact with the fans, prompt them with questions, and make this production something worth following.

Make the posts unique. If the only thing uploaded are links to new episodes, many social media sites will drop the impressions. They know social media is a form of free advertising, so there are limits for exposure to links to outside sources. Post images onto Facebook or Twitter- don't link them to the website image. Photo posts will be given a higher priority than links. Livestream options also currently receive top engagement on fan feeds, making live video promos the most advantageous exposure route currently. The second best exposure is through uploaded and produced videos. How often does the production post something? Some websites and social media experts recommend posting more often to get more views, but from my experience, I always find that fewer better posts increase the chance of attracting fans with more lasting impressions.

The background algorithms/dynamics change constantly for social media, so to focus on growing through word of mouth is always the best practice. As for other types of posts, be sure to keep up on the individual platform's policy and algorithm updates. Social media sites constantly update how they determine the order in which something appears, relying on mathematical calculations that weighs how impressionable one's post or account is. Every social network can either filter or boost someone's "post priority" for whatever reason they deem fit.

Live Events

One of the best ways to engage fans and audience members is by having live events. These offer a place for listeners to come and see the creators of the show, as well as the actors, and maybe get a few things signed or purchased. Live events are a great way to earn some extra funds and expose new people, as someone always brings a friend.

Live events can also be costly and complicated. Paying for a venue, insurance, coordinating actors' schedules, the merchandise displays, and the technical setup if you plan on doing a live read, can be overwhelming. It's an incredible amount of work for a single event. Personally, I would love to take the performances on the road and tour, but unfortunately being able to do so with as many working voice actors as we have, makes it not feasible.

11.3 The Community

Are you producing your own materials? You are not alone. There are others like you that want to create in this medium, and truly embrace the ideals of Audio Theater. Everyone might have different opinions on how to approach the creation of audio-only entertainment, but every one of them strive to be the best aural storyteller.

I am active and a part of several Facebook groups. In fact, I used these groups as a resource for input into the process of categorization. The Audio Drama community assists each other with technical questions, casting notices, and even crew calls and collaboration. I highly suggest joining one of these communities and joining in on the conversation. LINK to Group: https://www.facebook.com/groups/747178725350066/

Chapter Twelve

Theater for the Mind ™

12. The Movement

    The last thing that I want to talk about is the "Theater for the Mind ™" movement, and the what I've been calling the "Audio Theater Association."
    Because of the nature of this medium, and relative ease of access to technical equipment, virtually anyone can create audio-only entertainment. Over the last several years, the amount of independent productions has increased to such a scale that I can no longer continue to keep track of all the new series. Unfortunately, not all of them hold up in terms of quality. The *suspension of disbelief* and the *illusion of aural perception* can be easily shattered.

    While anyone can create Audio Theater or Audio Drama, something that I consider "Theater for the Mind" is an entirely different level. It's specifically designed to put a listener's mind into an aural "theater," and become part of the journey. The score is tailored to perfectly accompany and accent the story, the Foleyed actions of each character are created in a way to communicate every aspect of that person's actions, and the character dialogue flows smoothly because most of the actors are recorded at the same time. The audience is experiencing the dialogue of the characters as they are speaking, by understanding the aurally illustrated actions and exposition through dialogue and sound effects. The narration is minimal, present only when absolutely necessary.
    It's a journey tailored *for your mind*, putting the listener in the world.

That's Theater for the Mind.

The intention of this movement is to use "Theater for the Mind" (TFTM) as a Trademark, and in doing so, protect the brand, and associate it with productions that meet specific criteria. The eventual goal is to establish the "Audio Theater Association," which would vote on and freely license the TFTM trademark to use with qualifying productions. By having a formal association, it would allow rules and guidelines to be passed for a possible audio rating system similar to what the MPAA does for films.

That's the goal. Will it work? That remains to be seen. I have already applied for the trademark with the intention of using it for my brand, but I also want to see it be used by the growing medium as a collective. There are those in the community who don't like the idea of a "content filter," but in order for this particular style of the medium to advance and become accepted into a broader public spectrum, it needs to be scrutinized. The process will encourage more listeners to seek out other like-productions that contain a similar label. I'm often asked by fans, "What other stories do you recommend that are similar to the style of <u>We're Alive</u>?" to which I would like to be able to reply, search "Theater for the Mind."

There's still a lot that needs to happen before the Audio Theater Association can be established and the TFTM trademark licensed, and it will only really work if other productions adhere and accept the terms. Nevertheless, I will continue my efforts in moving forward to establish such an association.

12.1 Conclusion

Is this the end of the book already? [Scoffs] I hope you've enjoyed this collection of technical notes, suggestions, and what might be considered my own crazy aural musings. Hopefully this can inspire what could be the start of the next generation of audio theater producers.

Whether you use part of this text to create the next aural Shakespeare, or you're solely an avid listener interested in the craft, I will leave you with one last piece of advice.

Creating is hard... clearly it can be a lot of work, and at times may not feel rewarding, but if what you make can influence just one person in a positive way, then it's all worth it.

Art has the power to save any withering soul.

Additional Resources

xx. Equipment Index

NOTE: All Prices are listed as new and 2017 prices.

- **Sound Foam**
  - Foam Factory Inc (www.foambymail.com) - ($30 - $100) Various foam panel options. Sample: 1-1/2" Egg-crate Foam 48"x72" - 2-Pack ($63) - These are great to cover walls to reduce reflection. Buy from the factory, not retail.
- **Sound Blankets**
  - Vocal Booth To Go Sound Blankets with grommets - VB71G ($35) - 72"x80" - These blankets are designed and engineered for sound absorption.
- **Mics**
  - Wired Lavalier Mic (Mid) - Sony ECM44b ($150) - Durable for outdoor and portable usage.
  - Medium Shotgun Mic (Mid) - Audio Technica BP4073 ($700) - Recorded vocals for WA.
  - Vocal Condenser Mic (Top) Neumann u87 ($3,600) - Recorded vocals for Bronzeville.
  - Vocal Condenser Mic (Mid) Neumann TLM 103 ($1,000)
  - Vocal Condenser Mic (Low) Audio-Technica AT4033 ($400) - Recorded many commercials and audiobooks with this model.
  - Vocal Dynamic Mic (Mid) Shure SM7B ($400) - Classic recording mic.
  - Vocal Dynamic Mic (Low) Shure SM58 ($99) - Durable, sensitive, great lows, and omnidirectional. Use these all the time with podcasts, live shows, etc...
  - Binaural Head Recorder (High) Neumann KU 100 Dummy Head Microphone ($8000) - These are the best of the best in Binaural recording, is used on Darkest Night Podcast series.
- **Portable Audio Recorders**
  - Zoom H4N Handy Recorder* ($199) - 2 XLR Mic Pre-Amps and 2 Built-in Mics - The internal mics on this model aren't great.
  - Zoom H6 Handy Recorder* ($349) - 4 XLR Mic Pre-Amps and Swappable mic modules.
  - *BE WARNED: ALL portable audio recorders are brutal on batteries. Be sure to have a plug-in adapter handy just in case.
- **Mic Stand**
  - Hercules Single-Pole Stand (Mid) MS201B for Vocals ($59) -

Perfect for space, easy to collapse.
- Hercules Tripod Stand (Mid) MS533B for Foley ($69) - This model is more appropriate for Foley, as there are many adjustments and angles needed to capture certain sounds.
- **Music Stand**
  - Ultimate Support Music Stand JS-MS200 (Mid) - Holds three pages, collapsable and has holes through the metal to reduce reflection.
- **Headsets**
  - Sony MDR-7506 Headphones ($99) - Great studio monitors, and the design hasn't changed in years.
- **Monitors/Speakers**
  - JBL LSR305 5" studio monitors ($150 each, $300 pair)
  - KRK Rocket 5 studio monitors ($150 each, $300 pair)
  - JBL LSR308 8" studio monitors ($250 each, $500 pair)
- **Audio IO**
  - Focusrite Scarlett 2i2 USB (Low) - ($150) - 2 Pre-amp Mic Inputs and 2 Outputs - Great for a small, getting started home studio.
  - Focusrite Scarlett 18i20 USB (Mid) - ($500) - 8 Pre-amp Mic Inputs for a total of 18 Inputs / 20 Outputs - Perfect for a multi-cast recording room.
- **Computer**
  - Apple iMac 21.5" or larger, made after 2015 if you're buying new. Pre-owned can likely go back to 2013.
  - Apple MacBook Pro 2015+ - Screen space is limited for audio editing, and would recommend installing a second monitor.
- **Software**
  - Avid Pro Tools 12 - ($600 - Perpetual License, $235 - Annual License)
  - Avid Pro Tools 12 Educational - ($299 - Perpetual License, $99 - Annual License)
  - Reaper ($60 Discounted License, $225 Full Commercial License)
  - Audicity (Free)
- **Pro Tools Plugins**
  - IZotope RX Elements ($129) Standard ($399) Advanced ($1,200)
  - Audio Ease Speakerphone 2 ($495)
  - Audio Ease Altiverb 7 ($595)
  - Audio Ease Indoor ($795)
  - Avid Spaces ($500 or FREE with PT subscription)
  - SoundMiner ($199)
- **Sound Effects Libraries**
  - Sound-Ideas (Variable $) - Various sound effect packs

- Series 1000 (3k sound effects) - ($295 or $.10 per SFX)
- **Additional Software**
    - Google Drive cloud storage (100 GB $2/mo, 1 TB $10/mo, 10 TB $100/mo)
    - Scrivener (Reg $40-45, EDU $38)
    - Final Draft (Reg $250, EDU $130)
- **Data Storage**
    - G-Raid Drive - 4 TB GTGDT4 ($300) - Thunderbolt and USB 3.0

xx.1 Concepts and Phrases

Aural - The artistic interpretation of audio.

Aural branding - A combination of sounds that ties into an audio signature.

Aural Image - The visual property given by sound to illustrate the scene.

Aural Spectrum - Variance of sounds, sound dynamics.

Crowd-Funding - Raising money via fan donations in exchange for creating something.

Exposition - The details of the plot, typically used when describing dialogue that has a large amount of plot information.

Hard Sound Effects - Clips of audio that are already set and recorded.

"Off-scene" - When a character is doing something outside the scene(s), portrayed in front of the audience.

"On the nose" - Refers to when an idea is the most obvious and blatant choice; often referred to as 'cliche.'

Pickup - Recording an individual line or group of lines after the larger scene was already finished.

Plosives - Syllables that give off puffs of air that can distort a recording.

SFX - Sound Effects, referring to individual clips

Sides - Refers to small segments from scripts that actors read for auditions.

SPOV - Sound Point of View is the location where the sound is perceived to be heard by the audience.

VOX - Any sound that comes from a person's mouth.

Photo Credits

Dino Aranda:
8-1-1: Jodi
8-3-1: Kc
8-3-2: Rogelio and Kc

Shannon Leith:
9-1-1: Recording Stage
9-1-2: Equipment

Kc Wayland:
9-1-3: Lockdown Foley
9-1-4: Ceiling Curtains
9-1-5: Collapsed Ceiling Curtains
9-2-1: Signal Flow Illustration
9-2-2: Xlrs
10-10-1: Lady Shoes

Made in the USA
Columbia, SC
01 February 2021